KV-621-272

DOMESTIC VIOLENCE: LAW ENFORCEMENT RESPONSE AND LEGAL PERSPECTIVES

CRIMINAL JUSTICE,
LAW ENFORCEMENT AND CORRECTIONS

Additional books in this series can be found on Nova's website at:

https://www.novapublishers.com/catalog/index.php?cPath=23_29&
seriesp=Criminal+Justice%2C+Law+Enforcement+and+Corrections

CRIMINAL JUSTICE, LAW ENFORCEMENT AND CORRECTIONS

DOMESTIC VIOLENCE: LAW ENFORCEMENT RESPONSE AND LEGAL PERSPECTIVES

MARIO R. DEWALT
EDITOR

Nova
Nova Science Publishers, Inc.
New York

Copyright © 2010 by Nova Science Publishers, Inc.

All rights reserved. No part of this book may be reproduced, stored in a retrieval system or transmitted in any form or by any means: electronic, electrostatic, magnetic, tape, mechanical photocopying, recording or otherwise without the written permission of the Publisher.

For permission to use material from this book please contact us:
Telephone 631-231-7269; Fax 631-231-8175
Web Site: http://www.novapublishers.com

NOTICE TO THE READER

The Publisher has taken reasonable care in the preparation of this book, but makes no expressed or implied warranty of any kind and assumes no responsibility for any errors or omissions. No liability is assumed for incidental or consequential damages in connection with or arising out of information contained in this book. The Publisher shall not be liable for any special, consequential, or exemplary damages resulting, in whole or in part, from the readers' use of, or reliance upon, this material. Any parts of this book based on government reports are so indicated and copyright is claimed for those parts to the extent applicable to compilations of such works.

Independent verification should be sought for any data, advice or recommendations contained in this book. In addition, no responsibility is assumed by the publisher for any injury and/or damage to persons or property arising from any methods, products, instructions, ideas or otherwise contained in this publication.

This publication is designed to provide accurate and authoritative information with regard to the subject matter covered herein. It is sold with the clear understanding that the Publisher is not engaged in rendering legal or any other professional services. If legal or any other expert assistance is required, the services of a competent person should be sought. FROM A DECLARATION OF PARTICIPANTS JOINTLY ADOPTED BY A COMMITTEE OF THE AMERICAN BAR ASSOCIATION AND A COMMITTEE OF PUBLISHERS.

LIBRARY OF CONGRESS CATALOGING-IN-PUBLICATION DATA

Domestic violence : law enforcement response and legal perspectives / editor, Mario R. Dewalt.
 p. cm.
Includes bibliographical references and index.
ISBN 978-1-60876-774-8 (hardcover : alk. paper)
1.Family violence--Law and legislation--United States. 2. Victims of family violence--Services for--United States. 3. Police social work--United States. I. Dewalt, Mario R. II. United States. Dept. of Justice.
KF9322.D663 2009
345.73'02555--dc22

2009045953

Published by Nova Science Publishers, Inc. ✦ *New York*

CONTENTS

PREFACE

The purpose of this book is to describe to practitioners what the research tells us about domestic violence, including its perpetrators and victims, the impact of current responses to it and, more particularly, the implications of that research for day-to-day, real-world responses to domestic violence by law enforcement officers, prosecutors and judges. Domestic violence tends to be underreported: women report only one-quarter to one-half of their assaults to police, men perhaps less. The vast majority of physical assaults are not life threatening; rather, they involve pushing, slapping, and hitting. This book describes the problem of domestic violence and reviews factors that increase its risks. The authors examine perpetrator and victim characteristics, including gender, age, and certain personality traits. It also reviews responses to the problem and what is known about these from evaluative research and police practice. This book consists of public documents which have been located, gathered, combined, reformatted, and enhanced with a subject index, selectively edited and bound to provide easy access.

Chapter 1 - This guide begins by describing the problem of domestic violence and reviewing factors that increase its risks. It then identifies a series of questions to help you analyze your local domestic violence problem. Finally, it reviews responses to the problem and what is known about these from evaluative research and police practice.

Chapter 2 - The Judicial Oversight Demonstration (JOD) Initiative set out to improve the provision of comprehensive services to victims of domestic violence (DV), increase victim safety, and hold offenders more accountable. JOD activities were jointly funded and managed by the Office on Violence Against Women and the National Institute of Justice (NIJ). The Urban Institute conducted an independent, multisite evaluation under a cooperative agreement with NIJ. This report (part of a series of reports on JOD) discusses some of the evaluation's findings and lessons learned about implementing court-involved DV prevention programs.

Chapter 3 - According to the latest 2005 National Crime Victimization Survey (NCVS), during the period from 1993 to 2005, the average annual domestic violence rate per 1,000 persons (age 12 or older) for intimate partners and/or relatives was 5.9 for females and 2.1 for males. About one- third of the victims reported they were physically attacked; two-thirds were threatened with attack or death. A little more than half (50.5 percent) of the female victims suffered an injury, but only 4.5 percent were seriously injured. Slightly more than 3 percent were sexually assaulted. Fewer male victims — 41 .5 percent - reported injuries, of which less than 5 percent were serious injuries. Those males or females who were separated (or divorced) experienced more nonfatal domestic violence than those who were together. [27]

Chapter 4 - The Judicial Oversight Demonstration (JOD) was designed to test the feasibility and impact of a coordinated response to intimate partner violence (IPV) that involved the courts and justice agencies in a central role. A national evaluation of JOD began in 2000 with the start of demonstration activities and continued throughout and beyond the intervention period. This report presents an overview of the entire evaluation and presents specific findings from the three JOD sites and from comparison sites.

Chapter 5 - Domestic violence cases involving intimate partners pose challenges for the crimi-nal justice system as the cases move from arrest to adjudication to sentencing. The lengthy time period after arrest but before case dispo-sition (either by plea, trial ver-dict, or dismissal) puts domestic violence victims at high risk. Offenders often vio-late no-contact orders and seek out their victims during this pretrial period, raising the potential for more violence.

State courts in three demon-stration sites are rethinking how they handle domestic violence cases through the Judicial Oversight Demon-stration (JOD) project. The three sites are all seeking to increase victim safety while holding offenders accountable, but each site implemented the project in a slightly different way.

In: Domestic Violence: Law Enforcement Response...   ISBN: 978-1-60876-774-8

Editor: Mario R. Dewalt   © 2010 Nova Science Publishers, Inc.

Chapter 1

DOMESTIC VIOLENCE[*]

Rana Sampson

ABOUT THE PROBLEM-SPECIFIC GUIDES SERIES

The *Problem-Specific Guides* summarize knowledge about how police can reduce the harm caused by specific crime and disorder problems. They are guides to prevention and to improving the overall response to incidents, not to investigating offenses or handling specific incidents. Neither do they cover all of the technical details about how to implement specific responses. The guides are written for police—of whatever rank or assignment—who must address the specific problem the guides cover. The guides will be most useful to officers who:

- **Understand basic problem-oriented policing principles and methods.** The guides are not primers in problem- oriented policing. They deal only briefly with the initial decision to focus on a particular problem, methods to analyze the problem, and means to assess the results of a problem- oriented policing project. They are designed to help police decide how best to analyze and address a problem they have already identified. (A companion series of *Problem-Solving Tools* guides has been produced to aid in various aspects of problem analysis and assessment.)
- **Can look at a problem in depth.** Depending on the complexity of the problem, you should be prepared to spend perhaps weeks, or even months, analyzing and responding to it. Carefully studying a problem before responding helps you design the right strategy, one that is most likely to work in your community. You should not blindly adopt the responses others have used; you must decide whether they are appropriate to your local situation. What is true in one place may not be true elsewhere; what works in one place may not work everywhere.
- **Are willing to consider new ways of doing police business.** The guides describe responses that other police departments have used or that researchers have tested.

---

[*] This is an edited, reformatted and augmented version of a U. S. Department of Justice publication dated January 2007.

While not all of these responses will be appropriate to your particular problem, they should help give a broader view of the kinds of things you could do. You may think you cannot implement some of these responses in your jurisdiction, but perhaps you can. In many places, when police have discovered a more effective response, they have succeeded in having laws and policies changed, improving the response to the problem. (A companion series of *Response Guides* has been produced to help you understand how commonly-used police responses work on a variety of problems.)

- **Understand the value and the limits of research knowledge.** For some types of problems, a lot of useful research is available to the police; for other problems, little is available. Accordingly, some guides in this series summarize existing research whereas other guides illustrate the need for more research on that particular problem. Regardless, research has not provided definitive answers to all the questions you might have about the problem. The research may help get you started in designing your own responses, but it cannot tell you exactly what to do. This will depend greatly on the particular nature of your local problem. In the interest of keeping the guides readable, not every piece of relevant research has been cited, nor has every point been attributed to its sources. To have done so would have overwhelmed and distracted the reader. The references listed at the end of each guide are those drawn on most heavily; they are not a complete bibliography of research on the subject.

- **Are willing to work with others to find effective solutions to the problem.** The police alone cannot implement many of the responses discussed in the guides. They must frequently implement them in partnership with other responsible private and public bodies including other government agencies, non-governmental organizations, private businesses, public utilities, community groups, and individual citizens. An effective problem-solver must know how to forge genuine partnerships with others and be prepared to invest considerable effort in making these partnerships work. Each guide identifies particular individuals or groups in the community with whom police might work to improve the overall response to that problem. Thorough analysis of problems often reveals that individuals and groups other than the police are in a stronger position to address problems and that police ought to shift some greater responsibility to them to do so. Response Guide No. 3, *Shifting and Sharing Responsibility for Public Safety Problems*, provides further discussion of this topic.

The COPS Office defines community policing as "a policing philosophy that promotes and supports organizational strategies to address the causes and reduce the fear of crime and social disorder through problem- solving tactics and police-community partnerships." These guides emphasize problem-solving and police-community partnerships in the context of addressing specific public safety problems. For the most part, the organizational strategies that can facilitate *problem-solving* and *police- community partnerships* vary considerably and discussion of them is beyond the scope of these guides.

These guides have drawn on research findings and police practices in the United States, the United Kingdom, Canada, Australia, New Zealand, the Netherlands, and Scandinavia. Even though laws, customs and police practices vary from country to country, it is apparent that the police everywhere experience common problems. In a world that is becoming increasingly interconnected, it is important that police be aware of research and successful practices beyond the borders of their own countries.

Each guide is informed by a thorough review of the research literature and reported police practice and is anonymously peer-reviewed by line police officers, police executives and researchers prior to publication.

The COPS Office and the authors encourage you to provide feedback on this guide and to report on your own agency's experiences dealing with a similar problem. Your agency may have effectively addressed a problem using responses not considered in these guides and your experiences and knowledge could benefit others. This information will be used to update the guides. If you wish to provide feedback and share your experiences it should be sent via e-mail to cops pubs@usdoj.gov.

For more information about problem-oriented policing, visit the Center for Problem-Oriented Policing online at www.popcenter.org. This website offers free online access to:

- the Problem-Specific Guides series
- the companion Response Guides and Problem-Solving Tools series
- instructional information about problem-oriented policing and related topics
- an interactive problem-oriented policing training exercise
- an interactive Problem Analysis Module
- a manual for crime analysts
- online access to important police research and practices
- information about problem-oriented policing conferences and award programs.

ACKNOWLEDGMENTS

The *Problem-Oriented Guides for Police* are produced by the Center for Problem-Oriented Policing, whose officers are Michael S. Scott (Director), Ronald V. Clarke (Associate Director) and Graeme R. Newman (Associate Director). While each guide has a primary author, other project team members, COPS Office staff and anonymous peer reviewers contributed to each guide by proposing text, recommending research and offering suggestions on matters of format and style.

The project team that developed the guide series comprised Herman Goldstein (University of Wisconsin Law School), Ronald V. Clarke (Rutgers University), John E. Eck (University of Cincinnati), Michael S. Scott (University of Wisconsin Law School), Rana Sampson (Police Consultant), and Deborah Lamm Weisel (North Carolina State University.)

Members of the San Diego; National City, California; and Savannah, Georgia police departments provided feedback on the guides' format and style in the early stages of the project.

Cynthia E. Pappas oversaw the project for the COPS Office. Research for the guide was conducted at the Criminal Justice Library at Rutgers University under the direction of Phyllis Schultze. Katharine Willis edited this guide.

THE PROBLEM OF DOMESTIC VIOLENCE

This guide begins by describing the problem of domestic violence and reviewing factors that increase its risks.[§] It then identifies a series of questions to help you analyze your local domestic violence problem. Finally, it reviews responses to the problem and what is known about these from evaluative research and police practice.

Domestic disputes are some of the most common calls for police service. Many domestic disputes do not involve violence; this guide discusses those that do, as well as the measures that can be used to reduce them. In the United States, domestic violence accounts for about 20 percent of the nonfatal violent crime women experience and three percent of the nonfatal violent crime men experience.[1] Harm levels vary from simple assault to homicide, with secondary harms to child witnesses. Domestic violence calls can be quite challenging for police as they are likely to observe repetitive abuse against the same victims, who may not be able to or may not want to part from their abusers. Police typically view these calls as dangerous, partly because old research exaggerated the risks to police.[§§]

Domestic violence is but one aspect of the larger set of problems related to family violence. Related problems not directly addressed in this guide, each of which requires separate analysis, include:

- parent abuse
- child abuse
- child sexual abuse
- elder abuse
- sibling violence
- domestic violence by police officers.

In addition, police must address a range of disputes among intimates, former intimates, and family members that may or may not involve violence, including

- domestic disputes
- child custody disputes
- stalking
- runaway juveniles.

[§] Much of the recent research about domestic violence refers to the problem as "intimate partner violence." Mostly this guide keeps to the term domestic violence, not because it is more accurate, but simply because it is still so widely used by police. Also in this guide, the term domestic violence is intended to include violence perpetrated by current and former intimates or dating partners, including those of the opposite or same sex.

[§§] Originally researchers failed to separate domestic disputes from other types of "disturbance" calls and raw percentages stretched the findings beyond what they reasonably meant (Fridell and Pate, 1997). Of the 713 officers feloniously slain in the United States between 1983 and 1992, 33 percent (235 officers) were slain while intervening in a crime. Of those, 24 percent (56 officers) were slain during a domestic disturbance. In other words, about five officers a year in the United States over that 10-year period were killed during domestic disturbance calls. The frequency of the call likely makes claims of dangerousness in terms of injury to officers overblown as well.

Some of these related problems are covered in other guides in this series, all of which are listed at the end of this guide. For the most up-to-date list of current and future guides, visit www.popcenter.org.

General Description of the Problem

Domestic violence involves a current or former intimate (and in many states, a current or former dating partner). Domestic violence tends to be underreported: women report only one-quarter to one-half of their assaults to police, men perhaps less.[2] The vast majority of physical assaults are not life threatening; rather, they involve pushing, slapping, and hitting.[3] Most women victims of domestic violence do not seek medical treatment, even for injuries deserving of it.[4]

Surveys provide us with estimates of the level of domestic violence in the United States, but there are wide differences among them depending on the definitions of domestic violence used and populations surveyed.[5] Two large surveys provide some insight into the level of domestic violence in the United States. The first, the National Violence Against Women Survey (NVAWS),[§] Conducted in 1995 and1996, found that nearly one in four women and nearly one in 13 men surveyed experienced rape and/or physical assault by a current or former spouse/partner/dating partner at some time in their lifetime, with about one and one-half percent of women and about one percent of men having been so victimized in the 12 months before the survey.[6] The National Crime Victimization Survey's (NCVS) estimates, however, are about one-third lower for women and more than two-thirds lower for men. [§§] Differences in survey administration and methodology may account for the large differences in the numbers.[§§§]

Even the lower numbers of the NCVS suggest that intimate partner violence in the United States is extensive. However, NCVS trend data through 2001 shows that partner violence between current and former intimates has declined significantly. From 1993 through 2001, the rate of reported intimate violence dropped by about 50 percent in the United States.[7] From 1994 through 2001, the rate of every major violent and property crime declined by similar percentages.[8,§§§§] It is unknown whether domestic violence is paralleling these declines for the same or different reasons.

[§] NVAWS is a telephone survey of a representative sample of 8,000 U.S. men and 8,000 U.S. women.

[§§] The National Crime Victimization Survey (NCVS) collects data about criminal victimization from an ongoing nationally representative sample of U.S. households. The survey is administered every six months to about 100,000 individuals in approximately 50,000 households. Interviewers ask questions about crime victimization of all household members age 12 and older. The survey attempts to capture two types of crime, victimization that was reported to the police and victimization that was not reported to the police. (Rennison and Welchans, 2000).

[§§§] The NCVS, administered by census workers as part of a crime survey, does not conduct all of its interviews in private because all members of the household are interviewed for different portions of the survey; also in contrast, the NVAWS survey uses more questions to screen for intimate violence, perhaps drawing out more from those interviewed.

[§§§§] From 1994 through 2001, the rate of every major violent and property crime also steeply declined: homicide/manslaughter (down 40 percent); rape/sexual assault (down 56 percent); robbery (down 53 percent); aggravated assault (down 56 percent); simple assault (down 46 percent); household burglary (down 51 percent); motor vehicle theft (down 52 percent); theft (down 47 percent). (Rennison, 2001).

Domestic violence homicides have declined in similar proportions as well. In the United States, there were about half the number of intimate partner homicides (spouses, ex-spouses, boyfriends, and girlfriends) in 2002 as there were in 1976 with the largest portion of the decline in male victims (see Figure 1).[9]

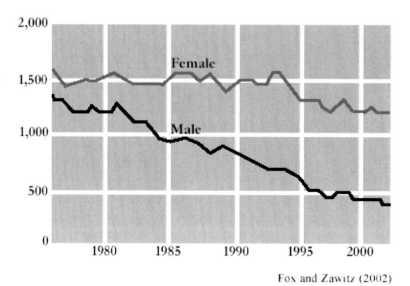

Fox and Zawitz (2002)

Figure 1. Homicides of intimates by gender of victim, 1976-2002 Number of victims

Some commentators suggest that the decline in homicides may be evidence that abused women have developed legitimate ways to leave their relationships (e.g., divorce, shelters, police, and courts). The reasons for the decline may be even more complex because there is wide variation by race, not just by gender. Between 1976 and 2002, the number of black male victims of intimate partner homicide fell by 81 percent as compared to 56 percent for white males. The number of black female victims of intimate partner homicide fell 49 percent as compared to 9 percent for white females.[10]

Women as Offenders

There is a robust debate among researchers about the level of relationship violence women are responsible for and the extent to which it is in self-defense or fighting back.[11] The NCVS and other studies have found that women are the victims in as much as 85 percent of domestic violence incidents.[12] However, there are also research findings that women in heterosexual relationships have the same, if not higher, rates of relationship violence as men.[13] Generally, studies about domestic violence fall into two categories: family conflict studies and crime victimization studies. Those that tend to show high rates of violence by women (or rates higher than men) are family conflict studies and contain questions about family conflicts and disputes and responses to these, including physical responses. These studies use a family conflict assessment tool. Those studies that show that male assaultive behavior predominates in domestic violence are criminal victimization surveys and/or studies that rely on the counting of crime reports.[14]

Critics suggest that studies finding about equal rates of violence by women in relationships are misleading because they fail to place the violence in context (Dekeseredy et al. 1997); in other words, there is a difference between someone who uses violence to fight back or defend oneself and someone who initiates an unprovoked assault. Also, the physical differences between some women and their male partners may make comparisons between equivalent types of violence (slapping, kicking, punching, hitting) less meaningful, particularly because many studies show that violence by women is less likely to result in injury. Researchers agree that women suffer the lion's share of injuries from domestic violence.[15]

Women living as partners with other women report lower rates of violence (11 percent) compared to women who live with or were married to men (30 percent).[16] About 8 percent of men living with or married to women report that they were physically abused by the women. About 15 percent of men cohabitating with men reported victimization by a male partner. These data suggest that men are engaged in more relationship violence.

Harms Caused by Domestic Violence

Domestic violence can include murder, rape, sexual assault, robbery, and aggravated or simple assault. In addition to the physical harm victims suffer, domestic violence results in emotional harm to victims, their children, other family members, friends, neighbors, and co-workers. Victims and their children experience the brunt of the psychological trauma of abuse, suffering anxiety, stress, sleep deprivation, loss of confidence, social isolation, and fear.[17] Batterers frequently also subject their victims to harassment (such as annoying or threatening phone calls), vandalism, trespassing, stalking, criminal mischief, theft, and burglary.[18]

Domestic violence also has economic costs. Victims may lose their jobs because of absenteeism related to the violence, and may even lose their homes because of loss of income. Some domestic violence victims must rely on shelters or depend on others to house them, and others become part of a community's homeless population, increasing their risk for other types of victimization.[§] Medical expenses to treat injuries, particularly of uninsured victims, create additional financial burdens, either for the victims or for the public.

Theories about Domestic Violence

Theories about why men or women batter and why some people are reluctant to end abusive relationships may seem abstract to police practitioners, but the theories have important implications for how police might effectively respond to the problem.

[§] In the United States estimates of the percentage of homelessness among women resulting from domestic violence vary, but it may be upwards of 20 percent (National Coalition for the Homeless, 2004). In the United Kingdom, about 16 percent of the homeless to whom local authorities provided housing were victims of domestic violence (Office of the Deputy Prime Minister, n.d.). A recent report from Australia found that domestic violence is a major contributing factor to homelessness. The study also found that more than one-third of those accessing government housing assistance for homelessness were women escaping domestic violence, and two-thirds of the children in the housing program were those who accompanied a female parent or guardian escaping domestic violence (Australian Institute of Health and Welfare, 2005).

Why Some Men Batter

Generally, four theories explain battering in intimate relationships.[19]

Psychological theory. Battering is the result of childhood abuse, a personality trait (such as the need to control), a personality disturbance (such as borderline personality), psychopathology (such as anti-social personality), or a psychological disorder or problem (such as post traumatic stress, poor impulse control, low self-esteem, or substance abuse).

Sociological theory. Sociological theories vary but usually contain some suggestion that intimate violence is the result of learned behavior. One sociological theory suggests that violence is learned within a family, and a partner-victim stays caught up in a cycle of violence and forgiveness. If the victim does not leave, the batterer views the violence as a way to produce positive results. Children of these family members may learn the behavior from their parents (boys may develop into batterers and girls may become battering victims). A different sociological theory suggests that lower income subcultures will show higher rates of intimate abuse, as violence may be a more acceptable form of settling disputes in such subcultures. A variant on this theory is that violence is inherent in all social systems and people with resources (financial, social contacts, prestige) use these to control family members, while those without resort to violence and threats to accomplish this goal.

Feminist or societal-structural theory. According to this theory, male intimates who use violence do so to control and limit the independence of women partners. Societal traditions of male dominance support and sustain inequities in relationships.

Violent individuals theory. For many years it was assumed that domestic batterers were a special group, that while they assaulted their current or former intimates they were not violent in the outside world. There is cause to question how fully this describes batterers. Although the full extent of violence batterers perpetrate is unknown, there is evidence that many batterers are violent beyond domestic violence, and many have prior criminal records for violent and non-violent behavior.[20] This suggests that domestic violence batterers are less unique and are more accurately viewed as violent criminals, not solely as domestic batterers. There may be a group of batterers who are violent only to their current or former intimates and engage in no other violent and non-violent criminal behavior, but this group may be small compared to the more common type of batterer.[21]

Why Some Women Batter

Some women batter their current or former intimates. Less is known about women who use violence in relationships, particularly the extent to which it may be in self-defense, to fight back, or to ward off anticipated violence. When asked in a national survey if they used violence in their relationships, many Canadian college women said they did. However, the majority of these women said it was in self-defense or to fight back and that the more they were victimized the more they fought back.[22] One researcher suggests that women should be discouraged from engaging in minor violence because it places them at risk for retaliation from men and men are more likely to be able to inflict injury.[23]

Clearly, there are women who use violence in relationships provocatively outside the context of fighting back or self- defense. The extent of this problem, as we noted earlier, remains unknown but is ripe for additional study.

The theories explaining male violence cited earlier may also have some relevance for women, although the picture is not clear.

Why Some Women are Reluctant to End Abusive Relationships

Police commonly express frustration that many of the battered women they deal with do not leave their batterers. Although many women do leave physically abusive relationships, others remain even after police intervene. There is no reliable information about the percentage of women who stay in physically abusive relationships. Researchers offer a number of explanations for the resistance by some to leave an abuser.[24]

Cycle of violence. Three cyclical phases in physically abusive intimate relationships keep a woman in the relationship: 1) a tension-building phase that includes minor physical and verbal abuse, 2) an acute battering phase, and 3) a makeup or honeymoon phase. The honeymoon phase lulls an abused woman into staying and the cycle repeats itself.

Battered woman syndrome. A woman is so fearful from experiencing cycles of violence that she no longer believes escape is possible.

Stockholm syndrome. A battered woman is essentially a hostage to her batterer. She develops a bond with and shows support for and kindness to her captor, perhaps because of her isolation from and deprivation of more normal relationships.

Traumatic bonding theory. A battered woman experienced unhealthy or anxious attachments to her parents who abused or neglected her. The woman develops unhealthy attachments in her adult relationships and accepts intermittent violence from her intimate partner. She believes the affection and claims of remorse that follow because she needs positive acceptance from and bonding with the batterer.

Psychological entrapment theory. A woman feels she has invested so much in the relationship, she is willing to tolerate the battering to save it.

Multifactor ecological perspective. Staying in physically abusive relationships is the result of a combination of factors, including family history, personal relationships, societal norms, and social and cultural factors.

Factors Contributing to Domestic Violence

Understanding the risk factors associated with domestic violence will help you frame some of your own local analysis questions, determine good effectiveness measures, recognize key intervention points, and select appropriate responses. Risk factors do not automatically mean that a person will become a domestic violence victim or an offender. Also, although some risk factors are stronger than others, it is difficult to compare risk factor findings across studies because of methodological differences between studies.

Age

The female age group at highest risk for domestic violence victimization is 16 to 24.[25] Among one segment of this high-risk age group—undergraduate college students—22 percent of female respondents in a Canadian study reported domestic violence victimization, and 14 percent of male respondents reported physically assaulting their dating partners in the year before the survey.[26] And although the victimization of teen girls is estimated to be high, it is difficult to "...untangle defensive responses from acts of initial violence against a dating partner."[27]

Socioeconomic Status

Although domestic violence occurs across income brackets, it is most frequently reported by the poor who more often rely on the police for dispute resolution. Victimization surveys indicate that lower-income women are, in fact, more frequently victims of domestic violence than wealthier women. Women with family incomes less than $7,500 are five times more likely to be victims of violence by an intimate than women with family annual incomes between $50,000 and $74,000.[28]

Although the poorest women are the most victimized by domestic violence,[29] one study also found that women receiving government income support payments through Aid for Families with Dependent Children (AFDC) were three times more likely to have experienced physical aggression by a current or former partner during the previous year than non-AFDC supported women.[30]

Race

Overall, in the United States, blacks experience higher rates of victimization than other groups: black females experience intimate violence at a rate 35 percent higher than that of white females, and black males experience intimate violence at a rate about 62 percent higher than that of white males and about two and a half times the rate of men of other races.[31] Other survey research, more inclusive of additional racial groups, finds that American Indian/Alaskan Native women experience significantly higher rates of physical abuse as well.[32,§]

Repeat Victimization

Domestic violence, generally, has high levels of repeat calls for police service.[33] For instance, police data in West Yorkshire (United Kingdom) showed that 42 percent of domestic violence incidents within one year were repeat offenses, and one-third of domestic violence offenders were responsible for two-thirds of all domestic violence incidents reported to the police. It is likely that some victims of domestic violence experience physical assault only once and others experience it repeatedly[34] over a period as short as 12 months.[35] British research suggests that the highest risk period for further assault is within the first four weeks of the last assault.[36]

---

§ It is unclear how much of the differences in victimization rates by race is the result of willingness to reveal victimization to survey interviewers (Tjaden and Thoennes, 2000).

Incarceration of Offenders

Offenders convicted of domestic violence account for about 25 percent of violent offenders in local jails and 7 percent of violent offenders in state prisons.[37] Many of those convicted of domestic violence have a prior conviction history: more than 70 percent of offenders in jail for domestic violence have prior convictions for other crimes, not necessarily domestic violence.[38]

Termination of the Relationship

Although there is a popular conception that the risk of domestic violence increases when a couple separates, in fact, most assaults occur during a relationship rather than after it is over.[39] However, still unknown is whether the severity (as opposed to the frequency) of violence increases once a battered woman leaves.

Pregnancy

Contrary to popular belief, pregnant women are no more likely than non-pregnant women to be victims of domestic violence.[40] In fact, some women get a reprieve from violence during pregnancy. The risk of abuse during pregnancy is greatest for women who experienced physical abuse before the pregnancy.[41] Some additional factors increase the risk during pregnancy: being young and poor and if the pregnancy was unintended.[42] Physical abuse during the pregnancy can result in pre-term delivery, low birth weight, birth defects, miscarriage, and fetal death.[43]

Multiple Risk Factors for Women and Men

Being young, black, low-income, divorced or separated, a resident of rental housing, and a resident of an urban area have all been associated with higher rates of domestic violence victimization among women.[44] For male victims, the patterns were nearly identical: being young, black, divorced or separated, or a resident of rental housing.[45] In New Zealand, a highly respected study found that the strongest predictor for committing partner violence among the many risk factors in childhood and adolescence is a history of aggressive delinquency before age 15.[46] The study also found that committing partner violence is strongly linked to cohabitation at a young age; a variety of mental illnesses; a background of family adversity; dropping out of school; juvenile aggression; conviction for other types of crime, especially violent crime; drug abuse; long-term unemployment; and parenthood at a young age.[47]

Other Risk Factors

Several other risk factors emerge from research:

-
- A verbally abusive partner is one of the most robust risk factors for intimate partner violence.[48]
- Women whose partners are jealous or tightly controlling are at increased risk of intimate violence and stalking.[49]
- There is a strong link between threat of bodily injury and actual bodily injury, suggesting that abuser threats should be taken seriously.[50]

Recently, there is much discussion among police about the link between pet abuse and domestic violence. Although some overlap is likely, particularly under the theory that many batterers are generally violent, not enough is known because of the types of studies undertaken. Some small surveys of domestic violence shelter residents suggest that some women might have left their abuser sooner but they worried about their pet's safety.[51]

Finally, although alcohol and drug use do not cause intimate partner battering, the risk of victim injury increases if a batterer is using alcohol or drugs.[52]

Understanding Your Local Problem

Notwithstanding its decline over the last decade, domestic violence stubbornly remains a frequent call for police, and efforts to further reduce it require general and specific information about the nature of the problem. You must combine the basic facts with a more specific understanding of your local problem. Analyzing the local problem carefully will help you design a more effective response strategy.

Stakeholders

In addition to criminal justice agencies, the following groups have an interest in the domestic violence problem and ought to be considered for the contribution they might make to gathering information about the problem and responding to it:

- domestic abuse protection, counseling, and advocacy organizations
- medical providers
- public health agencies
- employers
- schools (if school-aged children are affected)
- university faculty and research staff
- clergy.

Asking the Right Questions

The following are some critical questions you should ask in analyzing your community's domestic violence problem, even if the answers are not always readily available. Your answers to these and other questions will help you choose the most appropriate set of responses later on.

Aggregate data is an important source for analyzing your domestic violence problem, but it is useful only if domestic violence incidents are properly investigated and documented. It is important for investigating officers to understand the context and history of domestic assaults to determine if the incident is part of a series of abuse the victim has sustained and if it's likely to recur or escalate to more serious violence. For instance, in assessing individual incidents it is important to find out how long the abuse has been occurring, the frequency of the abuse, if the abuse is escalating, specific threats (even threats of suicide), whether threats can be carried out or there is an indication that they will be carried out, and whether victimization also involves other criminal behavior (i.e., harassing phone calls, vandalism, theft, burglary). You should analyze a variety of data sources such as calls for police service relating to domestic disputes, offense/incident reports of domestic violence, and databases from domestic abuse social service agencies.

Victims

- What percentage of the total number of calls for police service in your jurisdiction is for domestic violence?[§] What percentage of crime cases is for domestic violence (including stalking, vandalism, trespassing, harassment, restraining order violations, etc.)?
- What percentage of domestic dispute calls in your jurisdiction involves physical abuse? What percentage involves only verbal abuse?
- What percentage of domestic violence victims are women in your jurisdiction? What percentage are men?
- What percentage of domestic violence calls is unfounded?
- What percentage of domestic violence calls involves a repeat victim?[§§]
- What is the average time between calls from repeat victims?
- How many victims account for two calls to the police over a 12-month period? Three calls? Four calls? Five calls? More than five calls?
- What percentage of victims is pregnant at the time of assault?
- What percentage of domestic violence calls involves a current intimate? What percentage of calls involves a former intimate? What percentage of crime cases involves a current intimate versus former intimate?
- What percentage of domestic violence calls involves the following types of relationships: married and living together, live-in unmarried, separated, divorced, never married, never married but child in common, dating?
- When was the violence most serious (while dating, when living together, upon breakup)?
- What percentage of domestic violence victims actually leaves their abuser after police respond?
- What is the average age of reported domestic violence victims in the jurisdiction?
- What is the percentage of domestic violence victims who are homeless?

[§] Initial call takers may not have sufficient information to accurately determine whether or not domestic violence occurred. Consequently, call for service data will likely not be adequate to distinguish violent from non-violent domestic disputes. Police may need to refine call disposition codes to distinguish between different types of domestic disputes.

[§§] When assessing repeat victimization levels it is recommended that police use a rolling 12-month period (nothing less), which means looking for victimizations of the same person for the preceding 12 months, as opposed to simply looking for victimizations of the same person by calendar year (Bridgeman and Hobbs, 1997). Also, be alert to name changes among victims that might conceal a repeat victimization pattern. For further guidance, see Problem-Solving Tools Guide No. 4, Analyzing Repeat Victimization.

Offenders[§]

- In what percentage of cases are restraining orders violated?
- What parts of restraining orders are most violated (phone calls, distance from victim, etc.)?
- What percentage of offenders is arrested at the scene? What percentage is arrested at a later date? What is the average amount of time between the domestic violence crime report and the arrest when an offender left before the police arrived?
- What percentage of domestic violence incidents results in the arrest of both parties?
- What percentage of offenders has prior arrest records? What are the most common prior arrests for?
- What percentage of offenders is on probation, parole, or bail at the time of the incidents?
- What percentage of cases is disposed the day of arraignment?
- What percentage of arrested offenders is prosecuted?
- What percentage of misdemeanor and felony arrestees is kept in custody through the different stages of the adjudicatory process?
- What percentage of domestic violence felony arrests is dropped to misdemeanors by prosecutors?
- What percentage of offenders pleads guilty?
- What percentage of offenders is sentenced to prison for felony assault conviction?
- What percentage of offenders convicted of a misdemeanor is given jail time?
- Of those given jail time for a felony, what percentage re-assaults their former partner upon release?
- Of those given jail time for a misdemeanor, what percentage re-assaults their former partner upon release?
- What percentage of offenders is sentenced to alternatives to prison or jail (such as treatment programs or electronic monitoring)?
- What percentage of offenders sentenced to court- mandated treatment completes the treatment?
- What percentage of "treated" offenders re-offends against their former partner?

Incidents

- How many domestic violence calls per year involve physical violence? Is it on an increasing trend line, a decreasing trend line, or stable?
- What percentage of domestic violence calls to police is placed by victims? By neighbors, friends, employers, or children of victims?
- What percentage of domestic violence incidents involves the man as the primary aggressor? The woman?
- How many phone calls do domestic violence hotlines in your area receive annually? Is there a pattern to the calls (days of week, times of day, repeat victims calling)?

[§] You should review one worth of domestic violence cases from two years prior. For instance, if the current calendar year is 2006, review the results of domestic assault cases from the calendar year 2004. The two-year gap allows agencies to follow offenders from arrest to sentencing and even the participation in and completion of treatment.

Locations/Times

- When do domestic violence incidents commonly occur? During child custody exchanges? When the victim or offender returns home to collect belongings after the other party has moved out? On certain days of the week? Days of the month? Times of the day? Are patrol officers aware of these patterns?
- Where do domestic violence incidents commonly occur? Are there particular places such as apartment complexes or mobile home parks where incidents involving different victims and offenders commonly occur?

Current Responses

- What do the police department and other local agencies do to encourage victims to report domestic violence to the police?
- Are community support services adequate to address the counseling, housing, employment, childcare, substance abuse, emergency financial, and transportation needs of victims and child witnesses? Are these services easily accessible to victims?
- What percentage of domestic violence victims actually follows up with referral services?
- What is the average nightly number of domestic violence victims that local women's shelters house? What percentage of the victims in the shelters called the police to report the physical abuse? What is the average length of stay? What follow- up do these shelters provide once a victim leaves the shelter? Is there a sufficient number of shelter beds in the community for victims who exit abusive relationships?
- What is the current police agency policy regarding domestic violence incidents?
- What is the current prosecution policy regarding domestic violence incidents?
- Is treatment available? If so, what kind of treatment is it, and has it been evaluated?

Measuring Your Effectiveness

Measurement allows you to determine to what degree your efforts have succeeded, and suggests how you might modify your responses if they are not producing the intended results. You should take measures of your problem *before* you implement responses, to determine how serious the problem is, and *after* you implement them, to determine whether they have been effective. (For more detailed guidance on measuring effectiveness, see the companion guide to this series, *Assessing Responses to Problems: An Introductory Guide for Police Problem-Solvers.*)

Impact measures gauge the degree to which you reduced the harms caused by the problem. Process measures gauge the degree to which you implemented responses as planned. A good assessment employs both impact and process measures.

Impact Measures

The following are potentially useful measures of the effectiveness of responses to domestic violence:

- reduced number of actual incidents of domestic violence
- reduced number of domestic violence calls involving repeat victims
- reduced number of repeat offenders
- reduced frequency of battering by repeat offenders (longer time intervals between physical abuse)
- reduced percentage of domestic violence offenders who re-offend during or after treatment.

Process Measures

The following are potentially useful measures of the extent to which you implemented your planned responses:

- increased number of chronic or severe batterers incarcerated
- increased percentage of victims using referral services
- increased percentage of domestic violence calls to police being made by victims, as opposed to other parties
- increased information about repeat victimization from more comprehensive victim interviews and records review
- increased official follow-up with repeat victims and repeat offenders
- increased medical screening of women for domestic violence victimization
- increased percentage of domestic violence arrests resulting in a conviction
- reduced amount of time between arrest and conviction
- reduced percentage of incidents where both parties are arrested
- increased partnering with researchers to design evaluation of efforts
- increased availability of customized batterer treatment programs.

Responses to the Problem of Domestic Violence

Your analysis of your local problem should give you a better understanding of the patterns of domestic violence cases and calls in your jurisdiction. Once you have analyzed your local problem or important aspects of it and established a baseline for measuring effectiveness, you should consider possible responses to address the problem.

These strategies are drawn from a variety of sources, including descriptive materials, research studies, and police reports. It is critical that you tailor responses based on reliable analysis. In most cases, an effective strategy will involve implementing several different responses. Law enforcement responses alone are seldom effective in reducing or solving the problem. Do not limit yourself to considering what police can do: carefully consider others in your community who share responsibility for the problem and can help police better respond to it. In some cases, the responsibility of responding may need to shift toward those who have the capacity to implement more effective responses. (For more detailed information on shifting and sharing responsibility, see Response Guide No. 3, *Shifting and Sharing Responsibility for Public Safety Problems*).

General Considerations for an Effective Response Strategy

1. Implementing a comprehensive and collaborative response strategy. Comprehensive and collaborative approaches to reducing domestic violence are more likely to succeed than piecemeal approaches, but they require significant commitment from all participating. One research team wrote, "[a]n offense as complex as domestic violence is unlikely to be prevented by a single measure."[53] A thorough assessment of the current overall response to domestic violence can identify critical gaps in strategies, resources, and response protocols.

Although some communities have adopted a more integrated approach engaging advocates, police, and the criminal justice system,[§] for the most part, recidivism remains high. In the small studies of these integrated domestic violence approaches, there is evidence that victim satisfaction is high but insufficient evidence that recidivism and revictimization rates have decreased. One commentary suggests that the small core of persistent batterers (who are violent toward others as well as their intimates) are perhaps resistant to even highly coordinated efforts.[54]

To improve the likelihood that a comprehensive approach reduces recidivism and victimization requires a continuum of responses depending on the most reliable research and covering the different points in time most important to reducing domestic abuse: before an incident to keep it from occurring, during an incident to stop the immediate violence, and after an incident to reduce or prevent revictimization. It involves responses that focus on victims and potential victims and strategies that focus on offenders and potential offenders. As well, it involves the improved identification and reporting of cases of abuse between current and former intimates and dating partners.

The matrix below may help you organize the strategic focus, goals, and timing of your responses to domestic violence. This section is followed by information on the impact of specific responses to domestic violence strategies. Many of the responses will require the support and collaboration of other governmental agencies and community nonprofits.

2. Educating collaborative partners. Each partner in a domestic violence reduction collaborative brings a unique perspective and body of knowledge. It is important for members of domestic violence collaborations to operate with precise and accurate information about what does and does not work and about the dimensions of the problem in your community. Do not assume that other professional groups participating in the collaborative have the most up-to-date knowledge about the problem or are following prescribed protocols.

3. Tailoring the police response on the basis of offender and victim risk. Some researchers advocate a *graded response* to domestic violence. They view batterers along a continuum—some are easily dissuaded from rebattering, others require increased actions—and a graded or tiered approach to control offender behavior can be effective. For instance, we know that a percentage of batterers is deterred from rebattering simply by having the police called on them, so encouraging reporting is essential; others may be deterred with the additional application of a restraining order. More is required to keep other batterers from

---

[§] For a fuller description of the different types of integrated approaches adopted and their studies, see Buzawa and Buzawa, chapter 15 (2003).

rebattering, which suggests a need to refine assessments about who these batterers are.[55] Some researchers also suggest a graded approach to victim safety for similar reasons: some victims are at low risk of being revictimized and some are at higher risk.

Strategic Focus	Strategic Times for Responses	Goal	Police Role	Other Agencies, Organizations, Group
At-risk population	Before incidents	Prevention; persuade those at risk that, if abused, call the police	Alert and educate at-risk victim population; educate/warn at-risk offending population	Public health organizations; domestic violence coalitions; schools and educators; medical professionals
Peers and neighbors of at-risk individuals	Ongoing	Getting peers and neighbors to call the police if they learn of domestic abuse	Educate these groups about the importance of calling the police to reduce the violence	Public health organizations; domestic violence coalitions; educators
Injured women and men	During medical care	Screen the injured for domestic violence; raise awareness of available services; provide medical care	Engage the medical profession and link medical professionals with appropriate referral organizations	Medical professionals
Individual incident	During	Violence cessation	Stop the violence; identify primary aggressor; accurately identify abuse history	Medical and public health professionals
Immediately after incident	After; ongoing	Prevent revictimization	Assist with victim safety; develop tailored strategies for victim and offender based on risk/physical violence history; increase focus on high-risk offenders; ensure victim is linked with needed resources; increase focus on high-risk victims; ongoing monitoring	Domestic violence victim advocates, victims' friends and family, shelters, victim services, criminal justice system, treatment services

Figure 2. Matrix of Responses to Domestic Violence

Graded approaches to both victim and offender can be effective ways to reduce revictimization. British researchers conducted several evaluations and found that significant reductions in repeat victimization are achievable.[56] The key to reduction is that, at each level, police (and others) must focus equal attention on the victim *and* the offender. The victim and the offender must know about the actions police have and will take in relation to each other. Graded approaches must be applied quickly because the highest risk period for further assault is within the first four weeks of the last assault.[57]

Under a graded approach victims are assigned to one of three follow-up response levels based on the following:

- the harm the abuser caused or threatened
- the victim's account of previous incidents not reported to the police
- all incidents recorded in police databases involving the same victim with the same offender[§]
- the offender's previous violence to other victims.[58]

Each of the three levels to which a victim is assigned requires some follow-up. There is in an increase in the variety and intensity of safety measures used to protect the victim and to restrict the offender from rebattering if the offender's violence and criminal history indicates he is at an increased risk to re-offend.[59] Evaluations of graded approaches found reduced domestic violence calls and increased time intervals between violence.[60] The methods to protect the victim or deter the offender can include a variety of situational crime prevention opportunity blocking mechanisms, such as the following:

- increased police surveillance of victims' homes
- greater coordination with other parts of the criminal justice system
- pendant alarms for at-risk victims
- video cameras placed in high-risk victims' homes
- cocoon watch over victims[§§]
- target hardening of victims' vulnerable properties
- police watch of offenders
- police opposition to bail
- electronic ankle bracelet monitoring of high-risk released offenders
- alarm-activated recording devices with two-way speech capability (allowing victims to speak directly to the police, and vice versa).[§§§]

Tailoring police responses to particular offenders based on the seriousness and frequency of their offenses has been successfully applied in the context of conventional crime and may be as useful for dealing with domestic batterers.[§§§§] This is likely because much domestic violence is committed by repeat and chronic offenders who may be particularly vulnerable because they often are under various forms of legal supervision due to past offending.[61]

According to Buzawa and Buzawa, "The criminal justice system must develop the capabilities to identify those batterers for whom normal deterrence can be effective, perhaps the majority in terms of numbers of incidents... [i]t should also be able to differentiate, segregate, and incapacitate batterers who must be deterred by special approaches."[62]

[§] Incidents other than domestic violence are reviewed because they may be indicators of escalating aggressiveness (Hanmer et al. 1999).

[§§] With a victim's permission, neighbors, relatives, friends, or all three are asked to look out for the victim and immediately call if the offender returns.

[§§§] To view the 25 techniques of situational crime prevention, see www.popcenter.org/25techniques. htm in the Center for Problem-Oriented Policing. Click on a particular technique to view its description.

[§§§§] See Kennedy, Waring, and Piehl (2001) for a description of the pulling levers/focused deterrence application in the homicide context, and Spelman (1990) for a discussion of repeat offender programs. See Kennedy (2002) for a discussion of the application of the approach to domestic violence.

Specific Responses to Domestic Violence

4. Educating potential victims and offenders. Some police agencies participate in domestic violence awareness campaigns and school programming, such as classroom instruction to teens about dating violence and ways to handle conflict. Domestic violence prevention messages may target the general population or specific populations. For example, campaigns may be designed to encourage victim reporting, deter potential offenders, or raise the consciousness of potential witnesses of abuse (neighbors, friends, relatives).[§] However, the effect of these prevention strategies is unknown.[63] For instance, few of the programs developed to reduce teen dating violence have been evaluated, and of those that have, there have been mixed results.[64] Although some report an increase in knowledge in the targeted population and greater familiarity with available resources to help victims, this does not necessarily translate into a reduction in the incidence level of dating violence.

As a rule, prevention is more likely to work if highly targeted. General campaigns are not typically effective. Highly targeted campaigns that focus on a specific target group or geographic area can have some impact. Offender-oriented campaigns, which are designed to raise potential offenders' perceptions that there will be meaningful consequences to battering, are more likely to be effective than campaigns that appeal to potential offenders' morals.[§§]

Prevention efforts targeting potential victims should focus on those at higher risk, such as young women ages 16 to 24, as they experience the highest rates of intimate violence. Special efforts should be made to reach the poorest women in this age group as they are at an even higher risk. In addition, some recent immigrant communities, depending on the laws and privileges in the home country, may show a high level of domestic abuse, particularly if there is a lack of familiarity with assault laws in the adopted country.[§§§] One of the reasons crime prevention campaigns have had limited success is that potential victims do not see themselves as such; victim-oriented prevention campaigns must overcome this threshold issue.

5. Encouraging domestic violence victims and witnesses to call the police. Police and other members of a domestic violence reduction collaborative should encourage people to call the police if they are victims of, witnesses to, or know a victim of domestic violence. Prevention and education efforts should include this as a core message. A study of more than 2,500 domestic violence victims concluded that calling the police had a strong deterrent effect on revictimization, even when the police did not make an arrest, when the offender had a prior history of violence against the victim, and when the assault was sexual. Calling the police was beneficial even when the violence was severe. In addition, offender retaliation did not appear to be more likely even when a victim rather than a third party called police.[65,§]

[§] The Lancashire (United Kingdom) Police Constabulary placed messages about domestic violence on police vehicles, beer glass coasters in bars, utility bills, and lampposts, and used radio advertising to increase awareness of domestic violence.

[§§] For more in-depth information about prevention campaigns and the conditions under which they are most likely to be effective, see Response Guide No. 5, Crime Prevention Publicity Campaigns.

[§§§] For a review of the research pertaining to domestic violence and immigrant populations, see Buzawa and Buzawa (2003).

[§] The study, which examined felony and misdemeanor violence, male and female offenders, and couples in different types of relationships, tracked victims for three years.

6. Encouraging other professionals to screen for domestic violence victimization and make appropriate referrals. The American Medical Association adopted domestic violence screening and referral guidelines for medical practitioners.[66] Physicians should screen injured women patients to determine if domestic violence was the cause of the injury.[§§] Medical professionals should also discuss domestic violence with pregnant patients during prenatal checkups. Physicians' documentation of specific incidents of domestic abuse can be critical to the successful prosecutions of batterers.[§§§]

In spite of these professional recommendations, most physicians are reluctant to routinely screen women for domestic violence, citing a lack of training in how to conduct screenings and insufficient knowledge of appropriate responses and referrals when a patient discloses domestic violence.[67]

7. Providing victims with emergency protection and services after an assault. Battered women's shelters protect women from further harm after an assault, sometimes on referral from the police and sometimes not. Typical services include a domestic violence hotline, temporary housing, information and referrals to other social services, safety planning, victim advocacy for emergency benefits or at court proceedings, and referrals for legal services.[§§§§]

The first shelter for battered women and their children opened in London in 1972. There are currently more than 2,000 shelters in the United States.[68] In most communities, shelters raise community funds for operation; in some communities, police contribute a portion of their budget to aid in shelter operation. Shelters often rely on volunteers and a few paid personnel to provide round- the-clock assistance to battered women and their families. Little is known about the number of repeat victims served annually, the length of average stays, or the effectiveness of shelter services in preventing subsequent violence.

Although there are confidentiality issues to resolve or respect, police should seek to exchange information with domestic violence victim service providers as much as possible to learn more about the domestic violence victim population, some of whom do not seek out police assistance. This information exchange can aid in identifying the highest risk victims and offenders, targeting prevention efforts, designing safety plans, and learning more about the community's offenders.

Recently emerging are family justice centers, which house domestic violence victim services in one location to increase victim survival, independence, and recovery. Formerly, victim services were scattered in different places, sometimes at opposite ends of cities. If victims followed up with these fragmented services, they too often experienced the frustration of retelling the story of violence to every individual provider.[§]

[§] The American Academy of Pediatrics, the American Medical Association, and the American College of Obstetricians and Gynecologists all endorse screening.

[§§§] See Issac and Enos (2001) for guidelines for proper medical documentation of battered patients.

[§§§§] More than 60 U.S. law schools offer student advocacy services for domestic violence victims at court proceedings (Roberts, 2002b).

[§] The San Diego Family Justice Center provides victims with advocacy, childcare, clothing, counseling, court support, deaf/hard-of-hearing assistance, emergency housing, food, forensic documentation of injuries, housing for pets, internet access, law enforcement, legal assistance, locksmith services, medical services, military assistance, phones, phone cards, restraining orders, support groups, safety planning, spiritual support, transportation, and victim compensation (San Diego Family Justice Center).

8. Assessing the threat of repeat victimization. Gathering accurate information about past abuse, including unreported incidents, is critical in assessing a victim's current risk and tailoring appropriate offender interventions. Although there is no foolproof profile of a repeat batterer or repeat victim, having a complete and accurate picture of both the victim's and the offender's history of abuse is useful for predicting future risk. You may need to gather records from other jurisdictions where the victim or offender lived. You should also be alert for other related behaviors such as threats of violence, harassment, trespassing, vandalism, stalking, protective order violations, and prior use of a gun, as these behaviors offer clues as to whether abusive behavior is chronic and/ or escalating.

You should supplement official records with the victim's personal knowledge about the offender. Keep in mind that for a variety of social and psychological reasons, victims may be reluctant to reveal the extent of the battering, particularly to police.

Police may consider soliciting the assistance of trained medical professionals to help determine a victim's abuse history. A study of one initiative in which a doctor and a nurse (or paramedic) accompanied police on domestic violence calls found victims revealing much more about the extent to which their partner battered them than police typically elicit, suggesting that victims may feel more comfortable reporting repeat victimization to medical professionals. Even with the high levels of repeat victimization uncovered, few victims had sought counseling, shelter, or medical treatment for the prior assaults.[69]

There is great interest in developing an assessment instrument police can use to predict and help prevent domestic violence homicides. Although some such instruments exist, they tend to over-predict lethality. This is because only a very small portion of domestic violence victims are murdered and distinguishing between victims who will be murdered and those who will not remains elusive. For instance, even though offender unemployment is a risk factor, the vast majority of unemployed abusers do not murder their current or former intimates. Even when you combine unemployment with other risks it does not give you the profile of a murderer, but someone who is at an increased risk of battering.

9. Arresting offenders. Many U.S. police agencies adopted pro-arrest or mandatory arrest domestic violence policies in the 1980s and early 1990s. Propelling these policies were:

- legal decisions establishing civil liability against the police for failure to protect women victims of domestic violence[70]
- the women's movement's advocacy and activism on behalf of domestic violence victims. The women's movement challenged the view of domestic violence as a family problem that could or should be handled privately or differently from stranger assault
- widespread dissemination of pro-arrest results of a misdemeanor domestic assault research study.[71],[§]

Generally, pro-arrest laws and policies apply not only to spouses, but to unmarried partners, former intimates, and persons who had or raised a child together. In many jurisdictions the laws or policies apply to both heterosexual and homosexual relationships.

[§] More than 300 newspapers reported the results of the study, unprecedented coverage for that time (Fagan, 1996)

Police interventions in domestic violence incidents have expanded beyond merely separating and counseling the parties; they've become full-blown criminal investigations in which witnesses are interviewed, neighbors are canvassed, injuries are photographed, physical evidence is collected, future threats are assessed, and victims are referred to follow-up protective services and helped to plan for their future safety. In addition, some states permit police to seize firearms from alleged batterers,[72] and federal laws generally prohibit convicted misdemeanant batterers or those against whom there is a valid order of protection from possessing a gun.[73] All U.S. states now permit police to make warrantless arrests for both misdemeanor and felony assaults.[74]

The highly influential 1980s study of police interventions in domestic violence incidents in Minneapolis found deterrence value in arrest in misdemeanor domestic assaults, as compared to two other interventions — separation of parties or mediation of the dispute at the scene.[75] However, less well-reported replication studies in the late 1980s produced mixed results.[76] A more recent analysis combining five of the replication studies concluded there is only some *modest* deterrent effect from arrest.[77] However, even this modest effect should be viewed with caution for several reasons:

- These studies considered only misdemeanor, not felony, domestic assaults.
- Offenders' employment status appears to be an important variable: unemployed offenders have less at stake (they will not lose their jobs) if they re-offend and thus are less deterred by arrest.[78]
- A prior arrest record for any crime, and intoxication at the time of the incident, increase the risk that batterers will re-offend after arrest.[79]
- A small group of offenders, perhaps fewer than 10 percent, appear to continue battering regardless of the intervention, including arre st.[80,§§]

A more recent study of victims of both misdemeanor and felony assaults concluded the following:

- calling the police was a strong deterrent to repeat battering
- the effects of arrest were small and statistically insignificant but could not be ruled out completely
- if arrest does have an effect, it is likely to be modest, particularly in comparison to the effect of calling the police.[81,§§§]

Victim advocacy groups have generally not been swayed by findings of little or modest effect of arrest. For many advocates, batterer arrest is seen as an important symbol of a woman's legal right to be free of intimate partner violence[82] and, moreover, argue that police continue to arrest other types of offenders without strong evidence of its effectiveness. Arrest

---

§§ Nearly ten percent of the more than 3,000 studied battered repeatedly regardless of the intervention. This group of 250 batterers accounted for 7,380 battering incidents in the six months after the initial intervention. Interventions, even arrest, did not deter this small but violent group.

§§§ The researchers found that batterers who battered again had an increased likelihood of battering a third time, and offenders who were under the influence of alcohol or drugs at the time of the incident were more likely to re-offend. The researchers did not find that marital status, poverty, race, education or gender improved the effect of arrest, but because they did not have access to employment information, they could not rule out that arrest deters employed offenders but not unemployed offenders.

is believed to be an important message to children that abuse of their parent is illegal, and perhaps also a deterrent to male children as they become men.[§] This belief has not yet been properly studied, however.

10. Issuing and enforcing restraining orders. Restraining orders (also known as "stay away" or protective orders) are intended to prevent offenders from further harassing, threatening or contacting the victims. Courts have made restraining orders widely available to domestic violence victims, whether or not they file a police report.[§§] Courts may issue a temporary (time-limited) restraining order even when the "party being restrained" is not present or represented. Protective relief may be temporary or permanent.[§§§] Violation of these orders is now a criminal offense in all U.S. states.[83]

Domestic violence restraining orders are frequently violated although some offenders may be deterred by them. Some research findings suggest that a victim is more likely to seek a protective order if the partner had a criminal history of violent offending, which may be why so many orders are violated; those with robust abuse histories may be the least likely to be deterred by written limits[§§§§] so police are advised that more must be done in these cases.

11. Aggressively pursuing criminal prosecution of severe domestic violence cases and publicizing convictions. Police pro-arrest and mandatory arrest policies have generated significantly larger caseloads for prosecutors. Similarly, prosecution policies against dropping charges ("no-drop") even when the victim expresses such a desire (the functional equivalent of "mandatory arrest" for police) has further strained prosecutorial resources.[84,§§§§§] Although such police and prosecution policies can have the beneficial effect of reducing an offender's urge to retaliate against the victim because responsibility for the prosecution is no longer in the victim's hands,[§§§§§§] it is not yet clear whether such policies have limited further violence or have had the unintended consequence of discouraging some victims from calling police in the first instance.[85]

"No-drop" policies have some drawbacks. Victim discretion is further reduced, case backlogs increase, and time to disposition is lengthened, which can strain resources devoted to pretrial victim safety.[86] The increase in prosecutorial workload can force prosecutors to trade off the prosecution of other crimes for misdemeanor battering. It is now apparent that prosecutors in "no- drop" jurisdictions rarely prosecute all cases; they retain some level of discretion in case filing decisions, typically at the intake and case screening point.[87] Police

---

[§] Victims of domestic abuse have also called for police agencies to monitor, address, and more appropriately sanction officers engaging in domestic assault. Although some police agencies have been responsive, additional efforts are required for victims to have higher levels of confidence in police agencies' domestic violence response policies.

[§§] In most jurisdictions these are obtained from civil court; however, some jurisdictions also grant concurrent jurisdiction to criminal court. Criminal courts can also issue these once a criminal proceeding begins.

[§§§] Civil restraining orders were in fact developed to counter the reluctance of police, prosecutors, and criminal courts to treat domestic violence as a serious criminal matter (Buzawa and Buzawa, 2003).

[§§§§] For a good review of the research about protective orders, see Buzawa and Buzawa (2003).

[§§§§§] The rationale for "no-drop" policies is that the state has an independent interest in seeing domestic violence offenders prosecuted because of the harm caused to victims, victims' children, and potential victims.

[§§§§§§] Victim recanting remains high. As a result, many prosecutors rely on physical evidence such as photographs and medical reports of victims' injuries and out-ofcourt statements (e.g., 911 call tapes of in-progress assaults) to counter uncooperative and fearful victims. For an excellent review of prosecutorial response to the increased numbers of domestic violence cases and studies of prosecutorial case screening practices, see Buzawa and Buzawa chapter 11 (2003).

must therefore help prosecutors identify the most severe and chronic cases from among the many arrests and encourage prosecutors to prosecute such cases vigorously, make special efforts to protect the victim,[§] and publicize convictions so as to maximize the general deterrent effect.

12. Establishing special domestic violence courts. There are more than 200 domestic violence courts in the United States, and a growing number in the United Kingdom as well. The proliferation of these courts is part of a wider trend toward specialty courts: drug court, mental health court, drunk driving court, etc.[§§] Advocates for specialty courts believe they result in improved outcomes: an increase in specialty knowledge critical to case handling (including the dynamics of the underlying crime/behavior, whether it is battering, drinking, or schizophrenia, depending upon the court), timely attention to the case, and a concentration of appropriate resources that traditional courts do not have that can lead to more effective case handling.

Typically in specialty courts a single judge works with a community team to develop a case plan for the defendant and uses pending criminal sanctions to compel a defendant's compliance with treatment. The judge monitors compliance and imposes criminal sanctions if the defendant fails to keep to the case plan.

Early evaluations of domestic violence courts generally report on how these courts handle their workload, victim satisfaction, and issues of implementation. It remains unclear if these courts impact recidivism. Researchers who examined these courts in New York describe some of the more important unresolved issues:

> Many domestic violence advocates are hesitant to embrace the idea that domestic violence courts are "problem-solving courts." There are substantial differences between domestic violence courts and other problem-solving courts. Many of these differences stem from how success is measured and to whom services are offered. Drug courts can easily look to see whether defendants are successfully completing their court-mandated drug-treatment programs. But domestic violence courts are not targeted at "rehabilitating" defendants. Indeed, services are offered primarily to help victims achieve independence. The primary "service" offered to defendants is batterers programs. But in New York, batterers programs are used by domestic violence courts primarily as a monitoring tool rather than as a therapeutic device. This approach is based on the research about batterers programs, which is extremely mixed. It is unclear whether these programs have any impact at all in deterring further violence.[88]

13. Providing treatment for batterers. Some batterer treatment programs are voluntary; others are court- mandated. In some jurisdictions, prosecutors recommend these programs as part of pre-trial diversion; in others they are part of court-ordered mandatory sentencing. Many states now mandate batterer treatment.[89]

Batterer treatment programs may take a variety of forms. Many offer group treatment with a focus on anger management. Others include individual assessments and individual counseling, and substance abuse and/or mental health treatment.[90]

Unfortunately, few batterer treatment programs have undergone thorough evaluation, and those that have show a mix of positive and negative results.[91] Court-mandated treatment is more likely to result in batterers completing programs,[92] "but there is little evidence to support the effectiveness of one batterer program over another in reducing recidivism."[93]

The quality of the evaluations of batterer treatment programs have improved over time but continue to encounter both methodological and programmatic challenges as illustrated by two recent studies of batterer treatment programs, one in Broward County, Florida and the other in Brooklyn, New York.[94] In both, offender treatment was based on the Duluth treatment model, which is the most commonly used.[§] The Broward evaluation found that treatment attendance did not reduce battering, but that offenders who were married, employed, or homeowners were less likely to batter again (that is, these offenders had a "stake in conformity"). Also, younger men, particularly those with no stable residence, were more likely to rebatter.[95] In Brooklyn, the evaluation showed minor improvement for some of the batterers (that is, some reduction in the number of battering incidents for those attending a 26-week treatment program rather than the same program condensed into an eight- week schedule). In neither case were batterers' attitudes toward domestic abuse changed. Even these evaluation results are not fully reliable because both studies experienced data collection challenges as a result of a high drop-out rate by offenders, difficulty finding relocated victims for follow-up interviews, and inadequate offender attitude assessment tools. In addition, judges sometimes overrode random assignment of batterers, thereby tainting the makeup of the different groups studied.[96] Evaluations of other types of treatment programs, including cognitive- behavior therapy (another widely used approach), have also suffered from similar methodological flaws.

Several experts suggest that greater refinement in assigning batterers to appropriate programs could improve results. The most chronic batterers should receive the most intensive treatment.[97] A "one-size fits-all" approach to batterer intervention cannot accommodate the diverse population of batterers entering the criminal justice system."[98] The different types of batterers—family-only, one who is generally violent even to others, dysphoric (mood-disordered) /borderline—may require tailored treatment.[99]

Experts recommend that treatment programs be designed around explicit theories. In other words, each intervention proposed should have a specific underlying theory. Outcomes expected from each of the interventions should be clearly defined and then evaluated for short- and long-term impact. Designing treatment programs that fit this model requires close collaboration between service providers and researchers.[100] In addition, the timing of treatment may be an important element to success.

"Counseling ideally would begin almost immediately after a violent episode, when the offender feels most remorseful, most frightened of the criminal justice system, and most receptive to demands for change."[101]

Responses with Limited Effectiveness

14. Arresting both parties in a domestic violence incident. Arresting both participants in a domestic violence incident (so-called "dual arrest") under the principle of mutual combat is ineffective toward interrupting the pattern of violence between the two. In the context of

---

[§] The Duluth model suggests that batterers seek to control their partners (or ex-partners) and this must change for batterers' behavior to change (Pence and Paymar, 1993). The model "helps offenders to understand how their socialized beliefs about male dominance impede intimacy; that violence is intentional and a choice designed to control their intimate partner; that the effects of abusive behavior damage the family; and that everyone has the ability to change" (Minnesota Program Development, Inc.).

the longer history of the relationship—as opposed to the one incident—there is nearly always one primary aggressor. When police respond to a domestic violence call, self-defense may look like "mutual combat" and only detailed interviews of the parties (their prior abuse history) and witnesses may reveal the primary aggressor. In addition, at the scene of domestic abuse, "a victim may feel safe to express anger against the batterer in the presence of the police ... giving the impression that they are the perpetrators."[102] As a result, more than 20 states have enacted primary aggressor or "predominant aggressor" laws. Even these might not be enough to discourage dual arrest practices unless the law recognizes the importance of ascertaining the pattern/history and not just the aggression within a single incident. To complicate matters, there are couples in which both partners are violent. These are more likely to entail "recurrent acts of minor violence initiated by either party, but the type of violence generally seen by police (and in shelter and clinical samples) is more likely to involve serious and frequent beatings, as well as the terrorizing of women."[§]

APPENDIX: SUMMARY OF RESPONSES TO DOMESTIC VIOLENCE

The table below summarizes the responses to domestic violence, the mechanism by which they are intended to work, the conditions under which they ought to work best, and some factors you should consider before implementing a particular response. It is critical that you tailor responses to local circumstances, and that you can justify each response based on reliable analysis. In most cases, an effective strategy will involve implementing several different responses. Law enforcement responses alone are seldom effective in reducing or solving the problem.

Response No.	Page No.	Response	How It Works	Works Best If...	Considerations
General Considerations for an Effective Response Strategy					
1.	23	Implementing a comprehensive and collaborative response strategy	Addresses both victimization and offending; identifies gaps in strategies, resources, and response protocols	...the collaborative does an appraisal of the response to domestic violence to identify what is and gaps	Group should be educated about what works in reducing domestic violence victimization and revictimization and the limitations of some approaches; group commits to ongoing evaluation of efforts; collaboration with a university researcher may be useful; will probably require a champion who pursues a collaborative response strategy
2.	26	Educating collaborative partners	Increases likelihood of adoption of proven effective responses	...collaborative partners commit to relying on facts and research, rather than anecdotes	Requires high level of coordination

---

[§] For a good discussion of "dual arrest" research and the complexities within the primary aggressor issue, see Buzawa and Buzawa (2003).

Table (Continued)

Response No.	Page No.	Response	How It Works	Works Best If...	Considerations
3.	26	Tailoring the police response on the basis of offender and victim risk	Applies the most appropriate type and level of response to the particular victim and offender	...offender is told about the measures police put in place; graded responses are applied quickly because the highest risk period for further assault is within the first four weeks of the last assault	Accurate victimization and offending information is needed to select the most appropriate level of response
Specific Responses to Domestic Violence					
4.	28	Educating potential victims and offenders	Encourages victim reporting, de-motivates potential offenders, or raises the Consciousness of potential witnesses to abuse	...efforts are highly targeted and focused on a geographic area or certain high- risk groups	If evaluation mechanisms are not put in place, the campaign, which can be
5.	30	Encouraging victims and witnesses to call the police	Deters potential and actual offenders	...at-risk populations and their peers and neighbors believe that calling the police will be effective	Hard core batterers are not likely to be deterred just by calling, so more must be done
6.	30	Encouraging Other professional to screen for domestic violence victimization and make appropriate referrals	Increases likelihood of effective intervention in abusive relationships	...doctors have adequate training	Requires active participation of medical profession
7.	31	Providing victims with emergency protection and services after an assault	Provides safe place for victims; Improves information sharing between police and victim service providers; informs police about high-risk victims and offenders; links victims with other essential services	...there is a belief that each service provider, including the police, has a common interest in ensuring victim safety *and* de-motivating the offender	May require extensive Discussions by parties to define roles, responsibilities, and limits of partnership; collaboration requires agreement about confidentiality issues
8.	32	Assessing the threat of repeat victimization	Determines need for immediate protection of victim and apprehension of offender	...officers/ collaborators trained to assess revictimization threats	Requires training and timely and accurate intelligence information

Table (Continued)

Response No.	Page No.	Response	How It Works	Works Best If...	Considerations
9.	33	Arresting offenders	Incapacitates offender during high-risk periods and deters potential and actual offenders	...a graded response to battering is adopted depending on the likelihood of rebattering; used with situational crime prevention opportunity blocking frame work	Under some conditions arrest may increase risk of revictimization; some offenders undeterred by arrest
10.	36	Issuing and enforcing restraining orders	Removes excuses for offender and victim to come into contact with one another	...police recognize that defiance of a restraining order may be an indicator of future risk to the victim	Police see violation of a restraining order as the need for a victim safety plan, and the adoption of a graded response to both victim and offender depending on the circumstances
11.	36	Aggressively pursuing criminal prosecution of severe domestic violence cases and publicizing convictions	Incapacitates offender and deters potential and actual offenders	...police and prosecutors can agree beforehand what constitutes chronic and severe offenders; used as part of pulling levers/focused deterrence approach or other graded responses to batterers	Requires proper evidence collection; should also include Coordination and prosecutor participation around victim safety
12.	37	Establishing special domestic violence courts	Enhances knowledge of particular victims and offenders and ability to monitor compliance with court orders	...courts participate in an evaluation to improve knowledge about recidivism reduction; courts can discern between batterers who can be deterred and those who	May require extra court resources
13.	39	Providing treatment for batterers	Reduces batterers' court-ordered; date knowledge of propensity for violence	...treatment is treatment has proven effective - ness and is tailored to a specific type of batterer	Requires up-to-effectiveness of different treatment approaches
Responses With Limited Effectiveness					
14.	41	Arresting both parties in a domestic violence incident	Incapacitates both parties during high-risk period		Consumes scarce jail and court resources and not generally recommended for reasons discussed earlier in this guide

REFERENCES

American Medical Association Data on Violence Between Intimates (2000). Available at www.amaassn.org/ama/pub/category/13577.html. Adopted recommendations available at www.ama-assn.org/ama/ pub/category/1 3577.html#RECOMMENDATION.

Anderson, D., Chenery S. & Pease K. (1995). *Biting Back: Tackling Repeat Burglary and Car Crime. Crime Detection and Prevention Series*, Paper 58. London: Home Office.

Ascione, F. (2004). *Children and Animals: Exploring the Roots of Kindness and Cruelty.* West Lafayette (Indiana): Purdue University Press.

Australian Institute of Health and Welfare (2005). *Female SAAP Clients and Children Escaping Domestic and Family Violence 2003-2004.* Bulletin No. 30, AIHW Cat. No., AUS 64. Canberra. Available at www.aihw.gov.au/publications/aus/bulletin30 /bulletin 30.pdf.

Brewster, M. (2002). "Domestic Violence Theories, Research, and Practice Implications." In A. Roberts (ed.), *Handbook of Domestic Violence Intervention Strategies.* Oxford and New York: Oxford University Press.

Bridgeman, C., & Hobbs, L. (1997). *Preventing Repeat Victimisation: The Police Officers' Guide.* Police Research Group. London: Home Office.

Brookoff, D., O'Brien, K., Cook, C., Thompson, T. & Williams, C. (1997). "Characteristics of Participants in Domestic Violence: Assessment at the Scene of Domestic Assault." *JAMA: The Journal of the American Medical Association, 277*(17),1 369-1 373.

Bruno v. Codd, 47 N.Y. 2d 582, 393 N.E. 2d 976, 419 N.Y.S. 2d 901 (1979).

Bureau of Alcohol, Tobacco, Firearms, and Explosives (2004). Relevant regulations related to 18 U.S.C. 922(g) and (n), 27 CFR 178.32(a) and (b), and 924(a)(24). Available at www.atf.gov/pub/fire pub/i33103.   pdf and www.atf.gov/pub/fire-explo pub /i33 1 02.pdf.

Buzawa, E. & Buzawa, C. (2003). *Domestic Violence: The Criminal Justice Response* (3rd ed). Thousand Oaks, London, and New Delhi: SAGE Publications.

——— (1996). *Do Arrests and Restraining Orders Work?* Thousand Oaks, London, and New Delhi: SAGE Publications.

Carrington, K. & Phillips, J. (2003). *Domestic Violence in Australia—an Overview of the Issues*, E-Brief. Available at www.aph.gov.au/library/intguide/SP violence. htm.

Charlotte-Mecklenburg (North Carolina) Police Department (2002). *Baker One Domestic Violence Intervention Project: Improving Response to Chronic Domestic Violence Victims.* Finalist for the Herman Goldstein Award for Excellence in Problem-Oriented Policing. Available at www.popcenter.org/library/ goldstein/2002/02-09(F) .pdf.

Chenery, S., Holt, J. & Pease, K. (1997). *Biting Back II: Reducing Repeat Victimisation in Huddersfield. Crime Detection and Prevention Series*, Paper 82. London: Home Office.

Dekeseredy, W., Saunders, D., Schwartz, M. & Alvi, S. (1997). "The Meanings and Motives for Women's Use of Violence in Canadian College Dating Relationships: Results from a National Survey." *Sociological Spectrum,* Vol. *17(2),*199-222.

Fagan, J. (1996). *"The Criminalization of Domestic Violence: Promises and Limits."* National Institute of Justice Research Report. Available at www.ncjrs.org/ txtfiles /crimdom.txt.

Feder, L. & Forde, D. (2003). "The Broward Experiment." In Jackson, S., L. Feder, D. Forde, R. Davis, C. Maxwell, and B. Taylor (eds.), *Batterer Intervention Programs: Where Do*

We Go From Here?. National Institute of Justice, Special Report. Washington, D.C.: U.S. Department of Justice, National Institute of Justice. Available at www.ncjrs.gov/pdffiles1 /nij/195079.pdf.

Felson, R., Ackerman, J. & Gallagher, C. (2005). "Police Intervention and the Repeat of Domestic Assault." *Criminology*, Vol., *43*(3), 563-588.

Fox, A. & Zawitz, M. (2002). *"Homicide Trends in the United States."* Washington, D.C.: U.S. Department of Justice, Office of Justice Programs, Bureau of Justice Statistics. Available at www.ojp.usdoj.gov/bjs/ homicide/homtrnd.htm#contents.

Fridell, L. & Pate, A. (1997). "'Death on Patrol' Killings of American Law Enforcement Officers." In R. Dunham and G. Alpert (eds.), *Critical Issues in Policing* (3rd ed.), Waveland Press.

Gelles, R. (1996). "Constraints Against Family Violence: How Well Do They Work?" In Buzawa, E. and C. Buzawa (eds.), *Do Arrests and Restraining Orders Work?* Thousand Oaks, London, New Delhi: SAGE Publications.

Greenfeld, L., Rand, M., Craven, D., Klaus, P., Perkins, C., Ringel, C., Warchol, G., Matson, C. & Fox, J. (1998). *Violence by Intimates: Analysis of Data on Crimes by Current or Former Spouses, Boyfriends, and Girlfriends*, Bureau of Justice Statistics Factbook, Washington, D.C.: U.S. Department of Justice, Bureau of Justice Statistics. Available at www.ojp.usdoj.gov/bjs/pub/ pdf/vi.pdf.

Hanmer, J., Griffiths, S. & Jerwood, D. (1999). *Arresting Evidence: Domestic Violence and Repeat Victimization. Police Research Series*, Paper 104. London: Home Office, Police Research Group. Available at www.homeoffice. gov.uk/rds/prgpdfs/fprs104.pdf.

Healey, K., Smith, C. with O'Sullivan, C. (1998). *Batterer Intervention: Program Approaches and Criminal Justice Strategies*. Washington, D.C.: U.S. Department of Justice, National Institute of Justice. Available at www. ncjrs.gov/pdffiles/168638.pdf.

Hickman, L., Jaycox, L. & Aranoff, J. (2004). "Dating Violence among Adolescents: Prevalence, Gender Distribution, and Prevention Program Effectiveness." *Trauma, Violence & Abuse*, Vol. 5, No. 2. RAND Reprint, originally published by SAGE Publications.

Hotaling, G., Straus, M. & Lincoln, A. (1989). "Intrafamily Violence, and Crime and Violence Outside the Family." In O. Lloyd and M. Tonry (eds.), *Family Violence*. University of Chicago Press.

Issac, N. & Pualani Enos, V. (2001). *"Documenting Domestic Violence: How Health Care Providers Can Help Victims."* National Institute of Justice, Research in Brief. Washington, D.C.: U.S. Department of Justice, National Institute of Justice. Available at www. ncjrs.org/pdffiles1/nij/188564.pdf.

Jackson, S., Feder, L., Forde, D., Davis, R., Maxwell, C. & Taylor, B. (2003). "Analyzing the Studies." In *Batterer Intervention Programs: Where Do We Go From Here?*. National Institute of Justice, Special Report. Washington, D.C.: U.S. Department of Justice, National Institute of Justice. Available at www.ncjrs. gov/pdffiles1 /nij/195079.pdf.

Jackson, S., Feder, L., Forde, D., Davis, R., Maxwell, C. & Taylor, B. (2003). *Batterer Intervention Programs: Where Do We Go From Here?* National Institute of Justice, Special Report. Washington, D.C.: U.S. Department of Justice, National Institute of Justice. Available at www.ncjrs. gov/pdffiles1 /nij/195079.pdf.

Jasinski, J. (2001a). "Pregnancy and Violence Against Women: An Analysis of Longitudinal Data." *Journal of Interpersonal Violence, 16*(7), 71 2-733.

———— (2001b). "Pregnancy, Stress and Wife Assault: Ethnic Differences in Prevalence, Severity, and Onset in a National Sample." *Violence and Victims, 16*(3), 219- 232.

Kennedy, D. (2002). *"Controlling Domestic Violence Offenders."* Paper prepared for the Hewlett-Family Violence Prevention Fund. Available from author.

Kennedy, D., Waring, E. & Piehl, A. (2001). "Problem- oriented Policing, Deterrence, and Youth Violence: An Evaluation of Boston's Operation Ceasefire." *Journal of Research in Crime and Delinquency, 38*(3), 1 95-225.

Kruttschnitt, C., McLaughlin, B. & Petrie, C. (2003). *Advancing the Federal Research Agenda on Violence Against Women.* Washington, D.C.: National Research Council of the National Academies, The National Academies Press. Available at books.nap.edu/ openbook/030909 1098 /html/index.html.

Lloyd, S. (1998). *"Domestic Violence and Women's Employment."* NU Policy Research, electronic journal of the Institute of Policy Research at Northwestern University, available at www.northwestern.edu/ipr/ publications /nupr/nuprv03n1 /lloyd.html.

Lloyd, S., Farrell, G. & Pease, K. (1994). *Preventing Repeated Domestic Violence: A Demonstration Project in Merseyside.* Police Research Group, Crime Prevention Unit, Paper 49. London: Home Office. Available at www.homeoffice.gov.uk/rds/ prgpdfs/fcpu49.pdf.

Loue, S. (2001). *Intimate Partner Violence: Societal, Medical, Legal, and Individual Responses.* New York: Kluwer Academic/Plenum Publishers.

Maxwell, C., Garner, J. & Fagan, J. (2001). *The Effects of Arrest on Intimate Partner Violence: New Evidence from the Spouse Assault Replication Program.* Research in Brief, National Institute of Justice. Available at www.ncjrs.org/txtfiles1/nij /1881 99.txt.

Mazur, R. & Aldrich, L. (2003). "What Makes a Domestic Violence Court Work." *American Bar Association Judges' Journal,* Vol. *42*(2), ,5-9, 41-42.

Mears, D. (2003). "Research and Interventions to Reduce Domestic Violence Revictimization." *Trauma, Violence & Abuse,* Vol. *4*(2), 127-147.

Minnesota Program Development, Inc., *The Duluth Model,* www.duluth-model.org/recentresearch.htm (accessed June 23, 2006).

Moffitt, T. & Caspi, A, (1999). *Findings about Partner Violence from the Dunedin Multidisciplinary Health and Development Study.* National Institute of Justice, Research in Brief. Washington, D.C.: U.S. Department of Justice, National Institute of Justice. Available at www.ncjrs.org/txtfiles1/170018.txt.

National Center for State Courts (n.d.). Problem Solving Courts FAQs. Available at www.ncsconline.org/WC/ FAQs/SpeProFAQ.htm (accessed June 29, 2006).

National Coalition for the Homeless (2004). *Who is Homeless? National Coalition for the Homeless*, Fact Sheet #3, www.nationalhomeless.org/who.html (accessed June 23, 2006). Office of the Deputy Prime Minister (n.d.). Homelessness Statistics: September 2002 and Domestic Violence, www.communities (accessed August 22, 2006). up, Crime Detection and Prevention Series, Paper 90. London: Home Office. Available at www.homeoffice.gov.uk/rds/prgpdfs/fcdps90.pdf.

Pence, E. & Paymar, M. (1993). *Domestic Violence Information Manual: The Duluth Domestic Abuse Intervention Project.* Springer Publishing Company, Inc. Available at www.eurowrc.org/05.education/ education en/12.edu en.htm.

Rennison, C. (2003). *"Intimate Partner Violence, 1993- 2001."* Crime Data Brief. Washington, D.C.: U.S. Department of Justice, Office of Justice Programs,. Bureau of Justice Statistics. Available at www.ojp. usdoj.gov/bjs/pub/pdf/ipv01.pdf.

———— (2001, revised 09/18/02). *"National Crime Victimization Survey. Criminal Victimization* 2001: Changes 2000-2001 with Trends 1993-2001." Washington, D.C.: U.S. Department of Justice, Office of Justice Programs, Bureau of Justice Statistics. Available at www.ojp.usdoj.gov/bjs/pub/ascii/cv01. txt.

Rennison, C. & Welchans, S. (2000). *"Intimate Partner Violence."* Washington, D.C.: U.S. Department of Justice, Office of Justice Programs, Bureau of Justice Statistics. Available at www.ojp.usdoj.gov/bjs/pub/ pdf/ipv.pdf.

Roberts, A. (2002a). *Handbook of Domestic Violence Intervention Strategies.* Oxford and New York: Oxford University Press.

———— (2002b). "Police Response to Battered Women." In A. Roberts (ed.), *Handbook of Domestic Violence Intervention Strategies.* Oxford and New York: Oxford University Press.

Roberts, A. & Kurst-Swanger, K. (2002). "Court Responses to Battered Women and Their Children." In A. Roberts (ed.), *Handbook of Domestic Violence Intervention Strategies,* Oxford and New York: Oxford University Press.

Sampson, R. & Scott, M. (2000). *Tackling Crime and Other Public Safety Problems: Case Studies in Problem- Solving.* U.S. Department of Justice, Office of Community Oriented Policing Services, Fremont case study. Available at www.popcenter.org/Problems/ Supplemental Material/assaults/Tackling Crime.pdf.

San Diego Family Justice Center, www.familyjusticecenter. org (accessed June 27, 2006).

Sherman, L. & Berk, R. (1984). "The Specific Deterrent Effects of Arrest for Domestic Assault." *American Sociological Review, 49*(2), 261-272.

Smith, B., Davis, R., Nickles, L. & Davies, H. (2001). *"Evaluation of Efforts to Implement No-Drop Policies: Two Central Values in Conflict."* Unpublished Final Report. Available at www.ncjrs.org/pdffiles1/ nij/grants/187772.pdf (accessed August 22, 2006).

Spelman, W. (1990). *Repeat Offender Programs for Law Enforcement.* Washington, D.C.: Police Executive Research Forum.

Straus, M. (2005). "Women's Violence Towards Men is a Serious Social Problem." In D. Loeske, R. Gelles, and M. Cavanaugh (eds.), *Current Controversies on Family Violence* (2nd ed.). Thousand Oaks (California): SAGE Publications.

Thurman v. City of Torrington, 595 F. Supp 1521 (1984).

Tjaden, P. & Thoennes N. (2000). *Extent, Nature, and Consequences of Intimate Partner Violence.* Washington, D.C.: U.S. Department of Justice, Office of Justice Programs, National Institute of Justice and Centers for Disease Control. Available at www.ncjrs.org/ pdffiles1 /nij/181867.pdf.

U.S. General Accounting Office (2002). *Violence Against Women: Data on Pregnant Victims and Effectiveness of Prevention Strategies are Limited.* Report to the Honorable Eleanor Holmes Norton, House of Representatives. GAO-02-530. Washington, D.C.: GAO. Available at www.gao.gov/new.items/d02530.pdf.

Recommended Readings

- **A Police Guide to Surveying Citizens and Their Environments,** Bureau of Justice Assistance, 1993. This guide offers a practical introduction for police practitioners to two types of surveys that police find useful: surveying public opinion and surveying the physical environment. It provides guidance on whether and how to conduct cost-effective surveys.

- **Assessing Responses to Problems: An Introductory Guide for Police Problem-Solvers**, by John E. Eck (U.S. Department of Justice, Office of Community Oriented Policing Services, 2001). This guide is a companion to the *Problem-Oriented Guides for Police* series. It provides basic guidance to measuring and assessing problem-oriented policing efforts.

- **Conducting Community Surveys,** by Deborah Weisel (Bureau of Justice Statistics and Office of Community Oriented Policing Services, 1999). This guide, along with accompanying computer software, provides practical, basic pointers for police in conducting community surveys. The document is also available at www.ojp.usdoj.gov/bjs.

- **Crime Prevention Studies**, edited by Ronald V. Clarke (Criminal Justice Press, 1993, et seq.). This is a series of volumes of applied and theoretical research on reducing opportunities for crime. Many chapters are evaluations of initiatives to reduce specific crime and disorder problems.

- **Excellence in Problem-Oriented Policing:** *The 1999 Herman Goldstein Award Winners*. This document produced by the National Institute of Justice in collaboration with the Office of Community Oriented Policing Services and the Police Executive Research Forum provides detailed reports of the best submissions to the annual award program that recognizes exemplary problem- oriented responses to various community problems. A similar publication is available for the award winners from subsequent years. The documents are also available at www.ojp.usdoj.gov/nij.

- **Not Rocket Science? Problem-Solving and Crime Reduction**, by Tim Read and Nick Tilley (Home Office Crime Reduction Research Series, 2000). Identifies and describes the factors that make problem-solving effective or ineffective as it is being practiced in police forces in England and Wales.

- **Opportunity Makes the Thief: Practical Theory for Crime Prevention**, by Marcus Felson and Ronald V. Clarke (Home Office Police Research Series, Paper No. 98, 1998). Explains how crime theories such as routine activity theory, rational choice theory and crime pattern theory have practical implications for the police in their efforts to prevent crime.

- **Problem Analysis in Policing**, by Rachel Boba (Police Foundation, 2003). Introduces and defines problem analysis and provides guidance on how problem analysis can be integrated and institutionalized into modern policing practices.

- **Problem-Oriented Policing,** by Herman Goldstein (McGraw-Hill, 1990, and Temple University Press, 1990). Explains the principles and methods of problem-oriented policing, provides examples of it in practice, and discusses how a police agency can implement the concept.

- **Problem-Oriented Policing and Crime Prevention,** by Anthony A. Braga (Criminal Justice Press, 2003). Provides a thorough review of significant policing research about problem places, high-activity offenders, and repeat victims, with a focus on the applicability of those findings to problem-oriented policing. Explains how police departments can facilitate problem-oriented policing by improving crime analysis, measuring performance, and securing productive partnerships.

- **Problem-Oriented Policing: Reflections on the First 20 Years**, by Michael S. Scott (U.S. Department of Justice, Office of Community Oriented Policing Services, 2000). Describes how the most critical elements of Herman Goldstein's problem-oriented policing model have developed in practice over its 20-year history, and proposes future directions for problem-oriented policing. The report is also available at www.cops.usdoj.gov.

- **Problem-Solving: Problem-Oriented Policing in Newport News**, by John E. Eck and William Spelman (Police Executive Research Forum, 1987). Explains the rationale behind problem-oriented policing and the problem-solving process, and provides examples of effective problem-solving in one agency.

- **Problem-Solving Tips: A Guide to Reducing Crime and Disorder Through Problem-Solving Partnerships** by Karin Schmerler, Matt Perkins, Scott Phillips, Tammy Rinehart and Meg Townsend. (U.S. Department of Justice, Office of Community Oriented Policing Services, 1998) (also available at www.cops.usdoj.gov). Provides a brief introduction to problem-solving, basic information on the SARA model and detailed suggestions about the problem-solving process.

- **Situational Crime Prevention: Successful Case Studies**, Second Edition, edited by Ronald V. Clarke (Harrow and Heston, 1997). Explains the principles and methods of situational crime prevention, and presents over 20 case studies of effective crime prevention initiatives.

- **Tackling Crime and Other Public-Safety Problems: Case Studies in Problem-Solving**, by Rana Sampson and Michael S. Scott (U.S. Department of Justice, Office of Community Oriented Policing Services, 2000) (also available at www.cops.usdoj.gov). Presents case studies of effective police problem-solving on 18 types of crime and disorder problems.]

- **Using Analysis for Problem-Solving: A Guidebook for Law Enforcement**, by Timothy S. Bynum (U.S. Department of Justice, Office of Community Oriented Policing Services, 2001). Provides an introduction for police to analyzing problems within the context of problem-oriented policing.

- **Using Research: A Primer for Law Enforcement Managers,** Second Edition, by John E. Eck and Nancy G. LaVigne (Police Executive Research Forum, 1994). Explains many of the basics of research as it applies to police management and problem-solving.

OTHER PROBLEM-ORIENTED GUIDES FOR POLICE

Problem-Specific Guides series

1. **Assaults in and Around Bars, 2nd Edition.** Michael S. Scott. 2001. ISBN: 1-932582-00-2
2. **Street Prostitution, 2nd Edition.** Michael S. Scott. 2001. ISBN: 1-932582-01-0
3. **Speeding in Residential Areas.** Michael S. Scott. 2001. ISBN: 1-932582-02-9
4. **Drug Dealing in Privately Owned Apartment Complexes.** Rana Sampson. 2001. ISBN: 1-932582-03-7
5. **False Burglar Alarms.** Rana Sampson. 2001. ISBN: 1-932582-04-5
6. **Disorderly Youth in Public Places.** Michael S. Scott. 2001. ISBN: 1-932582-05-3
7. **Loud Car Stereos. Michael S. Scott. 2001.** ISBN: 1-932582-06-1
8. **Robbery at Automated Teller Machines.** Michael S. Scott. 2001. ISBN: 1-932582-07-X
9. **Graffiti. Deborah Lamm Weisel.** 2002. ISBN: 1-932582-08-8
10. **Thefts of and From Cars in Parking Facilities.** Ronald V. Clarke. 2002. ISBN: 1-932582-09-6
11. **Shoplifting. Ronald V. Clarke.** 2002. ISBN: 1-932582-10-X
12. **Bullying in Schools. Rana Sampson.** 2002. ISBN: 1-932582-11-8
13. **Panhandling. Michael S. Scott.** 2002. ISBN: 1-932582-12-6
14. **Rave Parties. Michael S. Scott.** 2002. ISBN: 1-932582-13-4
15. **Burglary of Retail Establishments.** Ronald V. Clarke. 2002. ISBN: 1-932582-14-2
16. **Clandestine Methamphetamine Labs, 2nd Edition.** Michael S. Scott. 2002. ISBN: 1-932582-15-0
17. **Acquaintance Rape of College Students.** Rana Sampson. 2002. ISBN: 1-932582-16-9
18. **Burglary of Single-Family Houses.** Deborah Lamm Weisel. 2002. ISBN: 1-932582-17-7
19. **Misuse and Abuse of 911. Rana Sampson.** 2002. ISBN: 1-932582-18-5
20. **Financial Crimes Against the Elderly.** Kelly Dedel Johnson. 2003. ISBN: 1-932582-22-3
21. **Check and Card Fraud.** Graeme R. Newman. 2003. ISBN: 1-932582-27-4
22. **Stalking.** The National Center for Victims of Crime. 2004. ISBN: 1-932582-30-4
23. **Gun Violence Among Serious Young Offenders.** Anthony A. Braga. 2004. ISBN: 1-932582-31-2
24. **Prescription Fraud.** Julie Wartell and Nancy G. La Vigne. 2004. ISBN: 1-932582-33-9

25. **Identity Theft.** Graeme R. Newman. 2004. ISBN: 1-932582-35-3

26. **Crimes Against Tourists.** Ronald W. Glensor and Kenneth J. Peak. 2004. ISBN: 1-932582-36-3

27. **Underage Drinking.** Kelly Dedel Johnson. 2004. ISBN: 1-932582-39-8

28. **Street Racing. Kenneth J. Peak and Ronald W. Glensor.** 2004. ISBN: 1-932582-42-8

29. **Cruising. Kenneth J. Peak and Ronald W. Glensor. 2004.** ISBN: 1-932582-43-6

30. **Disorder at Budget Motels. Karin Schmerler. 2005.** ISBN: 1-932582-41-X

31. **Drug Dealing in Open-Air Markets.** Alex Harocopos and Mike Hough. 2005. ISBN: 1-932582-45-2

32. **Bomb Threats in Schools.** Graeme R. Newman. 2005. ISBN: 1-932582-46-0

33. **Illicit Sexual Activity in Public Places.** Kelly Dedel Johnson. 2005. ISBN: 1-932582-47-9

34. **Robbery of Taxi Drivers.** Martha J. Smith. 2005. ISBN: 1-932582-50-9

35. **School Vandalism and Break-Ins.** Kelly Dedel Johnson. 2005. ISBN: 1-9325802-51-7

36. **Drunk Driving. Michael S. Scott, Nina J. Emerson, Louis B.** Antonacci, and Joel B. Plant. 2005. ISBN: 1-932582-57-6

37. **Juvenile Runaways. Kelly Dedel.** 2006. ISBN: 1932582-56-8

38. **The Exploitation of Trafficked Women.** Graeme R. Newman. 2006. ISBN: 1-932582-59-2

39. **Student Party Riots.** Tamara D. Madensen and John E. Eck. 2006. ISBN: 1-932582-60-6

40. **People with Mental Illness.** Gary Cordner. 2006. ISBN: 1-932582-63-0

41. **Child Pornography on the Internet.** Richard Wortley and Stephen Smallbone. 2006. ISBN: 1-932582-65-7

42. **Witness Intimidation.** Kelly Dedel. 2006. ISBN: 1-932582-67-3

43. **Burglary at Single-Family House Construction Sites.** Rachel Boba and Roberto Santos. 2006. ISBN: 1-932582-00-2

44. **Disorder at Day Laborer Sites. Rob Guerette. 2007.** ISBN: 1 -932582-72-X

45. **Domestic Violence. Rana Sampson. 2007.** ISBN: 1-932582-74-6

Response Guides series

- The Benefits and Consequences of Police Crackdowns. Michael S. Scott. 2003. ISBN: 1-932582-24-X

- **Closing Streets and Alleys to Reduce Crime:** Should You Go Down This Road? Ronald V. Clarke. 2004. ISBN: 1-932582-41-X
- **Crime Prevention Publicity Campaigns.** Emmanuel Barthe. 2006 ISBN: 1-932582-66-5
- **Shifting and Sharing Responsibility for Public Safety Problems.** Michael S. Scott and Herman Goldstein. 2005. ISBN: 1-932582-55-X
- **Video Surveillance of Public Places.** Jerry Ratcliffe. 2006 ISBN: 1-932582-58-4

Problem-Solving Tools series

- Assessing Responses to Problems: An Introductory Guide for Police Problem-Solvers John E. Eck. 2002. ISBN: 1-932582-19-3
- **Researching a Problem.** Ronald V. Clarke and Phyllis A. Schultz. 2005. ISBN: 1-932582-48-7
- Using Offender Interviews to Inform Police Problem Solving. Scott H. Decker. 2005. ISBN: 1-932582-49-5
- **Analyzing Repeat Victimization.** Deborah Lamm Weisel. 2005. ISBN: 1-932582-54-1

Upcoming Problem-Oriented Guides for Police

Problem-Specific Guides
Abandoned Vehicles
Bank Robbery
Bicycle Theft
Drive-By Shootings
Crowd Control at Stadiums and Other Entertainment Venues Child Abuse
Crime and Disorder in Parks
Pedestrian Injuries and Fatalities
Robbery of Convenience Stores
Traffic Congestion Around Schools
Transient Encampments
Thefts of and From Cars on Residential Streets and Driveways

Problem-Solving Tools
Designing a Problem Analysis System
Displacement
Implementing Responses to Problems
Understanding Risky Facilities
Using Crime Prevention Through Environmental Design in Problem Solving
Partnering with Community Developers to Address Public Safety Problems

Response Guides

Enhancing Lighting

Sting Operations

For more information about the *Problem-Oriented Guides for Police* series and other COPS Office publications, please call the COPS Office Response Center at 800.421.6770 or visit COPS Online at www.cops.usdoj.gov.

End Notes

[1] Rennison (2003).

[2] Tjaden and Thoennes (2000); Rennison and Welchans (2000).

[3] Tjaden and Thoennes (2000); Rennison and Welchans (2000).

[4] Tjaden and Thoennes (2000); Greenfeld et al. (1998).

[5] For an excellent discussion of the challenges these different definitions cause in making findings across research studies and surveys, see Mears (2003) and Buzawa and Buzawa (2003).

[6] Tjaden and Thoennes (2000).

[7] Rennison (2003).

[8] Rennison (2001).

[9] Fox and Zawitz (2002).

[10] Fox and Zawitz (2002).

[11] See Straus (2005) and Buzawa and Buzawa (2003) for a review.

[12] Rennison and Welchans (2000).

[13] Straus (2005); Moffit and Caspi (1999).

[14] Straus (2005).

[15] Tjaden and Thoennes (2000); Straus (2005).

[16] Tjaden and Thoennes (2000).

[17] Carrington and Phillips (2003).

[18] Charlotte-Mecklenburg Police Department (2002).

[19] For a summary, see Brewster (2002).

[20] Hotaling et al. (1989).

[21] For a thorough review of the research in support of this theory, see Kennedy (2002). Also see Hotaling et al. (1989) for the results of several studies and Buzawa and Buzawa (2003) for a general description of study findings about this topic.

[22] Dekeseredy et al. (1997).

[23] Straus (2005).

[24] For a summary, see Brewster (2002).

[25] Greenfeld et al. (1998); Rennison and Welchans (2000).

[26] Dekeseredy et al. (1997).

[27] Hickman et al. (2004). For a detailed discussion of the challenges of measuring teen dating violence and the results of different studies that have attempted to, see Hickman et al. (2004).

[28] Rennison and Welchans (2000).

[29] Rennison and Welchans (2000).

[30] Lloyd (1998).

[31] Rennison and Welchans (2000).

[32] Tjaden and Thoennes (2000).

[33] Hanmer et al. (1999).

[34] Tjaden and Thoennes (2000).

[35] Hanmer et al. (1999).

[36] Hanmer et al. (1999). Also see Buzawa and Buzawa (2003) describing a study one of the authors conducted with others in Quincy District Court (Massachusetts) finding a similar pattern.

[37] Greenfeld et al. (1998).

[38] Greenfeld et al. (1998).

[39] Tjaden and Thoennes (2000).

[40] Jasinski (2001a); Jasinski (2001b); for a summary of the research related to pregnancy and domestic violence, see U.S. General Accounting Office (2002).

[41] Jasinski (2001a); Jasinski (2001b); for a summary of the research related to pregnancy and domestic violence, see U.S. General Accounting Office (2002).

[42] Summary of research on pregnancy and domestic violence, U.S. General Accounting Office (2002).

[43] Jasinski (2001b).

[44] Rennison and Welchans (2000).

[45] Rennison and Welchans (2000).

[46] Moffitt and Caspi (1999).

[47] Moffitt and Caspi (1999).

[48] Tjaden and Thoennes (2000).

[49] Tjaden and Thoennes (2000).

[50] Tjaden and Thoennes (2000).

[51] Ascione (2004).

[52] Tjaden and Thoennes (2000).

[53] Lloyd et al. (1994).

[54] Buzawa and Buzawa (2003).

[55] Buzawa and Buzawa (1996).

[56] Hanmer et al (1999); Anderson et al (1995); Bridgeman and Hobbs (1997); Chenery et al (1997); Lloyd et al (1994); Pease (1998). For the application of a graded approach to reducing repeat domestic violence victimization in the United States, see the description of the Fremont Police Department approach in Sampson and Scott (2000).

[57] Hanmer et al. (1999). Also see Buzawa and Buzawa (2003) describing a study one of the authors conducted with others in Quincy District Court (Massachusetts) finding a similar pattern.

[58] Hanmer et al. (1999).

[59] Hanmer et al. (1999).

[60] Hanmer et al. (1999).

[61] Kennedy (2002).

[62] Buzawa and Buzawa (1996).

[63] U.S. General Accounting Office (2002).

[64] Hickman et al. (2004).

[65] Felson, Ackerman, and Gallagher (2005).

[66] See adopted recommendations in American Medical Association Data on Violence Between Intimates (2000).

[67] For a summary of the research on physician screening for domestic violence, see U.S. General Accounting Office (2002).

[68] Roberts (2002a).

[69] Brookoff et al. (1997).

[70] See *Bruno v. Codd* 47 N.Y. 2d 582, 393 N.E. 2d 976, 419 N.Y.S. 2d 901 [1979]; and *Thurman v. City of Torrington* 595 F. Supp 1521 [1984].

[71] Sherman and Berk (1984).

[72] Roberts and Kurst-Swanger (2002).

[73] Bureau of Alcohol, Tobacco, Firearms, and Explosives (2004).

[74] Roberts (2002a).

[75] Sherman and Berk (1984).

[76] For a discussion of the replication studies, see Gelles (1996) and Fagan (1996).

[77] Maxwell, Garner, and Fagan (2001).

[78] Maxwell, Garner, and Fagan (2001).

[79] Maxwell, Garner, and Fagan (2001).

[80] Maxwell, Garner, and Fagan (2001).

[81] Felson, Ackerman, and Gallagher (2005).

[82] Loue (2001).

[83] Buzawa and Buzawa (2003).

[84] Loue (2001).

[85] Buzawa and Buzawa (2003).

[86] Buzawa and Buzawa (2003) discuss the empirical research from two mandatory prosecution jurisdictions and the arguments for and the drawbacks to "no drop" policies.

[87] Smith et al. (2001); Buzawa and Buzawa (2003).

[88] Mazur and Aldrich (2003).

[89] Buzawa and Buzawa (2003).

[90] Brewster (2002).

[91] Brewster (2002).

[92] Brewster (2002).

[93] U.S. General Accounting Office (2002).

[94] Jackson (2003).

[95] Jackson (2003); Feder and Forde (2003).

[96] Jackson et al. (2003).

[97] Fagan (1996); Buzawa and Buzawa (1996).

[98] Healey et al. (1998).

[99] Fagan (1996); also see Healey et al. (1998) and Buzawa and Buzawa (2003).
[100] Kruttschnitt et al. (2003).
[101] Buzawa and Buzawa (2003).
[102] Healey et al. (1998).

In: Domestic Violence: Law Enforcement Response...
Editor: Mario R. Dewalt

ISBN: 978-1-60876-774-8
© 2010 Nova Science Publishers, Inc.

Chapter 2

THE EVALUATION OF THE JUDICIAL OVERSIGHT DEMONSTRATION: FINDINGS AND LESSONS ON IMPLEMENTATION[*]

Michael B. Mukasey, Jeffrey L. Sedgwick and David W. Hagyl

ABOUT THIS REPORT

The Judicial Oversight Demonstration (JOD) Initiative set out to improve the provision of comprehensive services to victims of domestic violence (DV), increase victim safety, and hold offenders more accountable. JOD activities were jointly funded and managed by the Office on Violence Against Women and the National Institute of Justice (NIJ). The Urban Institute conducted an independent, multisite evaluation under a cooperative agreement with NIJ. This report (part of a series of reports on JOD) discusses some of the evaluation's findings and lessons learned about implementing court-involved DV prevention programs.

WHAT DID THE RESEARCHERS FIND?

Challenges encountered by the JOD programs included: partner agencies' gaps in knowledge about the operations of other partners, unanticipated changes in the workloads of partner agencies, state and county hiring limitations that restricted recruiting for new positions, lack of adequate systems for sharing data across justice service providers, and overcoming obstacles to collaboration between justice agencies and community service providers (such as concerns about confidentiality).

Successful strategies included: a formal strategic planning process, an inclusive set of partners (incorporating a wide array of agencies including community-based organizations and service providers and, most importantly, local defense attorneys), active management of

---

[*] This is an edited, reformatted and augmented version of a U. S. Department of Justice publication dated June 2008.

the collaboration with regularly scheduled meetings and a full-time project director, training nd technical assistance by non-JOD partners with acknowledged expertise, and specialized staff dedicated to DV cases.

Impacts of JOD innovations included: fundamental changes in the coordination between the judiciary and other justice and community agencies (with the explicit involvement of judges in developing a coordinated response), increased consistency in the justice system response to DV cases, and changes in the response to DV that outlasted the demonstration time frame.

In this report, the terms intimate partner violence (IPV) and domestic violence (DV) are used interchangeably to mean violence that occurs between intimate partners.

The Judicial Oversight Demonstration (JOD) Initiative tested an innovative idea for improving the justice system's response to domestic violence (DV) cases: that a coordinated, focused and systematic response by the judicial system, law enforcement and probation agencies, and community service organizations could improve victim safety and hold offenders more accountable while encouraging them to change their abusive behavior.

In 1999, following an extensive search for sites with the resources, infrastructure and commitment needed to implement the envisioned demonstration, three sites — Dorchester, Mass., Milwaukee County, Wi., and Washtenaw County, Mich. — were selected to implement the JOD project. The demonstration activities were jointly funded and managed by the U.S. Department of Justice's Office on Violence Against Women (OVW) and the U.S. Department of Justice, Office of Justice Programs' National Institute of Justice (NIJ). Technical assistance to the sites, provided by the Vera Institute of Justice in New York City through a cooperative agreement with OVW, included onsite consultations, training, and educational opportunities within and across sites. The Urban Institute (UI) conducted an independent, multisite evaluation under a cooperative agreement with NIJ. Each demonstration site employed a local evaluator who assisted UI in gathering data for the evaluation and responded to local evaluation needs (see "Study Methods").

This Research for Practice report is the second in a series of reports about the experiences of the JOD sites in implementing the demonstration. It begins with a general description of JOD operations at the three study sites. (Specific details about the JOD operations at each site can be found in the first report, *Pretrial Innovations for Domestic Violence Offenders and Victims: Lessons From the Judicial Oversight Demonstration Initiative,* August 2007, available online at http://www.ncjrs.gov/ pdffiles1/nij/216041.pdf.) This report then presents findings from a process evaluation of the three JOD sites (that is, an evaluation of the processes used at the sites), and concludes with lessons learned about implementing JOD and similar initiatives.

STUDY METHODS

The implementation study and process evaluation of the Judicial Oversight Demonstration (JOD) used a variety of methods and data collection strategies. The primary methods were:

- *Site visits* that involved semistructured interviews with JOD partners; observations of court proceedings, project team meetings, and other activities (such as batterer intervention sessions); and meetings with groups of line staff (e.g., probation officers and law enforcement personnel in domestic violence [DV] units). Site visits were held quarterly during the initial phases of the demonstration and twice annually in the last year of the demonstration period.

- *Collection of quantitative data*, including: 1) aggregate descriptive data relating to the case before the court, court and treatment interventions, and system and client outcomes; 2) performance indicators to use in monitoring program operation and reporting accomplishments; and 3) documentation of services provided and court processing from the local evaluation staff. This entailed working with court and JOD staff to identify data elements, descriptive statistics, data retrieval and analysis strategies, and variables and categories needed to describe special JOD services or sanctions. Data from the different agencies involved in JOD at each site were gathered by the local evaluator and submitted to the Urban Institute (UI) monthly.

- *Participation of site staff and national partners* in conference calls, meetings and technical assistance workshops. The conference calls created opportunities for discussion of and reflection on how JOD was operating, including identification of problems, brainstorming of possible solutions, and revisions or modifications in the JOD project. The meetings and workshops included formal strategic planning sessions focused on individual sites as well as technical assistance workshops on specific topics such as victim advocacy, probation supervision and judicial oversight. OVW, NIJ, UI and the Vera Institute of Justice participated in the formal strategic-planning sessions in order to enhance their ability to work as partners with the sites.

- *Focus groups of offenders and victims in each site* to gain a more in-depth, personal perspective about how men and women involved in intimate partner violence (IPV) cases were affected by the actions of the JOD partner agencies, to ascertain their views about how they were treated by those agencies, and to help interpret the interview data. If victims or offenders indicated that they felt they were not treated fairly or given an opportunity to voice their opinions, that information might be useful in replicating the JOD model in other communities.

- *Site visits to comparison sites* (Ingham County, Mich., and Lowell, Mass.) at the beginning and end of the JOD demonstration period to document the criminal justice and community response to IPV cases in the communities that UI selected as part of the impact evaluation design. As did the site visits to the demonstration sites, the comparison site visits entailed interviews with a variety of agencies involved in IPV cases, including the court, prosecutors, law enforcement, probation, victim service agencies and batterer intervention program providers. These visits were important for interpreting the results of the impact evaluation and for documenting any changes that might have occurred in the comparison sites during the JOD demonstration period.

In combination, these methods for documenting the implementation of JOD complemented one another and provided UI with a thorough understanding of the overall operations in each JOD site (and the comparison sites) and the specific procedures implemented by each JOD partner agency.

An important component of the process evaluation was to document the context in which JOD was implemented. UI interviewed key stakeholders in the demonstration project, including project planners, judges, court administrators and other court staff, prosecutors, law enforcement officials, pretrial services staff, probation and parole staff, members of the defense bar, victim advocates, victim service providers, and community providers of other important services such as substance abuse and mental health treatment. The interviews with these participants collected data on: 1) their perceptions of and goals for JOD, 2) how the justice system in their communities handled DV cases prior to project implementation, and 3) what databases relating to DV cases existed and how they might be used for the evaluation and collection of existing reports, statistics, policy or procedure documents, and forms to supplement the interviews. Interim reports describe the implementation process in all sites.*

*DeStefano, Christine, Adele Harrell, Lisa Newmark, and Christy Visher, "Evaluation of the Judicial Oversight Demonstration Initiative: Baseline and Implementation Report," interim report for the National Institute of Justice, grant number 99–WT–VX–K005, Washington, DC: National Institute of Justice, 2001, NCJ 220871, available at http://www.ncjrs.gov/pdffiles1/nij/grants 220871.pdf; Harrell, Adele, Lisa Newmark, Christy Visher, and Christine DeStefano, "Evaluation of the Judicial Oversight Demonstration Initiative: Implementation Strategies and Lessons," interim report for the National Institute of Justice, grant number 99–WT–VX–K005, Washington, DC: National Institute of Justice, 2002, NCJ 220872, available at http://www.ncjrs.gov/pdffiles1/nij/ grants/220872.pdf.

A NEW APPROACH TO COMBATING INTIMATE PARTNER VIOLENCE

The JOD model included the following critical elements:

- *Uniform and consistent initial responses to DV offenses,* including: a) proarrest policies, b) the arrest of the primary aggressor, and c) a coordinated community response by law enforcement and victim advocates.

- *Coordinated victim advocacy and services,* including: contact by victim advocates as soon as possible after the DV incident, b) an individualized "safety plan" for the victim and the victim's children (if appropriate), and c) provision of needed services such as shelter, legal advocacy, medical assistance, economic support, etc.

- *Strong offender accountability and oversight,* including: a) intensive court-based supervision of offenders, referral to appropriate batterer intervention programs (BIPs), and c) administrative and judicial sanctions and incentives to influence offender behavior.

To achieve these objectives, a partnership among criminal justice agencies and community-based agencies that provide services to victims and hold offenders accountable was formed or identified in each JOD community to work in collaboration to respond to incidents of intimate partner violence (IPV) that enter the criminal court. This initiative differed from earlier coordinated community responses to intimate partner violence because it placed special focus on the role of the court in the partnership, as illustrated in exhibit 1.

Support for JOD innovations was grounded in recognition of the challenges IPV cases pose to criminal justice agencies and the need to take steps to better protect victims from repeat violence. The likelihood of subsequent violence, potentially lethal, is often present but is difficult to gauge. Prior research shows that abuse following court hearings for protection orders is predicted, not by the type and severity of the current charge, but by the history of recent abuse in the relationship and other factors, which points to the need for thorough record checks of defendants and comprehensive victim interviews at court intake.[1] Victims and their children often need emotional support and medical, legal and financial assistance to cope with what is often a long-standing pattern of abuse. Victims are often reluctant to testify, fearing retaliation or hoping for reconciliation, and they may be socially isolated and without economic or emotional support.

JOD was also developed to test the feasibility and effectiveness of closely monitoring offenders to hold them more accountable. By adopting a more intensive approach to managing DV cases, JOD would hold offenders accountable for their criminal behavior and require their participation in treatment and community service when appropriate. JOD was designed to implement the fundamental purposes of the 1994 Violence Against Women Act. It also incorporates key recommendations of the 1984 report of the Attorney General's Task Force on Family Violence:

- Family violence should be recognized and responded to as a criminal activity.
- Law enforcement officials, prosecutors and judges should develop a coordinated response to family violence.
- A wide range of dispositional alternatives should be considered in cases of family violence. In all cases, prior to sentencing, judges should carefully review and consider the consequences of the crime for the victim.
- In granting bail or releasing the assailant on his or her own recognizance, the court should impose conditions that restrict the defendant's access to the victim and strictly enforce the order.

Over the past decade, the criminal courts have begun to assume a leadership role in coordinated responses to domestic violence through innovations such as specialized DV courts. These courts have introduced increased judicial supervision supported by case management, victim advocacy, enhanced supervision by probation, and mandatory batterer intervention programs for eligible offenders. A dual focus on increased offender accountability and coordinated services for victims in DV cases was the essential feature of JOD.

The three demonstration sites, assisted by technical assistance teams, reviewed model policies, findings from the experiences of other jurisdictions, recent research, and other best practices previously identified for DV cases. They then developed programs geared to the needs of their individual jurisdictions. All demonstration sites included the following criminal justice and community elements:

- *Proactive law enforcement.* In law enforcement agencies around the country, written policies and procedures for responding to DV cases are now in place and officers are far more likely to have specialized training in responding to domestic violence than was true 15 years ago. The law enforcement components of the JOD initiative included innovations in training sites on arrest policies and protocols, enforcement of protection orders, and interagency communications.

- *Specialized prosecution.* JOD prosecutors expanded their use of independent evidence such as digital photographs of victim injury, hospital records, excited utterances (an exception to the hearsay rule), expert testimony, 911 audiotapes, and other evidence to support or replace victim testimony. The JOD projects included best practices such as special units, no-drop policies, vertical prosecution (processing of cases by a single prosecutor), and evidence-based prosecution. One site placed special focus on prosecuting bail violations such as bail jumping and witness tampering.

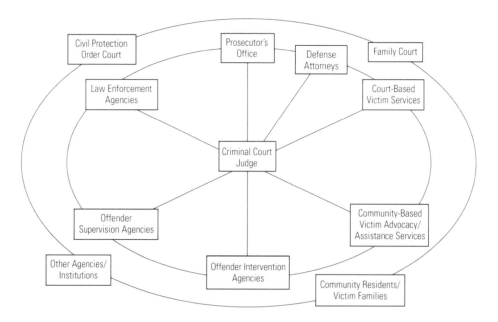

Exhibit 1. JOD Network of Partners

- *Specialized pretrial procedures.* Two of the three JOD sites focused on improvements to pretrial processes, including: standardization of bond conditions; group meetings in the week after arraignment to review bond conditions with defendants; creation of a new position, the domestic violence commissioner, to manage a special court that would process pretrial matters only; and intensive pretrial monitoring for offenders accused of a repeat DV offense.

- *Specialized DV dockets.* Some of the features of the JOD courts included: 1) intake units for particular kinds of cases involving domestic violence, 2) screening to coordinate case processing, 3) automated case tracking, 4) automated systems for identifying related cases, and 5) specialized calendars. The JOD demonstrations included specialized dockets, judicial review hearings for probationers, and a domestic violence intake court at one site.

- *Specialized probation and court-ordered batterer intervention services.* The JOD sites' demonstrations included: specialized probation officers for DV offenders, enhanced supervision of DV offenders, increases in staffing to reduce probation officer caseloads, referrals to only state- certified batterer intervention programs, and greater communication between probation officers and BIP staff to provide information for judicial review hearings.

- *Enhancement of victim services.* JOD sites expanded in-court victim services from both justice- based and community- based providers in a variety of ways, including: in-court victim advocates from local nongovernmental DV programs, civil legal assistance, services that promote autonomy, and private victim waiting rooms with childcare provided in courthouses.

- *Coordination of court and community agencies.* The complex and recurring nature of domestic violence requires a coordinated, systemic response from courts and other community-based agencies. The importance of communitywide coordination was affirmed by the Violence Against Women Act of 1994, in particular through the Grants to Encourage Arrest Policies and Enforcement of Protection Orders Program and the STOP (Services, Training, Officers, Prosecutors) Formula Grant Program, which requires states to engage in collaborative planning prior to awarding subgrants; allocate the funds among law enforcement, prosecution, courts and victim service agencies; and encourage coordinated community responses. Evaluation indicates that STOP subgrantees attributed the most significant changes in their communities to increased collaboration.[2]

The design of JOD and its specific elements in each site reflected principles that were identified in earlier demonstrations that focused on building coordinated community responses to domestic violence. From that work, six essential features of successful implementation of a coordinated approach to domestic violence emerged: 1) clear policies defining the roles and responsibilities of partners; 2) designated personnel in each agency responsible for coordination; 3) enhanced leadership and oversight, especially by judges; 4) cross-training of staff from multiple agencies; 5) vigorous prosecution; and 6) formal monitoring of partnership performance.[3] Mechanisms to ensure coordination in the JOD sites included: hiring a project director to coordinate and oversee implementation of JOD, an executive committee with working subcommittees that met regularly to identify and troubleshoot emerging issues, the development of standard policies and protocols to improve the consistency of case-handling practices, and enhanced communication among agencies through shared databases.

LESSONS LEARNED FROM IMPLEMENTING JOD

The "lessons learned" discussed here are drawn from the experiences of all three demonstration sites during the implementation of JOD. It is hoped that these lessons will provide useful direction to other jurisdictions that are considering similar innovative, comprehensive responses to intimate partner violence in their communities. The lessons fall generally into three categories:

- Barriers and challenges faced in implementing JOD.
- Strategies used by JOD sites to facilitate change.
- The impact of JOD on system responses to intimate partner violence.

These lessons are described in this report with one or two examples drawn from the site case studies. Further discussion of these lessons can be found in Volume 2 of the final report to NIJ on this research .4

JOD IMPLEMENTATION CHALLENGES

JOD partnerships began with a vision of collaborative operations in which agencies would work together seamlessly to protect victims and hold offenders accountable for their violence. Agreements were forged and commitments made. However, the process of bringing this collaborative vision to life encountered barriers and challenges that can serve as a lesson and guide to agencies embarking on similar coordinated responses to intimate partner violence. The challenges highlighted below required each of the JOD sites to work on issues not anticipated when the vision was formed.

Challenge 1: Gaps in Knowledge about the Operations of Other Partner Agencies

Despite the existing coordinated community response for domestic violence that was in place in all three sites prior to the demonstration, JOD partner agencies often did not under-stand the specific operations of their partners. For example, Dorchester planners discovered that, under union rules, cameras for collecting pictures to be used as evidence could be used only by detectives and not by the off icers who responded to an incident. Washtenaw County found that developing consistent policies and procedures across 11 law enforcement agencies, independent courts and probation agents required an enormous effort, in part because each lacked knowledge of the others' operations.

Challenge 2: Understanding the Effects of Changes on the Workload of Partner Agencies

A related challenge was the unforeseen impact of JOD activities on the workload of partner agencies. For example, Milwaukee introduced a crisis response team of advocates available to assist victims at the time of an incident without anticipating the extra burden on the police who would need to stay to ensure the safety of the advocate. Washtenaw County found probation agent workloads spiraling upward with the advent of judicial review hearings and added probation requirements, and decided to hire compliance specialists to assist the agents in monitoring IPV offenders.

Challenge 3: Dealing with Hiring Limitations Imposed by County and State Rules Governing Recruiting

All of the sites found that state and county rules governing recruiting and funding of new positions can slow the start of a new project and limit hiring options. All three sites were eager to begin JOD and developed ambitious plans for immediate change, only to encounter difficulties in staffing their projects. Both Dorchester and Milwaukee experienced delays in starting new activities, stemming from limitations on hiring key staff and turnover in key staff. In Milwaukee, the selection of the probation agent to staff the new pretrial monitoring unit was governed by Division of Community Corrections seniority rules, which resulted in the appointment of an agent whose lack of dedication to the initiative undermined the effectiveness of the new program. Dorchester encountered delays in hiring a project director because of county personnel rules governing hiring, a hiring freeze and seniority issues.

Challenge 4: Lack of Systems for Sharing Data across Justice Agencies and with Community Service Providers

A critical need in a program that emphasizes offender ccountability is the need for multiple agencies to share up-to-date information on offenders active in the criminal justice system. Data systems routinely kept by the courts and other justice agencies may not be adequate or in a form that can be used to provide information to partner agencies. This presented problems in all three JOD sites, none of which had systems shared by police, courts and probation agencies and none of which had consistent procedures for collecting information on compliance with batterer intervention programs. In all three sites, developing these data-sharing systems was technically complicated and sometimes controversial. In Dorchester, probation agents received computers for the first time as part of the JOD initiative, permitting automated tracking of compliance for review hearings. In Washtenaw, the county devoted extensive local funding to an interactive, Web-based system for sharing data on probationers but found that the system was difficult and time-consuming to use. In Milwaukee, the state-maintained probation database lacked a field for identifying IPV offenders. This made it difficult for officers to monitor these offenders, who were a small part of large, general probation caseloads.

Challenge 5: Building Collaboration between Justice Agencies and Community Service Providers

Collaboration between victim advocates from community-based organizations and justice agencies was central to the goals of JOD, but integrating community-based service providers into justice system operations proved difficult in all sites because of competing priorities between the two groups. Interagency differences among victim advocates needed to be accommodated through strategies for bridging the differences in goals, roles and expectations of the two groups. Issues arose around client confidentiality, encouraging victims to testify in court, and the weight to be given to victim preferences during prosecution. The sites had varying levels of success in meeting this challenge, and other communities are likely to face similar challenges.

SUCCESSFUL JOD STRATEGIES

The process evaluation identified a number of strategies used by the JOD sites to accomplish the goals of the project. The following list identifies those seen as critical to moving each site forward in the implementation of JOD.

Strategy 1: A Formal Strategic Planning Process

All three sites benefited from intensive strategic-planning sessions that included a kickoff meeting where site teams had an opportunity to present their plans to the other sites, agency officials, the technical assistance provider and the national evaluator. Later, sites engaged in 1- or 2-day intensive planning sessions, usually with a trained facilitator, to discuss initial plans for JOD with all local JOD partners. For all sites, these sessions were the first time that such a diverse group of justice and community agencies had come together to discuss a coordinated response to domestic violence in their communities. These planning sessions highlighted components of the initiative that required more attention, allowed agency partners to discuss their views on their role in the initiative, and led to the development of sub-committees and technical assistance on specific topics.

Strategy 2: An Inclusive Set of Partners

Projects typically began with a core group of agencies that had collaborated in project design and the preparation of the initial proposal to OVW for funding. It was critical, however, that this core group draw a wider group of agencies into project planning, giving them a voice in shaping policies and procedures. Of particular importance was the inclusion of the defense bar as full network partners in an effort to maintain a balance between advocacy on behalf of victims and fairness to defendants in court cases. The sites also found it important to continue adding partners as the partnership grew, and developed plans for adding outreach to specific cultural groups and broadening the types of victim assistance and batterer intervention programs available for court referrals. It was not always easy to integrate JOD into the existing coordinated community response because judges were reluctant to appear to be advocates for either the prosecution or the defense. Introducing the courts into existing victim service provider networks also challenged some existing understandings about agency roles and responsibilities.

Strategy 3: Active Management of the Collaboration with Regularly Scheduled Meetings and a Full-Time Project Director

Collective planning and ongoing meetings in all sites increased understanding among the participating agencies and increased the confidence of victim advocates, batterer intervention specialists and probation staff that their efforts to change offender behavior would be supported. Case-level collaboration also increased substantially. In each site, JOD management required regular team meetings, executive committee meetings, and meetings of subcommittees formed around specific issues.

A full-time project director was also critical to the full implementation of JOD. In all three sites, the project director was knowledgeable about one or more components of the criminal justice system or community responses to intimate partner violence. One project director was from the victim service field, another was from the probation department, and the third had years of management experience in the prosecutor's office. The JOD project directors had the confidence of the primary agency that was initiating JOD (the court or the prosecutor), and sufficient contacts throughout the criminal justice system and the community service network, to know whom to talk to when a specific problem arose. The project directors also ensured that grant deadlines were met, committee meetings were scheduled, and the overall implementation of JOD continued to move forward.

Strategy 4: Training and Technical Assistance by "Outsiders" with Acknowledged Expertise to Help Promote Change

All demonstration sites had extensive and ongoing training of personnel in the JOD partner agencies and provided technical assistance to partners in developing new policies and procedures. All sites benefited from general training on DV dynamics, cross-agency training on specific interagency protocols being developed, and specialized technical assistance and training on skills for specific positions, including judges, prosecutors, law enforcement officers, probation agents and others. OVW funded the Vera Institute to coordinate specialized training that greatly assisted the sites. For example, judges were offered the opportunity to attend Judicial Training Institutes sponsored by OVW, the Family Violence Prevention Fund, and the National Council of Juvenile and Family Court Judges. State-sponsored training was also offered. Law enforcement officers in JOD sites received training from local DV organizations and law enforcement consultants as part of the technical assistance provided by VERA throughout the demonstration period. Advocates and public defenders from each site received cross-disciplinary training. During JOD, the Milwaukee District Attorney's Office, in conjunction with a local service provider, the Task Force on

Family Violence, conducted training for probation agents on investigation strategies to help them better prepare for revocation hearings.

Strategy 5: Dedicate specialized staff to IPV cases. Specialized staff in the justice agencies is critical to developing a more effective response to intimate partner violence. IPV cases present specific challenges, including difficulties in collecting evidence for prosecution, the need to consider victim safety, the resistance of offenders to changing their behavior despite intervention, and the ambivalent feelings of those victimized by intimate partners. To act effectively, the police, prosecutors, courts and probation agencies need to understand, through training, the challenges of these cases and the strategies for responding effectively to intimate partner violence. In addition, they need to build ties to specialized staff in partner agencies to foster a team approach to managing cases.

IMPACT OF JOD ON SYSTEM RESPONSES TO IPV

The process evaluation identified three principal impacts of JOD on criminal justice and community responses to IPV cases.

Impact 1: Fundamental changes in the Coordination between the Judiciary and Other Justice and Community Agencies in IPV Cases

A major contribution of JOD in the three demonstration sites has been the explicit involvement of judges in developing a coordinated response to intimate partner violence and the commitment of judges to the issue of domestic violence. This shift has dramatically and permanently changed the culture of the court system in all three sites.

JOD judges were committed to the independence of the judiciary and their role as interpreters of the law. They avoided involvement in policy decisions on substantive matters that might come before them. At the same time, they were committed to systemic changes in the courts that were designed to improve the administration of justice, which meant holding offenders more accountable under the law. They realized the importance of being seen as fair and unbiased toward both the victim and the defendant, and they knew they must maintain a balance between the presumption of innocence and a willingness to hear the kinds of evidence that are relevant to domestic violence. The prospect of JOD challenged some traditional notions of the role of the judiciary, but all judges in the project emerged with a strong belief that JOD could simultaneously help ensure victim safety and justly hold offenders accountable.

JOD permitted experimentation with innovative court responses that likely would have not been attempted otherwise. In Milwaukee, JOD faced the challenge of integrating judges into a coordinated community response to domestic violence that had been managed for years by the Milwaukee Commission on Domestic Violence and Sexual Assault. Historically, the city's judges had been reluctant to become involved in the commission in order to avoid appearing biased toward DV victims. It soon became apparent, however, that to integrate JOD into the larger community, the participation of judges in the commission was needed and could be handled in a way that did not compromise their impartiality. This shift in the commission's governance formally joined the court to the larger community response to intimate partner violence and left in place a structure for further joint planning of policies and practices well into the future.

One site's experience with the impact of JOD on the judiciary and its operations illustrates a lesson learned. There was relatively strong opposition within the court system to making the changes in procedures required by JOD. Pleas for additional judges were slow to be heard and space for project staff was difficult to arrange. But the leadership of the judges, the skills of the project director, and positive interactions with JOD staff produced gradual acceptance. Eventually, there was a fundamental change. As a staff member of one JOD partner agency put it, "It was a combination of ... a solid idea, plus dollars, that made it possible ... against all odds."

Impact 2: Increased Consistency in the Justice System Response to IPV Cases

An important concept of justice is consistency in the standards applied to defendants and probationers. One expectation of a well-functioning justice system is that the responses of the police, courts, prosecutors and probation will be similar for similarly situated individuals and that variations should derive from differences in the offense and mitigating circumstances. JOD jurisdictions made huge strides in establishing consistent practices and policies that were negotiated by multiple partners. They also made efforts to make these policies clear to offenders.

Extensive efforts were made in the JOD sites to standardize procedures for IPV cases and to communicate clearly the actions of the court to both offenders and victims. (Some of the most notable examples are reviewed in this Research for Practice. Further discussion of these issues is available in Volume 2 of the final report to NIJ.)[5]

Responses to intimate partner violence varied across law enforcement agencies within the same county. For example, while one agency may have a mandatory arrest policy that results in jail time prior to arraignment, another law enforcement agency in a neighboring jurisdiction might issue a citation that requires the offender to pay a fine at the local police station. Standardized procedures for law enforcement officers are particularly difficult to develop and implement. In Washtenaw County, a uniform incident reporting form developed for IPV cases was eventually put into place in the majority of the law enforcement agencies in the county. In addition to getting officers to respond consistently to IPV incidents, the information collected greatly helped prosecutors in the development of their cases.

The judiciary has often struggled with consistent pretrial release conditions for IPV offenders, especially concerning when and for how long to impose a no-contact order. The judges in Washtenaw County negotiated a common script for the pretrial hearing that recommended imposition of a standard set of release conditions, including victim no-contact orders. Judicial meetings to discuss policies on pleas, sentencing and probation conditions, and their enforcement, occurred regularly. One effect of these changes was greater consistency in the response to these offenders, reducing the potential for bias and increasing the predictability of outcomes.

Judges in the JOD sites also had difficulty in deciding whether and when to lift a no-contact order, either during the pretrial period or during probation. Less progress was made toward consistent policies in this area as judges reacted differently to victims' requests to drop no-contact orders. Probation officers were frequently asked for information about an offender's compliance with court requirements to provide additional information for the judge's decision. As a compromise, several sites developed a no-violent-contact or no-nonconsensual-contact agreement that all parties signed.

JOD paid substantial attention to the probation function as a critical element of offender accountability. Probation officers have little flexibility in their work, are often overworked and underpaid, and rarely can implement special supervision procedures for particular types of cases. In response, probation agencies in JOD sites developed new procedures and protocols that attempted to impose some consistency on officers' interactions with offenders and with victims. These included protocols for officers' contacts with victims, revision of no-contact orders, and ending probation supervision. Specialized DV probation officers and, ideally, specialized DV probation units, improved consistency in the responses to offenders' violations of probation conditions.

Impact 3: Changes in the Response to Intimate Partner Violence that Will Outlast the Demonstration Period

All three demonstration sites chose to implement JOD throughout their communities rather than in a few police districts or with a selected subset of IPV cases. The demonstration became a full-scale assessment and overhaul of policies and practices related to the justice system and community response to IPV cases in which all partner agencies participated. Such an intensive process is likely to have lasting effects on the community. As of 2006, at least one year after the funding for JOD ended, a number of changes implemented during the demonstration have outlasted the demonstration period:

- *Post-conviction judicial review hearings with IPV probationers.* These hearings were strongly embraced by most judges and probation officers, despite the extra work and time involved. Judges can see for themselves whether offenders are making progress and they appreciate the chance to receive feedback from victims and the probation staff. Most probation officers appreciated the court's support of their supervision and reported that offenders faced with a review hearing were more willing to comply with referrals to batterer intervention programs and other probation requirements.

- *Improved practices for investigating and prosecuting IPV cases.* All three JOD sites refined evidence- collection procedures for law enforcement and prosecution investigators targeted to IPV cases. The use of digital cameras at the scene of the incident and the introduction of tapes of harassing calls from jailed defendants to their victims are just two of the innovative prosecution methods that resulted from JOD. In Milwaukee, the prosecutor's domestic violence unit documented their new practices in a manual for the investigation and prosecution of IPV cases.

- *Greater involvement of probation officers with victims and batterer intervention programs.* It is likely that permanent change has occurred in the ways that probation officers handle IPV defendants in JOD sites. Although not all sites have been able to retain specialized domestic violence probation officers, the lessons learned during the demonstration about enhanced monitoring have been included in training of new staff and formalized in written procedures. Moreover, probation off icers in the JOD sites now recognize the value of communicating with IPV victims and have benefited from specialized training for victim contacts. In addition, probation officers have developed collaborative relationships with batterer intervention program providers (who have improved their case tracking and reporting procedures), thus enabling probation and the court to have more timely information on the offender's com- pliance with probation conditions.

CONCLUSION

The process evaluation of JOD describes the broad changes in the demonstration sites as they implemented a model of coordinated justice and community response to intimate partner violence. Such a model was untested in the nation prior to the JOD site awards. All of the sites experienced challenges to the implementation of JOD yet, when faced with problems, were able in most instances to devise creative solutions and move forward. In addition, the dedication of the site teams to the goals of the demonstration enabled the sites to develop new strategies to facilitate changes in their communities' responses to intimate partner violence, even "against all odds.' Their accomplishments are further supported by the permanent changes in the system response to intimate partner violence after the demonstration was concluded in the three sites.

The National Institute of Justice is the research, development, and evaluation agency of the U.S. Department of Justice. NIJ's mission is to advance scientific research, development, and evaluation to enhance the administration of justice and public safety.

The National Institute of Justice is a component of the Office of Justice Programs, which also includes the Bureau of Justice Assistance; the Bureau of Justice Statistics; the Community Capacity Development Office; the Office for Victims of Crime; the Office of Juvenile Justice and Delinquency Prevention; and the Office of Sex Offender Sentencing, Monitoring, Apprehending, Registering, and Tracking (SMART).

End Notes

[1] Harrell, Adele, and Barbara E. Smith, "The Effects of Restraining Orders on Domestic Violence Victims,' in Eve Buzawa (ed.), Protection Orders for Domestic Violence Victims, Beverly Hills, CA: Sage, 1996; Harrell, Adele, Barbara Smith, and Lisa Newmark, "Court Processing and the Effects of Restraining Orders for Domestic Violence Victims,' final report to the State Justice Institute, Washington, DC: The Urban Institute, 1993.

[2] Burt, Martha R., Adele Harrell, Lisa J. Raymond, Britta Iwen, Kathryn Schlichter, Bonnie Katz, Lauren E. Bennett, and Kim M. Thompson, "1999 Report: Evaluation of the STOP Formula Grants Under the Violence Against Women Act of 1994,' final report for the National Institute of Justice, grant number 95–WT–NX–0005, Washington, DC: National Institute of Justice, 1999, NCJ 181797, available at http://www. ncjrs.gov/pdffiles1/nij/ grants/1 81797. pdf.

[3] Hofford, Merideth, and Adele Harrell, "Family Violence: Interventions for the Justice System,' Bureau of Justice Assistance Program Brief, grant number 89–DD–CX–K001, Washington, DC: Bureau of Justice Assistance, 1993, NCJ 144532.

[4] Harrell, Adele, Lisa Newmark, and Christy Visher, "Final Report on the Evaluation of the Judicial Oversight Demonstration, Volume 2: Findings and Lessons on Implementation,' final report for the National Institute of Justice, grant number 1999–WT–VX–K005, Washington, DC: National Institute of Justice, 2007, NCJ 219383, available at http://www.ncjrs.gov/pdffiles1/nij/ grants/21 9383. pdf.

[5] Ibid.

In: Domestic Violence: Law Enforcement Response...   ISBN: 978-1-60876-774-8
Editor: Mario R. Dewalt   © 2010 Nova Science Publishers, Inc.

Chapter 3

PRACTICAL IMPLICATIONS OF CURRENT DOMESTIC VIOLENCE RESEARCH: FOR LAW ENFORCEMENT, PROSECUTORS AND JUDGES[*]

United States Department of Justice

1. Overview of Domestic Violence
1.1. How Widespread is Nonfatal Domestic Violence?

According to the latest 2005 National Crime Victimization Survey (NCVS), during the period from 1993 to 2005, the average annual domestic violence rate per 1,000 persons (age 12 or older) for intimate partners and/or relatives was 5.9 for females and 2.1 for males. About one- third of the victims reported they were physically attacked; two-thirds were threatened with attack or death. A little more than half (50.5 percent) of the female victims suffered an injury, but only 4.5 percent were seriously injured. Slightly more than 3 percent were sexually assaulted. Fewer male victims — 41 .5 percent - reported injuries, of which less than 5 percent were serious injuries. Those males or females who were separated (or divorced) experienced more nonfatal domestic violence than those who were together. [27]

Victimization rates vary among different subpopulations. The highest reported rates are for Native American women. [154]

1.2. What Percentage of Calls to Police are to Report Domestic Violence?

Domestic-violence-related police calls have been found to constitute the single largest category of calls received by police, accounting for 15 to more than 50 percent of all calls. [68, 114] Not all domestic violence calls are for activities that constitute crimes. Several New York studies, for example, found that 65 percent of such calls in upstate New York pertained

---

[*] This is an edited, reformatted and augmented version of a U. S. Department of Justice publication dated June 2009.

to criminal conduct. In New York City, the police department found that 35 percent of reports pertained to specific chargeable index or other criminal offenses. [165, 184] In San Diego, approximately 25 percent of calls for service in domestic violence cases result in an arrest. [196]

Implications for Law Enforcement

Given the large numbers adversely affected by domestic violence and that victims' prime countermeasure - leaving their abusers - may not stop the abuse, law enforcement agencies must commit time, resources and attention to domestic violence as they do to confront any other major crime. For this reason, all law enforcement agencies should have a domestic violence policy that specifies, at a minimum, that written reports be completed on all domestic violence calls and, if no arrest is made, the reports fully explain the circumstances why not. (Research basis: Disparate national surveys, supplemented by local police department studies.)

> **Performance Measure:** A total of 77 percent of police departments have written operational procedures for responding to emergency domestic violence calls, and larger departments are most likely to have such written procedures. Most procedures include requiring the dispatcher to ask about weapons, check for protection orders, and advise the caller to stay on the line until police arrive. [213] (Research basis: Representative sample of 368 drawn from 14,000 law enforcement agencies across the nation.)

Implications for Prosecutors and Judges

Given the large numbers adversely affected by domestic violence and that victims' prime countermeasure - leaving their abusers - may not stop the abuse, and given the amount of time committed to responding to domestic violence calls and arresting and prosecuting alleged offenders, prosecutors and judges must commit sufficient resources and attention to ensure that domestic violence cases are handled efficiently and effectively. (Research basis: Disparate national surveys, supplemented by local police department and prosecution studies.)

1.3. What Time of Day Does Domestic Violence Occur?

According to the NCVS, most offenses (60 percent) occur between 6 p.m. and 6 a.m. at the victim's home. [27]

Implications for Law Enforcement

Although all potential responding law enforcement officers must be trained and prepared to deal with domestic violence, if the agency has only a limited number of victim advocates, related auxiliary personnel, or volunteers to assist on domestic violence calls, priority should be given to the 6 p.m. to 6 a.m. time period. (Research basis: National survey data from 1993 to 2004.)

1.4. How Widespread is Stalking?

Estimates of stalking vary, depending upon how it is defined. A 1995-1996 National Violence Against Women Survey (NVAWS) found that 5 per 1,000 females (18 and older) and 2 per 1,000 males report being stalked annually, using a conservative definition that requires victims to suffer a high level of fear. Eighty percent of stalking victims are women, and 87 percent of stalkers are male. Women were stalked by spouses or ex-spouses (38 percent), current or former intimates (10 percent), dating partners (14 percent), other relatives (4 percent), acquaintances (19 percent), and strangers (23 percent). The percentages add to more than 100 percent because some women reported being stalked by more than one person. Males were more likely than females to be stalked by strangers (36 percent) and acquaintances (34 percent). [131, 207] Furthermore, research suggests a close association between stalking and murders of women by intimate partners. One study, for example, found more than half (54 percent) of female intimate partner murder victims had reported stalking to police prior to their murders by the stalkers. [156]

Implications for Law Enforcement

It is important for law enforcement officers to correctly identify stalking behavior in order to accurately analyze victim risk and to use stalking laws appropriately. Even if the stalker is not charged, stalking constitutes a red flag for potential lethality. (Research basis: National study of 141 murders and 65 attempted murders of women, and confirmation in other stalking studies.)

Implications for Prosecutors and Judges

Whether stalkers are specifically charged or not, it is important for prosecutors and judges to correctly identify stalking behavior and recognize its significance in order to give victims maximum protection against potentially lethal abusers. (Research basis: National study of 141 murders and 65 attempted murders of women, and confirmation in other stalking studies.)

1.5. How Widespread are Sexual Assaults of Intimate Partners?

If there is physical abuse in domestic violence, studies suggest that there is probably sexual abuse as well. A Texas study found that almost 70 percent of women seeking protective orders were raped, most (79 percent) repeatedly. [157] Although reporting a lower rate, an earlier Massachusetts study found 55 percent of female restraining order petitioners reported to interviewers that they had been sexually assaulted by their abusers, although *no one* had included this in her affidavit requesting a protective order. [143] Female victims similarly underreported sexual abuse in a Colorado study. Although 20 to 50 percent of women seeking protective orders had been subjected to a variety of abuse, including forced sex within the preceding year, only 4 percent listed forced sex on the complaint form requesting the temporary restraining order. [105]

Implications for Law Enforcement

Investigators should be alert to possible sexual as well as physical abuse in interviewing or investigating domestic assaults. Judgment must be used as to how and when to approach potential victims of sexual assaults. (Research basis: National survey as well as disparate individual studies from multiple regions.)

Implications for Prosecutors and Judges

Prosecutors should be aware that sexual abuse is often part of domestic violence, although victims may not report it or be prepared to cooperate in its prosecution. Even if prosecutors cannot file or prosecute, evidence of sexual assaults should be taken into account when prosecutors and judges consider abuser risk and victim vulnerability in terms of filing other charges and making appropriate sentencing recommendations, bail decisions, issuing protective orders, and sentencing abusers after pleas or convictions. (Research basis: National survey as well as disparate individual studies from multiple regions.)

1.6. How Widespread is Fatal Domestic Violence?

According to the Supplementary Homicide Reports of the FBI's Uniform Crime Reporting Program in 2005, 1,181 females and 329 males were killed by their intimate partners. [27] The number of men killed has dropped by almost three-quarters since 1976, whereas the number of women killed has only dropped by a quarter. The number of white females killed has declined the least - only 6 percent. Intimate partner homicides constituted 11 percent of all homicides between 1976 and 2005, 30 percent of all female murders (1 976-2004), and 3 percent of all male murders (1976-2005). The proportion of female homicide victims killed by an intimate partner is increasing. Unlike nonfatal domestic violence, most intimate partner homicides (54 percent) involve spouses or ex-spouses, although intimate partner homicides for unmarried couples are approaching the rate for married or divorced couples.

Intimate partner homicides may also involve third parties, including children, bystanders, employers and lawyers, among others. For example, according to the Washington State Domestic Violence Fatality Review, between 1997 and 2004, there were 313 domestic violence fatality cases in that state involving 416 homicides, including 23 children, 32 friends/family members of primary intimate partner victims, 19 new boyfriends of primary intimate victims, one co-worker of the primary intimate victim, three law enforcement officers responding to the intimate partner homicide, 9 abusers killed by law enforcement, and 10 abusers killed by a friend or family member of victims. Additionally, 93 abusers committed suicide after killing their victim(s). [199]

Implications for Law Enforcement

To reduce female homicides generally, law enforcement must give priority to the protection of female intimate partners. (Research basis: National data collected by the Federal Bureau of Investigation.)

Implications for Prosecutors and Judges

To reduce female homicides generally, prosecutors and judges must give priority to the protection of female intimates. Reduction of female intimate homicides will also reduce collateral homicides of children, other family members, and responding law enforcement officers as well as reducing abuser suicides. (Research basis: National data collected by the Federal Bureau of Investigation, and multiple state and local fatality reviews.)

1.7. How Widespread are Multiple Forms of Domestic Violence against the Same Victims?

Analysis of NVAWS data revealed that 18 percent of the women who experienced abuse experienced *systemic abuse*, meaning they were likely to suffer physical attacks (with and without weapons) and strangulation; of these women, 24.4 percent also experienced sexual assault, and 47.8 percent experienced stalking. [153] A study of dating violence similarly found substantial overlap between physical and sexual victimization. [222]

Implications for Law Enforcement

A full investigation may indicate additional, even more serious incidents of domestic violence than the one to which the law enforcement officers respond. (Research basis: A national survey and a five-year longitudinal study of college students from schools considered representative of state colleges attended by 80 percent of all U.S. college students.)

Implications for Prosecutors

A post-arrest investigation by the prosecutor may indicate additional, even more serious incidents of domestic violence than the one specifically noted by law enforcement officers. Rarely does the reported abuse incident represent a single isolated, atypical act. Appropriate charges should be filed that cover the range of criminal behaviors of abusers. In light of the United State's Supreme Court case, *Crawford* v. *Washington*, 541 U.S. 36 (2004), and its increased demand for live victim testimony, prosecutors must work with law enforcement to uncover any evidence of abuser intimidation of victims that would inhibit the victim's testimony. Such evidence may also be used in preparing victim impact statements. (Research basis: A national survey and a five-year longitudinal study of college students from schools considered representative of state colleges attended by 80 percent of all U.S. college students.)

Implications for Judges

Although called upon to respond to discrete criminal charges, judges must insist that they receive sufficient information to reveal any pattern of systemic, abusive behaviors in order to accurately understand the victim's vulnerability. (Research basis: A national survey and a five- year longitudinal study of college students from schools considered representative of state colleges attended by 80 percent of all U.S. college students.)

2. REPORTING AND ARRESTS

2.1. To What Extent is Domestic Violence Reported to Law Enforcement and What Percentage Actually Reaches the Courts?

As with any crime, not all incidents of domestic violence are reported to law enforcement, not all incidents reported to law enforcement are forwarded to prosecutors, and even fewer are prosecuted.

Both the older NVAWS and the more contemporary NCVS reports agree that victims do not report all cases of their victimization to police. According to the NVAWS, only 27 percent of women and 13.5 percent of men who were physically assaulted by an intimate partner reported their assault to law enforcement. Less than 20 percent of women victims reported intimate partner rapes to police. Reporting rates for stalking were higher, with 52 percent of women and 36 percent of men reporting stalking incidents to law enforcement. A succession of NCVS surveys over the past several decades find much higher reporting rates (but for far fewer victimizations). According to these surveys, reporting to police of nonfatal partner victimization has increased for all victims (male and female) to more than 62 percent, with no gap between male and female victim reporting rates. The highest reporting rate is for black females (70.2 percent) and the lowest is for black males (46.5 percent). [27]

Comparing hundreds of police domestic violence incident reports with victim statements at four sites in three different states, researchers found that a proportion of victims deny abuse documented by police. Researchers found 29 percent of victims reported "no assault," contradicting police findings. Ironically, their alleged assailants were more likely to admit to the assaults, with only 19 percent reporting "no assault." However, suspects were more likely than victims to minimize the severity of the assaults. [63] Researchers also found that some victims do not report repeated incidents of abuse to police. A review of NCVS data from 1992 through 2002 found that, although 60 percent of the victims had been assaulted by their intimate partners before, only half of the latest survey assaults were reported to police, and these included reports made by persons other than the victim. Prior unreported domestic violence may be more serious than the incident actually reported. [63]

Reasons given in the 2005 NCVS for not reporting abuse incidents included a belief that the abuse was a private or personal matter (22 percent for females, 39 percent for males), fear of reprisal (12 percent for females, 5 percent for males), a desire to protect the suspect (14 percent for females, 16 percent for males), and a belief that police won't do anything (8 percent for females and for males). [27, 63]

Once reported, police arrest rates vary, depending on the jurisdiction and how each defines domestic violence. Arrests for domestic violence per 1,000 persons ranged from 3.2 in Omaha, Neb. (2003), to 12.2 in Wichita, Kan. (2000). [135]

Prosecution rates similarly vary. A review of 26 domestic violence prosecution studies from across the country found prosecutions per arrest ranged from 4.6 percent in Milwaukee in 1992 to 94 percent reported in Hamilton, Ohio, in 2005. The average rate was 63.8 percent, and the median rate was 59.5 percent. [71]

Implications for Law Enforcement and Prosecutors

> **Performance Measure:** On the basis of victim reporting rates to law enforcement alone, law enforcement officers should be responding annually to at least 4 to 5 incidents per 1,000 females (12 and older) and 1 to 2 per 1,000 males (12 and older). On the basis of actual rates as determined by victim surveys, law enforcement officers should be responding annually to 8 to 9 incidents per 1,000 females, and 2 to 3 per 1,000 males. Therefore, if the incidence of domestic violence reported in victim surveys is significantly above the level that victims actually report to law enforcement, greater community outreach and barriers to reporting must be addressed. Law enforcement officers must encourage the rest of the community to do its part, and prosecutors must work with law enforcement if incidents are not making it into the courts. (Research basis: Confirmed by multiple national surveys over past decades, although exact rates [as opposed to the national average] may vary by region, population density, ethnicity of population, and so on.)

Implications for Judges

Judges typically see only a small minority of domestic violence cases that actually occur. (Research basis: Multiple studies across the country based on victim surveys, police arrest records and court cases.)

2.2. At What Point Do Victims Report Domestic Violence?

Victims do not generally report their initial intimate partner victimization but typically suffer multiple assaults or related victimizations before they contact authorities or apply for protective orders. [63, 105, 133] A Texas protective order study, like others conducted across the country, found that 68 percent of the victims taking out orders had been physically abused by their partners in the two years before they took out orders. [26] A Massachusetts arrest study found that a majority (55 percent) of sampled intimate partner victims who called police reported that either the frequency or the severity of ongoing abuse was increasing in the period before the call. Another 11 percent reported no increases in either frequency or severity but increased controlling behaviors such as restrictions on freedom of movement, access to money, medical or counseling services, or social support. [23] The NCVS found that victims were more likely to report reassaults than initial assaults. [63]

Implications for Law Enforcement

In questioning victims, law enforcement officers should always inquire about unreported *prior* assaults for evidence of crimes that may be charged, depending on the jurisdiction's statute of limitations. These inquiries are also necessary to develop an accurate offender history to determine offender risk and to advise the victim. Prior abuse history may also be helpful in determining the primary or predominant aggressor. (Research basis: Both national studies and multiple, disparate individual-jurisdiction studies agree that battering that is likely to come to the attention of law enforcement constitutes repeated activity, much of it not reported to law enforcement initially.)

Implications for Prosecutors

In questioning victims, prosecutors should always inquire about prior unreported domestic violence for evidence of crimes that may be charged, depending on the jurisdiction's statute of limitations, and/or are necessary to develop an accurate offender history to determine appropriate prosecution and sentencing recommendations. (Research basis: Both national studies and multiple, disparate individual-jurisdiction studies agree that battering that is likely to come to the attention of law enforcement constitutes repeated activity, much of it not reported to law enforcement initially.)

Implications for Judges

Judges should not assume that the civil petition or criminal case before them represents isolated, unique behaviors on the part of the involved parties, particularly the abuser. Although this assumption may not be relevant until after the specific petition or case has been decided, it must be considered in terms of fashioning remedies and sanctions. (Research basis: Both national and multiple, disparate individual-jurisdiction studies agree that battering that is likely to come to the attention of the criminal justice system represents repeated activity.)

2.3. Which Victims are Likely to Report Domestic Violence?

Some victims are more likely to report their victimization or revictimization than others. Research indicates that women who have more experience with the criminal justice system especially those with protective orders or who have experienced more severe abuse histories - are more likely to call police. [23, 27, 120, 141]

The seriousness of injury may not increase victim reporting, however, because of incapacity, the increased likelihood that a third party will call in these cases, or the fact that seriously injured victims are less likely to have protective orders. [23] Younger women, those in dating relationships, and those with little prior contact with the criminal justice system are less likely to call police. [23, 27]

Implications for Law Enforcement

When a victim reports domestic violence, it probably indicates repeated prior abuse incidents. Law enforcement officers should be trained in how to assist victims and encourage them to secure protective orders if for no other reason than victims with protective orders are more likely than those without such an order to alert police to subsequent victimization incidents. Existence of protective orders adds to the body of evidence for future prosecution. (Research basis: Both national surveys and multiple local studies conclude that victim reporting is not uniform or consistent. Although one might argue that protective orders generate violations by criminalizing otherwise legal behavior, both national and multiple local studies found higher reporting rates of a variety of domestic violence crimes for victims with protective orders.)

2.4. Does the Quality of the Law Enforcement Response Influence Whether Domestic Violence is Reported?

Research indicates that actions of law enforcement, such as follow-up home visits after incidents, can encourage victim reports of domestic violence. [37] It appears that victim confidence in police response leads to more reports of new violence. [41, 68] This is reinforced by a study of a police department domestic violence unit, which documented that repeated victim contact with law enforcement officers assigned to a specialized domestic violence unit significantly increased the likelihood of victim reports of revictimization. [130]

On the other hand, research also shows that victims who reported prior victimization and thought the criminal justice response was insufficient or endangered them are less likely to report subsequent victimizations. [23] However, even if the victim opposed the arrest of her abuser, she is generally just as likely to report revictimizations as are victims who did not oppose the initial arrest. [23, 130]

Implications for Law Enforcement

Law enforcement officers should not be deterred from arresting abuse suspects for fear of prejudicing future victim reporting of revictimization. Law enforcement responses can increase victim reports of reabuse (even as they decrease the likelihood of reabuse). Therefore, increased reporting of victimization does not necessarily mean that law enforcement efforts are failing to reduce actual domestic abuse, and decreased reporting may not indicate successful law enforcement efforts. (Research basis: An increase in reported findings, based on three experimental studies as well as multiple observational studies from disparate localities.)

2.5. Who Else Reports Domestic Violence?

Most domestic violence reports are called in by victims, with victim report rates ranging from 59 percent [228] to 93 percent. [68] The review of NCVS reassaults between 1992 and 2002 found that 72 percent of the reassaults were reported by the victims, and 28 percent by third parties. [63] Third parties include family members, relatives and sometimes the suspects themselves. In Chicago's domestic violence misdemeanor court, 26 percent of the calls were made by third parties on their own, and another 7.3 percent called at the direct behest of the victim. [107] Third parties are more likely to call police if the incident involved major injuries or a weapon. [23, 27] Other family members are significantly more likely to report abuse of elderly women (60 years and older) abused by other family members, usually sons, daughters or grandsons. [139]

Implications for Law Enforcement

Tapes of 911 domestic violence calls should be routinely maintained and accessible, as they may contain possible excited utterance evidence, because a majority of calls reporting incidents are made by victims (some of whom may be reluctant to testify later). In addition, the identities and contact information for third-party domestic violence callers should be elicited when possible in case they are potential witnesses. Dispatchers should be trained on these matters. (Research basis: Multiple national and local observational studies.)

Implications for Prosecutors

Prosecutors should ask law enforcement to catalog and maintain 911 tapes of domestic violence calls (since they may contain possible excited utterance evidence) because a majority of reported incidents are made by victims, some of whom may be reluctant to testify later. In addition, the identities and contact information for third-party domestic violence callers should be elicited when possible, in case they are potential incident witnesses. Dispatchers should be trained toward these ends, and this information should be forwarded to prosecutors. (Research basis: Multiple national and local observational studies.)

2.6. Are There Other Major Sources for Reports of Domestic Violence?

Unlike most crime victims, victims reporting domestic violence can use a parallel track, namely, civil courts where they can petition for protective/restraining orders. In many jurisdictions, more victims report intimate assaults and related crimes to civil courts than to law enforcement. [135] Research from both ends of the country, Massachusetts [32, 134] and the state of Washington [121], however, indicates that the abuse reported in this civil setting is not significantly different from that reported to law enforcement.

Implications for Law Enforcement and Prosecutors

Civil protective order files offer law enforcement and prosecutors an essential tool in identifying domestic violence victims and perpetrators, gauging victim risk, and correctly calibrating appropriate charges and sentences. They may also indicate prior uncharged crimes that may be prosecuted along with more recent charges, particularly if the same victim and/or witnesses are involved in both sets of charges. They may also be used as evidence for violations of probationary sentences. Petitioner affidavits of abuse have been upheld as admissible evidence for probation violation in *Tweedie* v. *Garvey*, 94_CV_30139 (U.S. D. Springfield, MA, 1994). (Research basis: Disparate observational studies across the country as well as reported data from multiple states.)

Implications for Judges

Notwithstanding the court arena, civil or criminal, the abuse reported is typically as serious in one as in the other. The major differences are the responses courts can offer. For this reason, judges should inform or ensure that victims are informed that they may file criminal complaints in addition to petitioning courts for civil orders. Each process offers victims different benefits (and poses different challenges). (Research basis: Disparate observational studies across the country as well as reported data from multiple states.)

2.7. What Kinds of Domestic Violence are Reported to Law Enforcement and are Prosecuted?

Notwithstanding varying numbers and types of crimes that constitute domestic violence in state codes and the U.S. Code, almost two-thirds to three-quarters of domestic violence cited in law enforcement incident reports are for assaults. [23, 68, 120, 196, 228] Although prosecutors screen cases, a study of domestic violence prosecutions in California, Oregon, Nebraska and Washington found that assaults constituted 59 to 81 percent of all prosecuted domestic violence cases. [196]

The percentage of felony assaults varies widely, reflecting specific state felony enhancement statutes. The highest percentage of felony assault domestic violence charges documented (41 percent) is in California, where injurious domestic assaults are classified as felonies. [228] However, most studies find much smaller percentages of felony assault charges - for instance, 13.7 percent in Charlotte, N.C. [68], and only 5.5 percent in Massachusetts [23] - as most physical injuries are minor and most cases do not involve the use of weapons.

These studies accord with the findings of the NCVS. [27] The NVCS, based on victim self- reports, not police characterizations, found simple assaults against female intimate partners to be more than four times greater (4.4) than aggravated assaults in 2005. Most assaults (80.5 percent) did not involve weapons. [27]

Implications for Law Enforcement

If the ratio of arrest reports for lesser offenses (such as disorderly conduct or breach of the peace) is significantly greater than that for assaults, it may indicate that patrol officers are not correctly identifying or assessing the underlying criminal behavior. Additional training or supervision may be required. (Research basis: Numerous observational studies from across the country as well as findings of national victim surveys, 1993-2004.)

Implications for Prosecutors

If the ratio of arrest reports for lesser offenses (such as disorderly conduct or breach of the peace) is significantly greater than that for assaults, it may indicate that local law enforcement is not correctly identifying the underlying criminal behavior. Prosecutors must work with officers to correctly determine the necessary elements of specific domestic violence crimes, including assault, stalking and marital rape. Alternatively, if the majority of domestic assaults are routinely pled down to lesser offenses by prosecutors, prosecutors may be endangering victims as well as failing to hold abusers fully accountable for their violence. Federal misdemeanor firearm prohibitions - 18 U.S.C. §922(g)(9), for example - only apply to assault convictions. Where enhancement statutes are available, prosecutors should carefully review prior convictions to charge defendants as repeat offenders where appropriate. (Research basis: Numerous observational studies from across the country as well as findings of national victim surveys, 1993-2004.)

Implications for Judges

Reducing assault charges to nonassault charges allows convicted abusers to retain firearms otherwise prohibited pursuant to federal law, 18 U.S.C. § 922(g)(9), which prohibits abusers convicted of misdemeanor assaults from possessing firearms or ammunition. Qualifying offenses must include the use or attempted use of physical force or the threatened use of a deadly weapon. Judges can facilitate application of the federal prohibition by making specific findings of these necessary elements required in the federal law. (Research basis: Numerous observational studies from across the country as well as findings of national victim surveys, 1993-2004.)

2.8. Do Arrest Rates Correspond to Actual Rates of Domestic Violence and Stalking Based on Victim Surveys?

Domestic violence arrest rates as a percentage of written incident reports vary greatly because incident report writing practices vary across jurisdictions. A better, more consistent measure is the *arrests per capita* over the course of a year. At least one study documents that actual per capita arrests for domestic violence across an entire (albeit small) state exceeded the national estimates of domestic violence as determined by the NCVS. A Rhode Island study found in 2004 that per capita domestic violence arrests were 10.5 per 1,000 females (including both male and female suspects of female victims) and were 2.9 per 1,000 males (including both male and female suspects of male victims), higher than the national estimated incidence rates of 8.6 per 1,000 females and 2.5 per 1,000 males. [136] Other, disparate jurisdictions have similarly demonstrated high per capita arrest rates: Wichita, Kan. 12.1/1,000 (2000); Chicago, 6.9/1,000 (1997); and Nevada, 5.4/1,000 (2001). [135]

> **Performance Measure for Law Enforcement:** If domestic violence is broadly defined and if law enforcement agencies mandate and enforce arrest upon probable cause, over the course of a year, law enforcement can reach the same percentage of victims who identify themselves as abused in national crime victim surveys. Departments should establish benchmarks based on the NCVS to assess their performance. (Research basis: This performance measure is based on actual arrest figures from Rhode Island, a state with mandatory arrest for protective order violations and assaults with injuries, and where domestic violence includes any crime committed by family or household members,cohabitants, current or former intimate partners, and dating partners. Jurisdictions' definitions will necessarily vary and are based on state laws as documented in Klein, 2004, pp. 90-91.)

2.9. Do Stalking Arrests Correspond to Actual Stalking Rates as Reported by Victims?

Stalking arrests are rare, nowhere near the estimated number of stalkers. [207] A pioneering study determined that, although 16.5 percent (in a sample of 1,731) of all domestic violence incident reports filed in Colorado Springs, Colo., involved stalking, in all but one incident the suspect was charged with a lesser offense - harassment, violation of a protective order, or another nonstalking domestic violence offense. [210]

Implications for Law Enforcement

If stalking arrests constitute a negligible proportion of all domestic violence arrests, departments should undertake a legal, policy and practice review to determine barriers to the enforcement of stalking statutes. Law enforcement officers should receive training on stalking behavior and statutes. Not only may charging abusers with stalking more accurately reflect their behavior but also stalking charges are more likely to constitute felonies in many jurisdictions than are alternative domestic offense charges. (Research basis: National surveys supplemented by multiple domestic violence arrest studies from disparate jurisdictions across the country.)

2.10. Is Arrest the Best Response?

A major re-examination of a series of fairly rigorous experiments in multiple jurisdictions finds that arrest deters repeat reabuse, whether suspects are employed or not. In none of the sites was arrest associated with increased reabuse among intimate partners. [155] Another major study, based on 2,564 partner assaults reported in the NCVS (1992-2002), found that whether police arrested the suspect or not, their involvement had a strong deterrent effect. The positive effects of police involvement and arrest do not depend on whether the victim or a third party reported the incident to law enforcement. Neither do they depend on the seriousness of the incident assault, whether a misdemeanor or a felony. [63]

A Berkeley arrest study found similarly that all actions taken by responding officers - including arrest, providing victims with information pamphlets, taking down witness statements, and helping victims secure protective orders - were associated with reduced reabuse. By contrast, the highest reabuse rates were found where the responding officers left it to the victim to make a "citizen arrest," swearing out a complaint herself. [228] Research has also shown that police response also significantly increases the likelihood that victims will secure protective orders. [130, 151, 152]

Research also finds that, by and large, the vast majority of victims report satisfaction with the arrest of their abuser when interviewed after the fact. In Massachusetts, 82 percent were either very or somewhat satisfied, and 85.4 percent said they would call police again for a similar incident. [23] Similarly, a study of courts in California, Oregon, Nebraska and Washington found that 76 percent of the victims said they wanted their abuser arrested. [196] Also important to note is that police arrests in spite of victims' objections do not reduce the likelihood of victims reporting new abuse to police. [5]

Implications for Law Enforcement

Arrest should be the default position for law enforcement in all domestic violence incidents. (Research basis: Multiple studies in diverse jurisdictions. The police arrest studies were combined carefully, and intimate partner abuse cases were separated from family abuse cases.)

Implications for Prosecutors and Judges

One of the best ways prosecutors can encourage law enforcement to arrest abuser suspects is to follow through where possible by filing charges against those arrested. Judges encourage the arrest of abusers by ensuring that domestic violence cases that reach court are heard and not dismissed out of hand. (Research basis: The efficacy of arrests has been widely researched; the influence of prosecutors on law enforcement arrest behavior has been found in studies in which pro-arrest departmental policies mitigated anti-arrest personal views of individual officers. [59])

2.11. What Should Law Enforcement's Response be if the Suspect Is Gone When They Arrive?

A large percentage of alleged abusers leave the crime scene before law enforcement arrives. Where noted, absence rates range from 42 to 66 percent. [23, 50, 117, 196, 227, 228] Pursuing alleged abusers, including the issuance of warrants, is associated with reduced revictimization. [50] Pursuing absent suspects may be of particular utility because limited research finds that suspects who flee the scene before police arrive are significantly more likely to have prior criminal histories and to reabuse than those arrested at the scene. [23] Similarly, another study finds higher reabuse *if the victim is gone* when officers arrive. [228]

Implications for Law Enforcement
Law enforcement officers should make the arrest of abusers who flee the scene a priority. (Research basis: Numerous studies confirm that a large proportion of abusers flee the scene; only one study has looked at differences in records of those who fled the scene and those who didn't.)

Performance Measure: According to a national survey, 68 percent of police departments have specific policies that cover policies and procedures for responding law enforcement officers if the perpetrator is gone when they arrive. [213] In a study of the south shore communities of Massachusetts, researchers documented that police arrested 100 percent of abusers present at the scene and arrested or issued warrants for a majority (54 percent) who left the scene, for a total arrest or warrant rate of about 75 percent. [23] Similarly, a statewide New York study found that half of the domestic violence suspects fled the scene, but local police ultimately arrested 60 percent of those who fled. [165] (Research basis: State law varies regarding the power of police to arrest after the incident. Time limits are not restricted in Massachusetts or New York, where these results were documented.)

Implications for Prosecutors
Prosecutors should encourage law enforcement officers to file warrants for abusers who flee the scene and prepare reports for subsequent prosecution when arrests are made. Similarly, prosecutors should assist victims to file criminal complaints if necessary to allow for the prosecution of abusers who have left the scene before police arrived. (Research basis: Numerous studies confirm that a large proportion of abusers flee the scene. Only one study has looked at differences in records of those who fled the scene and those who didn't.)

2.12. Who is the Primary/Predominant Aggressor?

A substantial percentage of victims of domestic violence hit their perpetrators back. [72] In Massachusetts, 37.3 percent of the female victims fought back in the incident in which their male abuser was arrested. However, most (59.1 percent) of those females who fought back found that this made their abuser more violent. [23] A substantial number of victims will not self- disclose their victimization. [93] Consequently, determination of primary or predominant aggressor may not be self-evident. Nonetheless, data on police action in 2,819 jurisdictions in 19 states reveal that only 1.9 percent of incidents resulted in dual arrests for intimate partner violence and intimidation. In other words, less than 4 percent of all intimate partner arrests were dual arrests in which law enforcement could not determine a primary or predominant aggressor. [117]

Studies suggest that officers' determination of primary or predominant aggressor is particularly problematic when the intimate partner violence occurs between same-sex couples. Although police are equally likely to make arrests in same-sex as in heterosexual partner abuse cases, a study of more than 1,000 same-sex intimate partner violence reports from departments across the country found that officers were substantially more likely to arrest both parties in same-sex cases. Specifically, 26.1 percent of female same-sex cases and 27.3 percent of male same-sex cases resulted in dual arrests, compared to only 0.8 percent with male offenders and female victims, and 3 percent with female offenders and male victims. [175]

Research on the impact of primary aggressor policies, either mandated by state statute or by individual law enforcement agencies, reveals that such policies significantly reduce the percentage of dual arrests from an average of 9 percent to 2 percent of domestic violence arrests. [117]

Implications for Law Enforcement

If the rate of dual arrests exceeds that found on average across the country, law enforcement departments should develop and implement specific primary aggressor policies and protocols. (Research basis: The most significant dual-arrest study was based on examination of all assault and intimidation cases in the 2000 National Incident-Based Reporting System (NIBRS) database as well as more detailed examination of these data from 25 diverse police departments across the country.)

Implications for Prosecutors

If presented with a dual-arrest case, prosecutors should conduct an independent analysis to determine the predominant aggressor and proceed against that suspect alone. Determination of primary/predominant aggressor is briefly described by the American Prosecutors Research Institute on its Web site: http://www.ndaa.org/apri/programs/vawa/dv101.html. (Research basis: The most significant dual-arrest study documenting its rarity was based on examination of all assault and intimidation cases in the 2000 NIBRS database as well as more detailed examination of these data from 25 diverse police departments across the country.)

Implications for Judges

In dual-arrest cases, judges should insist that prosecutors provide evidence that one of the parties was the primary or predominant aggressor and the other the victim. This may be particularly important, as advocates caution that female victims who are arrested along with their abusers may nonetheless plead guilty in order to be able to return home to care for minor children. Furthermore, it appears that law enforcement finds it particularly challenging to determine the primary/predominant aggressor with same-sex couples. (Research basis: The most significant dual-arrest study was based on examination of all assault and intimidation cases in the 2000 NIBRS database as well as more detailed examination of these data from 25 diverse police departments across the country.)

3. PERPETRATOR CHARACTERISTICS

3.1. What is Their Gender?

Although some sociological research [202] based on self-reporting finds equal rates of male and female partner *conflict* (including mostly minor physical assaults), behavior that is likely to violate most state and federal criminal and civil (protective order) statutes is typically perpetrated by males. [153]

Perpetrators that come to the attention of the criminal justice system are overwhelmingly male. For example, 86 percent of abusers brought to court for restraining orders in Massachusetts were male, [2] as were those arrested for domestic violence in California [228] and Charlotte, N.C. (as much as 97.4 percent for the most serious cases). [68] In Rhode Island, 92 percent of abusers placed on probation for domestic violence were male. [68, 141] A Cincinnati court study found 86.5 percent of 2,670 misdemeanor domestic violence court defendants to be male. [11] The overwhelming majority of their victims were women: 84 percent in both Charlotte, N.C., [68] and Berkeley, Calif. [228] The 2000 NIBRS multistate study found that 81 percent of the suspects were male and their victims were female. [117]

Jurisdictions with higher numbers of female suspects and male victims usually include higher numbers of non-intimate family violence cases. [139, 196] The latter typically involve older victims and their adult children perpetrators. A study of elder abuse across the state of Rhode Island, for example, found that two-thirds of elder female victims were abused by family members as opposed to intimate partners, including 46.2 percent by adult sons and 26.9 percent by adult daughters, 8.6 percent by grandsons and 1.6 percent by granddaughters. [139]

Implications for Law Enforcement

If the ratio of male to female suspects and victims differs substantially from those found above, departments should be alert to potential gender bias in their response to domestic violence. Ongoing training and supervision can address overrepresentation of female versus male arrests. (Research basis: Multiple studies of abusers and their victims brought to the attention of the criminal justice system [including civil protective orders] confirm the gender ratio as opposed to studies focusing on non-intimate and family conflict.)

Implications for Prosecutors

Prosecutors should be alert to gender bias in the response of local law enforcement agencies and re-screen cases if the percentage of female suspects accused of abusing male victims exceeds that commonly found across the nation. (Research basis: Multiple studies of abusers and their victims brought to the attention of the criminal justice system [including civil protective orders] confirm the gender ratio as opposed to studies focusing on non-intimate and family conflict.)

Implications for Judges

If, upon reviewing domestic violence dockets, judges find much higher rates of female-on-male abuse cases than those typically found across the country as a whole, they should be alert to potential gender bias on the part of police and/or prosecutors and ensure that they are presented with sufficient evidence to confirm the correct designation of victims and their abusers. (Research basis: Multiple studies of abusers and their victims brought to the attention of the criminal justice system [including civil protective orders] confirm the gender ratio as opposed to studies focusing on non-intimate and family conflict.)

3.2. What Age are They?

Most studies find most perpetrators to be between 18 and 35 years old, with a median age of about 33 years, although they range in age from 13 to 81. [11, 23, 68, 228] A large U.S. west coast study of abusers subject to police incident reports or protective orders found that 33 percent were between 20 and 29 years old, and slightly more (33.4 percent) were between 30 and 39 years old. [121]

3.3. Are They Likely to Be Known to Law Enforcement Already?

Most studies agree that the majority of domestic violence perpetrators that come to the attention of criminal justice or court authorities have a prior criminal history for a variety of nonviolent and violent offenses against males as well as females, and of a domestic or nondomestic nature. For example, a study of intimate partner arrests in Connecticut, Idaho and Virginia of more than 1,000 cases each found that almost 70 percent (69.2) had a prior record and that 41 .8 percent of those had been convicted of a violent crime, including robbery and rape. [117]

The percentage of officially identified perpetrators with criminal histories ranges from a low of 49 percent for prior arrest within five years in an arrest study in Portland, Ore. [130], to 89 percent for at least one prior nonviolent misdemeanor arrest for domestic violence defendants arraigned in a Toledo, Ohio, Municipal Court. [216] Not only did most of the abusers brought to the Toledo Court for domestic violence have a prior arrest history but the average number of prior arrests was 14. Similarly, 84.4 percent of men arrested for domestic violence in Massachusetts had prior criminal records, averaging a little more than 13 prior charges (resulting from five to six arrests) - including four for property offenses, three for offenses against persons, three for major motor vehicle offenses, two for alcohol/drug offenses, one for public order violations, and 0.14 for sex offenses. [23] A study of the Cook County (Chicago) misdemeanor domestic violence court found that 57 percent of the men charged with misdemeanor domestic violence had prior records for drug offenses, 52.3 percent for theft, 68.2 percent for public order offenses, and 61.2 percent for property crimes. On average, they had 13 prior arrests. [107]

Even if abusers have no prior arrest records, they may be known to local police. In North Carolina, for example, researchers found from police files that 67.7 percent of the domestic violence arrestees had prior contact with the local criminal justice system, 64.5 percent were officially known by local police, and 48.3 percent had prior domestic violence incident reports. [68]

Studies of abusers brought to court for protective orders find similarly high rates of criminal histories, ranging from slightly more than 70 percent in Texas [26] to 80 percent in Massachusetts. [134]

Implications for Law Enforcement, Prosecutors and Judges

Given the large overlap between domestic violence and general criminality, law enforcement should carefully check domestic violence suspects' status in regard to outstanding warrants, pending cases, probationary or parole status, and other concurrent criminal justice involvement, including suspect involvement as a confidential informant for ongoing investigations. With regard to the latter, in the event the informant is involved in a domestic violence incident, he should be precluded from working with the department without the authorization of department supervisors. In prosecuting or sentencing defendants for other crimes, prosecutors and judges should look for concurrent domestic violence that was previously prosecuted, is pending, or that may be charged. (Research basis: Multiple studies from jurisdictions across the country confirm these findings, although the extent of prior records may vary, depending on jurisdictional law enforcement, court practices and resources.)

3.4. Are They Likely to Be Drug and/or Alcohol Abusers?

As with criminality in general, there is a high correlation between alcohol and substance abuse and domestic violence for abusers. This is not to say that substance abuse causes domestic violence. The Memphis night arrest study found that 92 percent of assailants used drugs or alcohol on the day of the assault, and nearly half were described by families as daily substance abusers for the prior month. [19] Other studies found a lower but still substantial incidence of substance use. For example, a California arrest study found alcohol or drugs, or both, were involved in 38 percent of the domestic violence incident arrests. [228] A large Seattle arrest and protective order study found that alcohol/drug use was reported in 24.1 percent of incidents involving police. [120, 121] It was higher in North Carolina, where 45 percent of suspects were identified as being intoxicated. [68]

A domestic violence fatality review study in New Mexico documented that alcohol and drugs were present in 65 percent of 46 domestic violence homicides between 1993 and 1996: 43 percent abused alcohol and 22 percent abused drugs. [170] Two surveys, one of state correctional facilities in 1991 and the other of jails in 1995, found more than half of those jailed or imprisoned for domestic violence admitted drinking and/or using drugs at the time of the incident. [93] Self-reports from batterers in Chicago revealed that 15 to 19 percent admitted to having a drug problem, and 26 to 31 percent scored more than one on the CAGE (Cut down drinking, drinking Annoyed others, felt Guilt over drinking, and needed a morning Eye-opener drink) test indicating alcohol abuse. [12] Among defendants prosecuted in Chicago's domestic violence misdemeanor court, 60.7 percent were found to have "ever had an alcohol or drug problem." [107]

Interviews with more than 400 North Carolina female victims who called police for misdemeanor domestic assaults found that abuser drunkenness was the most consistent predictor of a call to police. According to the victims, almost a quarter (23 percent) of the abusers "very often" or "almost always" got drunk when they drank, more than half (55 percent) were binge drinkers, 29.3 percent used cocaine at least once a month, and more than a third (39 percent) smoked marijuana. Furthermore, almost two-thirds of abusers were drinking at the scene of the incident, having consumed an average of almost seven drinks, resulting in more than half of them (58 percent) being drunk. [126] The national crime victims survey found substantial, but lesser rates of substance abuse. Between 1993 and 2004, victims reported that 43 percent of all nonfatal intimate partner violence involved the presence of alcohol or drugs, another 7 percent involved both alcohol and drugs, and 6 percent involved drugs alone. [27]

Both a batterer and an alcohol treatment study similarly reveal a consistent, high correlation between alcohol abuse and domestic violence. In one study, for example, for 272 males entering treatment for battering or alcoholism, the odds of any male-to-female aggression were 8 to 11 times higher on days they drank than on days they did not. [56]

Implications for Law Enforcement

Law enforcement officers should note the use of alcohol or drugs in domestic violence incident reports, not to mitigate abusive behavior but to indicate heightened abuser risk for continued abuse. (Research basis: The correlation is found in multiple studies across the country.)

Implications for Prosecutors and Judges

The presence of drug and/or alcohol abuse makes continued offending more likely. Although sobriety may not eliminate the risk for reabuse, research suggests it may be a necessary ingredient. When recommending or setting release or sentence conditions, requiring abstinence from alcohol and drugs may be appropriate. (Research basis: Correlation is found in multiple studies across the country.)

3.5. Are They Likely to be Mentally Ill or Have Certain Personality Traits?

Batterers are no more likely to be mentally ill than the general population. [89] Although various researchers have attempted to classify abusers - ranging from agitated "pit bulls" and silent "cobras" [128] to "dysphoric/borderline" and "generally violent and anti-social" [122] - attempts to use these classifications to predict risk of reabuse have proven unhelpful. [112] However, researchers agree that batterers may differ markedly from each other. [29, 123, 193] Although some batterers may appear to be emotionally overwrought to responding police officers, other batterers may appear calm and collected. [128] Other research suggests that batterers can be classified as low-, moderate- and high-level abusers and that, contrary to common belief, batterers remain within these categories. [28] Similarly, in the treatment literature, the multistate study of four batterer intervention programs consistently found that approximately a quarter of court-referred batterers are high-level abusers, unlikely to respond to treatment. [84, 85, 88]

Implications for Law Enforcement

Abuser demeanor at the scene, especially compared to overwrought, traumatized victims, can be misleading. (Research basis: Multiple studies have failed to validate any classification of battering propensity based on personality types or mental illnesses, and multiple observational studies reveal different patterns of behaviors among batterers.)

Implications for Prosecutors and Judges

Battering does not appear to be a mental aberration and is not responsive to mental health counseling. Although batterers may suffer from depression or low self-esteem after being arrested or restrained, these conditions have not been found to have caused the abuse. (Research basis: Multiple studies have failed to validate any classification of battering propensity based on personality types or mental illnesses, and multiple observational studies reveal different patterns of behaviors among batterers.)

3.6. Do Abusers Stick with One Victim?

Deprived of their victim, many abusers will go on to abuse another intimate partner or family member. Others may abuse multiple intimate partners and family members simultaneously. [32] The Rhode Island probation study, for example, found that in a one-year period, more than a quarter (28 percent) of those probationers who were rearrested for a new crime of domestic violence abused a different partner or family member. [141] The Massachusetts study of persons arrested for violating a civil restraining order found that almost half (43 percent) had *two or more victims over six years*. [18] This confirms an earlier state study finding that 25 percent of individuals who had protective orders taken out against them in 1992 had up to eight new orders taken out against them by as many victims over the subsequent six years. [2]

Studies have generally found that abusers who go on to abuse new partners are not substantially different from those who reabuse the same partner, with the exception that they tend to be younger and are not married to their partners. [2, 141]

Implications for Law Enforcement, Prosecutors and Judges

If the abuser is no longer with the victim of the last domestic violence incident, new intimate partners are vulnerable to becoming new targets of abuse. Whether the batterer remains with the same victim or not, battering behavior brought to police and prosecutors' attention is likely to reflect chronic, patterned, non-isolated behavior that is victim specific. In charging decisions, sentencing recommendations, and fashioning protective orders or criminal sanctions, prosecutors and judges must be concerned with future intimate-partner victims as well as immediate victims, even if the immediate intimate-partner victims are no longer available to the abusers. (Research basis: Although longitudinal studies of batterers are few, multiple studies that follow batterers for only a year or two also confirm the serial nature of battering for some abusers.)

3.7. How Many Abusers are Likely to Do It Again?

Depending on how reabuse is measured, over what period of time, and what countermeasures either the victim (e.g., getting a protective order or going into hiding) or the criminal justice system takes (arresting or locking up the abuser), a hard core of approximately one-third of abusers will reabuse in the short run, and more will reabuse in the long run.

In Rhode Island, 38.4 percent of abusers were arrested for a new domestic violence offense within two years of being placed on probation supervision for a misdemeanor domestic violence offense. [141] A half-dozen batterer program studies published between 1988 and 2001 and conducted across the United States documented reabuse, as reported by victims, ranging from 26 to 41 percent within five to 30 months. [4, 48, 54, 84, 85, 88, 89, 98] Five studies published between 1985 and 1999 of court-restrained abusers in multiple states found reabuse rates, as measured by arrest and victim reports for the period of four months to two years after their last abuse offense, to range from 24 to 60 percent. [4, 26, 105, 133, 134]

Where studies have found substantially lower rearrest rates for abuse, it appears the lower rate is a result of police behavior, not abuser behavior. In these jurisdictions, victims report equivalent reabuse, notwithstanding low rearrest rates. For example, studies of more than 1,000 female victims in Florida, New York City and Los Angeles found that, whereas only 4 to 6 percent of their abusers were arrested for reabuse within one year, 31 percent of the victims reported being physically abused during the following year (one-half of those reporting being burned, strangled, beaten up or seriously injured) and 16 percent reported being stalked or threatened. [61, 190] Similarly, in a Bronx domestic court study, whereas only 14 to 15 percent of defendants convicted of domestic violence misdemeanors or violations were rearrested after one year, victims reported reabuse rates of 48 percent during that year. [185]

Reabuse has found to be substantially higher in longer term studies. A Massachusetts study tracked 350 male abusers arrested for abusing their female intimate partners over a decade, 1995 to 2005. The study found that 60 percent were rearrested for a new domestic assault or had a protective order taken out against them, even though some went three to four years between arrests. [138, 224] An equivalently high rearrest rate for domestic violence was also documented in Colorado between 1994 and 2005. During that time, of 84,431 defendants arrested for domestic violence, according to the state bureau of investigation, more than 50,000 (nearly 60 percent) were arrested for domestic violence charges more than once. In other words, the domestic violence rearrest rate was almost 60 percent for arrested abusers over an average of five years. [125]

Implications for Law Enforcement

It is safe to assume that, more often than not, the typical abuser who comes to the attention of law enforcement has a high likelihood of continuing to abuse the same or a different victim, both in the short term and over the subsequent decade at least. (Research basis: Although observational studies vary on reports of reabuse [depending on how it is measured], there is widespread consensus that reported reabuse is substantially less than actual reabuse experienced by victims, which is typically found to be more than 50 percent. The few longitudinal studies of more than a year or two suggest that many abusers continue to abuse, notwithstanding gaps of several years between initial and subsequent reported incidents.)

Implications for Prosecutors and Judges

It is safe to assume that, more often than not, the typical abuser who makes it to the Prosecutor's office has a high likelihood of continuing to abuse the same or a different victim, both in the short term and over the subsequent decade at least. While prosecuting specific, discrete incidents, prosecutors should recommend sentences that address long-term patterns of criminal behavior and are based on abuser risk for reabuse. Judges should fashion civil or criminal remedies/sanctions that maximize protection of current and/or future victims from the abuser. It is inappropriate to consider a repeat abuser as a "first" offender just because several years may have passed between abuse offenses. (Research basis: Although observational studies vary on reports of reabuse [depending on how it is measured], there is widespread consensus that reported reabuse is substantially less than actual reabuse experienced by victims, which is typically found to be more than 50 percent. The few longitudinal studies of more than a year or two suggest that many abusers continue to abuse, notwithstanding gaps of several years between initial and subsequent reported incidents.)

3.8. Are Abusers at Risk for Committing New Nondomestic Violence Crimes?

Given their extensive prior criminal histories, abusers typically do not confine their reoffending to domestic violence alone. Studies concur that abusers are also likely to commit new nondomestic violence crimes in addition to domestic-violence-related crimes. Two New York City studies, one in the Bronx Misdemeanor Domestic Violence Court and the other in the Brooklyn Felony Domestic Violence Court, found that 58 percent of those arrested for domestic violence were rearrested for any crime within 30 months of the study arrest in the former study [164], and 44 percent within two years of arrest in the latter. [183] Most of the new arrests (according to official complaints) were for nondomestic-violence-related crimes such as drug possession/sale or property offenses.

Similarly, whereas 51 percent of Massachusetts abuser arrestees were rearrested for new domestic violence over the following 10 years, 57 percent were rearrested for nondomestic violence, including 15 percent who were not also arrested for new domestic violence. [138] Among Cook County domestic violence misdemeanants, 26.1 percent were arrested within 2.4 years on average for new domestic violence, whereas 46.5 percent were arrested for any offense. [12] It is not surprising that research from the National Youth Survey found that most men (76 percent) who engage in domestic violence report also engaging in one or more deviant acts concurrently, including illegal behavior such as stealing or illicit drug use. [167] Nor is it surprising that abuser violence was not limited to their households. In Cook County (Chicago), the majority of prosecuted misdemeanor domestic violence offenders (55.6 percent) were found to have been violent with others as well as their partners. [107]

Implications for Law Enforcement, Prosecutors and Judges

Aggressively pursuing, prosecuting and sentencing abusers not only may protect victims and their children but also may reduce nondomestic offenses often committed by abusers. (Research basis: Although multiple, disparate studies document that abusers identified by the criminal justice system are likely to have nondomestic criminal histories, at least one study of nonarrested young married or cohabiting men also found that domestic violence and other deviant behaviors were associated both concurrently and prospectively.)

3.9. When Are Abusers Likely to Reabuse?

Studies agree that for those abusers who reoffend, a majority do so relatively quickly. In states where no-contact orders are automatically imposed after an arrest for domestic violence, rearrests for order violations begin to occur immediately upon the defendant's release from the police station or court. For example, in both a Massachusetts misdemeanor arrest study and a Brooklyn, N.Y., felony arrest study, the majority of defendants rearrested for new abuse were arrested while their initial abuse cases were still pending in court. [23, 164] The latter included a 16-percent arrest rate for violation of no-contact orders and a 14-percent arrest rate for a new felony offense. [164] Similarly, a little more than one-third of the domestic violence probationers in Rhode Island who were rearrested for domestic violence were rearrested within two months of being placed under probation supervision. More than half (60 percent) were arrested within six months. [141] A multistate study of abusers referred to batterer programs found that almost half of the men (44 percent) who reassaulted their partners did so within three months of batterer program intake, and two-thirds within six months. The men who reassaulted within the first three months were more likely to repeatedly reassault their partners than the men who committed the first reassault after the first three months. [81, 83, 84] In the Bronx, similarly, reoffending happened early among those convicted for misdemeanor or domestic violence violations. Of those rearrested for domestic violence, approximately two-thirds reoffended within the first six months. [185]

Implications for Law Enforcement

Arrest is only the first step in stopping abuse. Countermeasures must begin immediately, once the suspect is released pending trial. Focusing on those already arrested for domestic violence provides law enforcement with the means to target a high-risk population of abusers who are disproportionately likely to commit new abuse-related and other offenses. (Research basis: Multiple studies from disparate jurisdictions have all found relatively quick reabuse by abusers who reabuse within the first year or two.)

Implications for Prosecutors and Judges

Arrest is only the first step in stopping abuse. Once arrested, prosecutors must immediately pursue measures to safeguard victims pending trial and thereafter. If abusers are automatically released pending trial, the most vulnerable victims will be reabused by the worst abusers. This reabuse may also inhibit subsequent victim cooperation with prosecutors, resulting in subsequent dismissals for lack of prosecution. This in turn may further encourage abusers to continue their abuse. (Research basis: Multiple studies from disparate jurisdictions have all found relatively quick reabuse by those that reabuse within the first year or two.)

3.10. Which Abusers are Likely to Do It Again in the Short Term?

When officers respond to a domestic violence call, they typically do not have a lot of information about the parties involved, their psychological profiles, family and child development histories, and the like. Fortunately, the research consistently finds that the basic information usually available to officers provides as accurate a prediction of abuser risk to the victim as do more extensive and time-consuming investigations involving more sources (e.g., clinical assessments). [111, 112, 113, 189] As a Bronx study on batterer treatment concluded, intensive individual assessments of attitudes or personality are not required to make reasonable judgments regarding abusers' risk of reabuse. [183]

3.11. Is Gender an Important Risk Factor?

Of course, the most powerful predictor of risk of domestic violence is gender. All of the research concurs that males are more likely to reabuse than females. [183]

3.12. Is Age an Important Risk Factor?

Younger defendants are more likely to reabuse and recidivate than older defendants. [23, 141, 183, 185, 216, 228] This has been found to be true in studies of arrested abusers and batterers in treatment programs as well as court-restrained abusers. [111, 112, 134, 153, 228]

3.13. Is Prior Arrest History an Important Risk Factor?

If the abuser has just *one* prior arrest on his criminal record for *any* crime (not just domestic violence), he is more likely to reabuse than if he has no prior arrest. [23, 39, 85, 172, 185] A multistate study of more than 3,000 police arrests found that offenders with a prior arrest record for any offense were more than *seven* times more likely to be rearrested than those without prior records. [117]

The length of prior record is predictive of reabuse as well as general recidivism. [163] In looking at all restrained male abusers over two years, Massachusetts research documented that if the restrained abuser had just one prior arrest for any offense on his criminal record, his reabuse rate of the same victim rose from 15 to 25 percent; if he had five to six prior arrests, it rose to 50 percent. [134] In the Rhode Island abuser probation study, abusers with one prior arrest for any crime were almost twice as likely to reabuse within one year, compared to those with no prior arrest (40 percent vs. 22.6 percent). If abusers had more than one prior arrest, reabuse increased to 73.3 percent. [141] Of course, prior civil or criminal records specifically for abuse also increase the likelihood for reabuse. [23, 68, 216, 228]

Related to the correlation between prior arrest history and reabuse, research also finds similar increased risk for reabuse if suspects are on warrants. In the Berkeley study, researchers documented that having a pending warrant at the time of a domestic violence incident for a prior nondomestic violence offense was a better predictor of reabuse than a prior domestic violence record alone. [228] Similarly, in the one study that addressed this issue, suspects who were gone when police arrived were twice as likely to reabuse as those found on the scene by police. [23]

Similarly, one large statewide study found that if the suspect before the court for domestic violence was already on probation for anything else, or if another domestic violence case was also pending at the time of a subsequent arrest for domestic violence, that defendant was more likely to be arrested again for domestic violence within one year. [141]

Implications for Law Enforcement

The absence of a prior domestic violence arrest is not as powerful a predictor of no reabuse as the absence of a prior arrest for anything. On the other hand, a prior arrest record for any crime may be as accurate a predictor for subsequent domestic violence as a prior record for domestic violence. Law enforcement officers should attempt to track down the suspect who leaves the scene and aggressively serve warrants to protect victims from higher risk abusers. (Research basis: Multiple studies in disparate jurisdictions find that both prior criminal history and prior domestic violence correlate with reabuse, and vice versa, although the predictive power of prior domestic violence history may be less revealing if domestic violence arrest rates are low in that specific jurisdiction. Although only the limited studies speak to reabuse in correlation with abuser flight, they are consistent with more plentiful arrest studies that find support for the efficacy of arresting abuse suspects.)

Implications for Prosecutors and Judges

The absence of a prior domestic violence arrest is not as powerful a predictor of no reabuse as the absence of a prior arrest for anything. On the other hand, a prior arrest record for any crime is as accurate a predictor of subsequent domestic violence as a prior record for domestic violence. Therefore, in making charging decisions sentencing recommendations, prosecutors should understand that if an abuser has a prior record for any crime, the prosecutor should assume him to be a high-risk domestic violence offender, not a low-risk "first" offender. Prosecutors should carefully review defendants' prior arrest records for warrant status and bail status at the time of the domestic violence arrest to accurately gauge defendant risk. Judges should understand that if an abuser has a prior record for *any* crime, he is a high-risk domestic- violence offender, not a low-risk "first" offender. Judges should demand access to prior criminal and abuse histories before fashioning civil orders, making pretrial release decisions, or sentencing abusers. (Research basis: Multiple studies in disparate jurisdictions find both prior criminal history and prior domestic violence correlate with reabuse, and vice versa, although the predictive power of prior domestic violence history may be less revealing if domestic violence arrest rates are low in that specific jurisdiction.)

3.14. Is Substance Abuse an Important Risk Factor?

Acute and chronic alcohol and drug use are well-established risk factors for reabuse as well as domestic violence in general. [118, 221] Prior arrests for drug and alcohol offenses also correlate with higher rates of reabuse. [78] Just one prior arrest for any alcohol or drug offense (e.g., drunk driving or possession of a controlled substance), for example, doubled the reabuse rate from 20 percent (no prior drug/alcohol arrest) to 40 percent (at least one arrest for drugs/alcohol) in a restraining order study over two years. [134]

Defendant alcohol and substance abuse, similarly, are predictive of reabuse and recidivism. [23, 134, 141, 228] The multistate batterer program referral study found heavy drinking to be a significant predictor for reabuse. For the same reason, it found that abuser participation in drug treatment predicted repeated reassaults. [113] Batterers who complete batterer intervention are three times more likely to reabuse if they are found to be intoxicated when tested at three-month intervals. [83, 84, 85, 88] Many [63, 117, 172], but not all, studies [23] have found abuser or victim abuse of drugs or alcohol *at the time of the incident* to be a consistent risk marker for continued abuse.

Implications for Law Enforcement
Seemingly unrelated nonviolent offenses such as drunk driving or drug possession, which suggest substance abuse by the abuser, should be considered as risk markers for continued abuse. (Research basis: Multiple, disparate studies suggest that any disagreement regarding the relationship between domestic abuse and substance abuse has to do with whether or not substance abuse "causes" domestic violence, not with the existence of the correlation.)

Implications for Prosecutors and Judges
Seemingly unrelated nonviolent offenses like drunk driving or drug possession, which suggest substance abuse by the abuser, should be considered as risk markers for continued abuse. Substance and alcohol abuse should be considered when prosecutors make prerelease and sentencing recommendations and when judges set bail, pronounce sentences, and fashion civil protective orders and conditions of probation supervision. (Research basis: Multiple, disparate studies suggest that any disagreement regarding the relationship between domestic abuse and substance abuse has to do with whether or not substance abuse "causes" domestic violence, not with the existence of the correlation.)

3.15. Are Victims Accurate Predictors of Reabuse?

Victim perception of risk has been found to significantly improve the accuracy of prediction over other risk factors [44], increasing *sensitivity* - the proportion of true positives that are correctly identified by the test - from 55 to 70 percent. [112] However, the same researchers found that women's perceptions have to be interpreted. Women who felt very safe were less likely to be repeatedly reassaulted than those that felt somewhat safe. However, women who were uncertain or felt somewhat unsafe were more likely to be reassaulted repeatedly than those who felt they were in great danger. The reason for this apparent contradiction is that women who felt in greatest danger took effective countermeasures during the study. In other words, the research suggests that if women are not certain they will be safe, they err by giving the benefit of the doubt to their abuser. For these reasons, these researchers concluded that the best predictions of repeated reassaults were obtained by using risk markers, including women's perceptions. [44, 112] The researchers' concern for victims with regard to assessed risk of abuse is borne out by a study of more than 1,000 women who sought protective orders or shelter, or whose abusers were arrested in Los Angeles or New York City. Almost a quarter of the victims who thought their risk of reassault was low were, in fact, reassaulted within one year. [190]

Victims' perception of risk also affects their reaction to criminal justice intervention. Arrest research finds that victims who were not revictimized for more than two years were twice as likely to have opposed arrest, compared to those who were revictimized. Those victims who thought police and court intervention did not go far enough were also accurate. Those who said police actions were too weak were three times more likely to experience revictimization, and those victims who said courts failed them were seven times more likely to experience revictimization. [23]

Implications for Law Enforcement

Asking victims if they fear reassault or severe reassaults provides one of the best ways to predict reabuse or potential lethality - and requires the least resources and time commitment - but cannot be relied on exclusively as a predictor. Although women are unlikely to exaggerate their risk, they often underestimate it. (Research basis: A national homicide study involving hundreds of victims of attempted homicides, as well as the general reabuse studies, confirms these findings.)

Implications for Prosecutors and Judges

Victim input should be an important part of any risk calculation considered by prosecutors and judges. If victims are in doubt as to their safety, prosecutors and judges should assume the worst. (Research basis: Extensive examination of multiple domestic violence risk studies shows agreement on this point.)

3.16. Are There Other Common Risk Factors Associated with Reabuse?

Several studies have found other consistent risk markers for reabuse, many associated with the variables described above. These include increased risk associated with abusers who flee the scene of domestic violence [23]; abusers who are unemployed [13, 25, 142, 154, 172], economically disadvantaged and living in disadvantaged neighborhoods [153], or living in a household with firearms [25, 142]; or abusers who are not the fathers of children in the household. [25, 142]

Implications for Law Enforcement

Law enforcement officers recording the status of the above variables in their initial reports will provide valuable data for the determination of risk in future bail hearings, charging decisions and sentencing reports. (Research basis: These specific risk factors generally have been found in multiple studies but may vary in relevance and power across jurisdictions.)

Implications for Prosecutors and Judges

Prosecutors and judges should review the status of the above variables for determination of risk to be used in bail hearings, charging decisions, sentencing recommendations and decisions, and fashioning civil protective orders and conditions of probation supervision. (Research basis: These specific risk factors generally have been found in multiple studies but may vary in relevance and power across jurisdictions.)

3.17. What Factors are Not Associated With Reabuse?

Generally, the seriousness of the presenting incident does not predict reabuse, whether felony or misdemeanor, including whether there were injuries or not, or what the specific charge is. [23, 39, 134, 141, 145, 172] Abuser personality types have not been found to be associated with increased risk of reabuse. [113] Actuarial data offer improvement over clinical data. [189] Victim characteristics, including relationship with abuser, marital status, and whether the parties are living together or separated, have not been found to predict reabuse. [23] At least one study has found that victim cooperation does not predict recidivism. [145]

Implications for Law Enforcement

Criteria for charges should not be confused with criteria for determining future risk. Abusers cited for misdemeanors are as likely to be dangerous as those charged with felonies. (Research basis: Wide agreement among multiple studies across the nation involving different abuser populations.)

Implications for Prosecutors

Criteria for charges should not be confused with criteria for determining future risk. Abusers charged with misdemeanors are as likely to be dangerous as those charged with felonies. If the offense against a dangerous defendant is not chargeable as a felony, prosecutors should explore the applicability of enhancement statutes for repeat offenses, multiple charges if appropriate, or maximum allowable sentencing recommendations. (Research basis: Wide agreement among multiple studies across the nation involving different abuser populations.)

Implications for Judges

Criteria for charges should not be confused with criteria for determining future risk. Abusers charged with misdemeanors are as likely to be dangerous as those charged with felonies. Although constrained by statute, judges should seek to minimize offender risk to the maximum extent allowable by law. (Research basis: Wide agreement among multiple studies across the nation involving different abuser populations.)

3.18. Do the Widely Used Risk Instruments Accurately Predict Reabuse?

All of the common risk instruments in use are insufficient. The best instruments have been found to falsely predict 40 to 43 percent of abusers in both directions. [24, 190] For example, a study of a risk instrument used by police in Berkeley, Calif., found that those abusers classified at highest risk for reoffending did have the highest rate of reoffending but also that the instrument generated 43 percent false positives for predicting reabuse. Those abusers gauged as having the lowest risk of reoffending had 2 percent false negatives. [228]

Implications for Law Enforcement and Prosecutors

Given high base rates of reabusing, the default presumption should be that the defendant is likely to reoffend until proven otherwise. Risk instruments do not significantly improve upon victim perception and basic actuarial data. (Research basis: Not only is there wide agreement among multiple studies but it is also agreed that the same instrument may have different results in different jurisdictions.)

3.19. Which Abusers are Most Likely to Try to Kill Their Victims?

Predicting lethality is much more difficult than predicting reabuse and recidivism because, fortunately, it is much rarer. Also, the risk of lethality may increase because of situational circumstances and not because of static abuser characteristics. Nonetheless, researchers have found some key factors that increase the likelihood of homicide or significant injuries.

3.20. How Critical is the Presence of Firearms and Other Weapons?

According to a CDC study, more female intimate partners are killed by firearms than by all other means combined. [176] Firearms in the household increase the odds of lethal versus nonlethal violence by a factor of 6.1 to 1. Women who were previously threatened or assaulted with a firearm or other weapon are 20 times more likely to be murdered by their abuser than are other women. [25, 142] Prior firearm use includes threats to shoot the victim; cleaning, holding, or loading a gun during an argument; threatening to shoot a pet or a person the victim cares about; and firing a gun during an argument. [17, 191]

A significant Massachusetts study of 31 men imprisoned for murdering their female partners (and willing to talk to researchers) found that almost two-thirds of the guns used by men who shot their partners were illegal because the suspect had a prior abuse assault conviction or a protective order was in effect at the time of the killing. [1]

Implications for Law Enforcement

One of the most crucial steps to prevent lethal violence is to disarm abusers and keep them disarmed. Departments should implement a program to identify firearms in abusers' possession, remove them as soon as legally permissible, and make sure the abuser remains disarmed. If police agencies are involved in firearm licensing, they should aggressively screen for domestic violence, even if it is not discovered initially by inquiries in the FBI's National Instant Criminal Background Check System (NICS). (Research basis: Multiple studies - national, state and local - support this policy, as do state-by-state correlations between the existence of restrictive gun laws for batterers, state registries to enforce them and lower domestic homicide rates. [217])

Implications for Prosecutors

One of the most crucial steps to prevent lethal violence is to disarm abusers and keep them disarmed. Prosecutors should take all steps possible to have firearms removed by the court as soon as abusers are arrested and obtain guilty verdicts so that federal firearm prohibitions apply (18 U.S.C. § 922(g)(9)). Victims should be advised to obtain protective orders, or the prosecutor should ask the court to order criminal no-contact orders against defendants so that federal firearm prohibitions apply (18 U.S.C. § 922(g)(8)). Prosecutors should collaborate with the U.S. Attorney to refer appropriate firearms violators for federal prosecution, especially where federal penalties are more substantial than state penalties. (Research basis: Although multiple studies document the association between firearms and domestic violence homicides, only one study examined the association between each state's restrictive gun laws for batterers, state registries to enforce them and lower domestic homicide rates. [217])

Implications for Judges

One of the most crucial steps to prevent lethal violence is to disarm abusers and keep them disarmed. Judges should take all steps possible to have firearms prohibitions enforced and refuse to approve alternative sanctions that preclude federal firearm prohibitions (18 U.S.C. §922(g)(9)). Victims in criminal cases should be advised to obtain protective orders if firearms cannot be removed through the criminal process (18 U.S.C. §922(g)(8)), and vice versa. In 2007, in *Weissenburger* v. *Iowa District Court for Warren County* (No. 47/05-0279, filed October 26, 2007), the Iowa Supreme Court reminded judges they are legally obligated to enforce federal domestic-violence firearm prohibitions, notwithstanding contrary (or silent) state statutes. (Research basis: Multiple studies - national, state and local - support this policy, as do stateby-state correlations between the existence of restrictive gun laws for batterers, state registries to enforce them and lower domestic homicide rates. [217])

3.21. What are Other Lethality Risk Markers?

In a national study, other lethality markers that multiply the odds of homicide five times or more over nonfatal abuse have been found to include: (a) threats to kill, 14.9 times more likely; (b) prior attempts to strangle, 9.9 times; (c) forced sex, 7.6 times; (d) escalating physical violence severity over time, 5.2 times; and (e) partner control over the victim's daily activities, 5.1 times more likely. [25, 142] Research has also found that male abusers are more likely to kill if they are not the fathers of the children in the household. [17, 25, 142] A Chicago study similarly found that death was more likely if the abuser threatened his partner with or used a knife or gun, strangled his partner or grabbed her around her neck, or both partners were drunk. [17]

A series of interviews with 31 men imprisoned for partner murders revealed how quickly abusers turned lethal. Relationships with short courtships were much more likely to end in murder or attempted murder; these relationships were also likelier to end much sooner than those with longer term courtships. Half of the murderers had relationships of no more than three months with the partners they murdered, and almost a third had been involved for only one month. [1]

In terms of female murders of male partners, the research suggests that abused women who killed their partners had experienced more severe and increasing violence over the prior year. They tended to have fewer resources, such as employment or high school education, and were in long-term relationships with their partners at the time. [17]

Implications for Prosecutors

Prosecutors must insist that law enforcement investigators provide them with appropriate information about prior activities, especially those associated with increased risk for lethality. (Research basis: Multiple studies have found similar risk factors for lethality. Although applying risk factors can create false positives, their consideration will avoid false negatives that prove deadly for victims.)

Implications for Judges

For judges to make safe decisions about bail, sentencing or fashioning civil orders, they must insist on appropriate information about abusers' prior activities, including those associated with increased risk for lethality. (Research basis: Multiple studies have found similar risk factors for lethality. Although applying risk factors can create false positives, their consideration will avoid false negatives that prove deadly for victims.)

3.22. What Are the Risk Markers for Severe Injury?

Medical researchers have looked at severe injuries, those causing victims to seek hospital emergency room treatment. They have found that alcohol abuse, drug use, intermittent employment or recent unemployment, and having less than a high school education distinguish partners of women seeking medical treatment from domestic violence injuries from partners of women seeking treatment for nondomestic violence injuries. In one study, researchers found that 63.7 percent of the abusive partners were alcohol abusers, 36.7 percent abused drugs, a slight majority (51.6 percent) were drinking at the time of the assault, and 14.8 percent admitted to drug use at the time. [144] A similar hospital study found that cocaine use and prior arrests distinguished the violent partners from the nonviolent partners of women admitted to hospitals for treatment of injuries. [95]

Implications for Law Enforcement, Prosecutors and Judges

Prior threats to kill, prior strangulation and sexual assaults, as well as drinking and drugging histories and current use, should be taken very seriously when considering offender dangerousness. (Research basis: Conclusions from repeated studies somewhat overlap, indicating the same or similar risk factors for injury and lethality, including hospital studies of severe injuries of victims not necessarily involved in the criminal justice system.)

4. Victim Characteristics

4.1. Are Victim Characteristics and Actions Important Factors in Assessing the Likelihood of Abuse?

Victims come in all shapes, sizes, ages and relationships, but these differences are largely irrelevant in terms of their victimization. Victim characteristics - other than gender and age - have generally not been found to be associated with the likelihood of abuse. [23] For example, although many studies have associated pregnancy with increased risk for domestic violence, research suggests that the increased risk is related to the youth of women, not their pregnancy. [219]

Those victims who leave their abusers have been found to be as likely to be reabused as those who remain with them. [141] Those victims who maintain civil restraining orders or criminal no- contact orders against their abusers are as likely to be reabused as those who drop the orders. Only one study [120], comparing women with orders and those without, found that women with permanent as opposed to temporary orders were less likely to have new police-reported domestic violence. However, the researchers in this study excluded violations of the orders themselves, including violations of no-contact or stay-away orders.

Implications for Law Enforcement

Victims face a dilemma - staying or leaving, and securing, maintaining or dropping a protective order may all result in reabuse. Law enforcement officers should assist victims in safeguarding themselves and their children while recognizing their limitations in controlling their abusers. (Research basis: Multiple protective order studies in different jurisdictions over different time periods.)

> **Performance Measure:** A little more than a quarter of both small and large law enforcement agencies require officers to review safety plans with victims, and almost three-quarters of agencies arrange transport of victims to shelters or medical facilities, when needed.

Implications for Prosecutors and Judges

Victims face a dilemma - staying or leaving, and securing, maintaining or dropping a protective order may all result in reabuse. Prosecutors and judges should assist victims in recognizing their limitations in controlling their abusers and safeguarding themselves and their children. Prosecutors must establish effective collaboration with victim advocacy and service agencies in order to refer victims as needed. In addition, prosecutors should advise victims that prosecution, along with civil protective orders, may further victim protection. (Research basis: Findings that protective orders reduce reabuse don't include the order violations themselves, undervaluing the detrimental impact of order violations on victims who have secured them. The research on prosecution efficacy can be found under the question, "Does prosecuting domestic violence offenders deter reabuse?" in the Prosecution Responses section.)

4.2. To what Extent Do Victims Engage in Alcohol and Drug Abuse?

Victim abuse of drugs and alcohol is also associated with domestic violence victimization. [153] In the most dramatic findings, victims (or their families) reported in the Memphis night arrest study that 42 percent of victims were drinking or drugging the day of their assault. [19] The New Mexico fatality review study documented that a third of the female victims had alcohol in their system at the autopsy, with a blood alcohol content of twice the legal limit allowable for driving; a little less than a quarter had drugs in their system. [170] Among women treated in emergency rooms for injuries caused by their abusers, those who suffered from substance abuse were found to have increased risk of violence from partners. However, if the partners' use of alcohol and drugs are controlled for, victim substance abuse is not associated with increased risk of violence. [144] Another hospital study also found that victims who were injured by partners were more likely than other injured women in an emergency room to test positive for substance abuse. [95]

Victim substance abuse has also been found to be associated with abuser use. For example, whereas one in five North Carolina victims reported either being high or binge drinking at the time of abuse, almost three-quarters (72 percent) of these victims were in relationships with men who were high or were binge drinking. [126]

Victim substance abuse has also been identified as a consequence of the ongoing abuse. In other words, victims abuse drugs as a form of self-medication to deal with their abuse trauma. [153]

Implications for Law Enforcement

Victims' abuse of drugs and/or alcohol may make them more vulnerable to continued abuse, requiring greater law enforcement scrutiny or surveillance. Information given to victims should include substance abuse treatment referral information. (Research basis: Multiple single- jurisdiction observational studies of victims as well as findings from a national victim survey of a representative sample of 8,000 women between November 1995 and May 1996.)

Implications for Prosecutors and Judges

Victims' abuse of drugs and/or alcohol may make them more vulnerable to continued abuse. Prosecutors should look at victim vulnerability first and worry about tactical considerations, such as what kind of witness they may make, second. Furthermore, prosecutors should be prepared to file a motion *in limine*, and judges should conduct a hearing, to determine whether to exclude evidence related to a victim's "bad" character (e.g., substance abuse) that does not directly relate to the abuse incident prosecuted and/or the victim's ability to perceive or remember the incident. (Research basis: Multiple single-jurisdiction observational studies of victims as well as findings from a national victim survey of a representative sample of 8,000 women between November 1995 and May 1996.)

4.3. Why Do Some Victims Behave as They Do?

A significant proportion of victims of intimate partner violence and sexual assault suffer from trauma. [3, 153] Studies have found up to 88 percent of battered women in shelters suffer from post-traumatic stress disorder (PTSD). [6] Other studies have found that as many as 72 percent of abuse victims experience depression [212] and 75 percent experience severe anxiety. [76] A meta-analysis across multiple samples of battered women found a weighted mean prevalence of 48 percent for depression and 64 percent for PTSD. [77]

Even victims who do not have PTSD have been found to be severely adversely affected by their abuse. [153] Victims brought to emergency rooms of hospitals, for example, are more socially isolated, have lower self-esteem and have fewer social and financial resources than other women treated for injuries in the same hospital emergency rooms who were not injured by their partners. [95, 153]

Research also suggests that some victims of intimate partner abuse have experienced multifaceted violence that stretches across their life span, beginning in childhood. [143] Such prior victimization is associated with greater risk of more serious (adult) partner violence, particularly *systemic abuse,* which includes physical, sexual and stalking abuse. [153] In short, some of the adult victims who suffer the greatest abuse may be the least able to protect themselves.

Implications for Law Enforcement
Law enforcement officers may find that the most severely traumatized victims behave the least as law enforcement officers expect of them. These victims may be among the least able to cooperate with law enforcement. (Research basis: Multiple victim studies have documented PTSD rates, although many studies obviously seek out samples likely to include the most severely abused victims, such as those in shelters.)

Implications for Prosecutors and Judges
Prosecutors should be prepared to assist and support traumatized victims and/or make appropriate referrals to other service providers. Prosecutors should be prepared to identify, and judges should allow appointment of, expert witnesses if they are needed to educate juries and judges as necessary if a victim's reaction to trauma appears problematic or counterintuitive. (Research basis: Multiple victim studies have documented PTSD rates, although many studies obviously seek out samples likely to include the most severely abused victims, such as those in shelters.)

4.4. Do Male Domestic Violence Victims Differ from Female Victims?

Research on domestic violence victims brought to the attention of law enforcement and the courts find that male victims differ substantially from female victims. [153] First and foremost, male victims of any specific domestic violence incident are more likely than female victims to be *future suspects* for domestic violence. In one of the only studies to track abusers and victims over time, the Charlotte, N.C., law enforcement study found that 41 percent of males who were identified as *victims* and who were involved in new incidents of domestic violence within two years were subsequently identified by police as *suspects*. This compares with only 26.3 percent of females with such role reversals. On the other hand, males identified as suspects were much less likely to be identified later as victims than were female suspects (26 percent vs. 44.4 percent). [68]

Similarly, male victims of domestic violence homicides are much more likely than female victims to have been identified previously as abusers of their eventual killers. [131, 199, 218] Several treatises suggest that the abuse experienced by male victims of female intimates is contextually different than that experienced by women victims of male intimates. [177, 198] Just as male victims differ, so do females convicted of abusing male partners. [162]

Implications for Law Enforcement

Specific incidents of domestic violence may not reveal longer term domestic violence patterns, particularly if the suspect is a female and the victim is a male. Police should acknowledge this and encourage suspects who are more typically victims to report future victimization, notwithstanding their current suspect status. (Research basis: The North Carolina process evaluation of the Charlotte-Mecklenburg police specialized domestic violence unit is unique in looking at subsequent status of victims and suspects in repeat incidents. The study looked at all police complaints involving domestic violence in 2003 that were followed for the next two years, totaling 6,892 domestic violence complaints. The findings are analogous to numerous findings regarding the prior status of male homicide victims as abusers.)

Implications for Prosecutors and Judges

Specific incidents of domestic violence may not reveal longer term domestic violence patterns, particularly if the suspect is a female and the victim is a male. Prosecutors and judges should be sensitive to this fact in charging and recommending sentences for such defendants and in issuing protective orders or fashioning sentences. Typical batterer intervention programs, for example, may not be relevant for abusers engaged in isolated, reactive or defensive behavior. (Research basis: The North Carolina process evaluation of the Charlotte-Mecklenburg police specialized domestic violence unit is unique in looking at subsequent status of victims and suspects in repeat incidents. The study looked at all police complaints involving domestic violence in 2003 followed for the next two years, totaling 6,892 domestic violence complaints in all. The findings are analogous to numerous findings regarding the prior status of male homicide victims as abusers. The analysis of batterer programs for court-referred female defendants is based on limited qualitative research that focused on content relevance based on defendant abuse histories.)

5. LAW ENFORCEMENT RESPONSES

5.1. Are Specialized Law Enforcement Domestic Violence Units Effective in Responding to Domestic Violence?

> **Performance Measure:** A total of 11 percent of police departments have specialized domestic violence units, according to a national survey of a representative sample of 14,000 law enforcement agencies. Most domestic violence units work within investigative units and are most common in larger departments. A majority of departments (56 percent) with 100 or more officers have specialized domestic violence units. Although only 4 percent of departments maintain domestic violence information on their Web sites, three-quarters of those departments also have specialized domestic violence units. [213] (Research basis: A representative sample drawn from 14,000 law enforcement agencies across the nation.)

5.2. Do They Influence Prosecutions and Convictions of Abuse Suspects?

Specialized domestic violence units, emphasizing repeat victim contact and evidence gathering, have been shown to significantly increase the likelihood of prosecution, conviction and sentencing. [130] Specialized domestic violence units are generally associated with more extensive inquiries by police department call takers - asking if weapons are involved, advising callers to stay on the line until police arrive, asking if children are present, whether the suspect uses drugs/alcohol, whether restraining orders are in effect, and whether the suspect is on probation or parole. [213] Domestic violence units are also more likely to amass evidence to turn over to prosecutors. The specialized unit in Mecklenburg County, Charlotte, N.C., collected evidence in 61 .8 percent of its cases, compared to only 12.5 percent of cases collected by patrol officers. In addition, whereas 30 percent of victims handled by regular patrols declined to prosecute, only 8 percent of victims handled by the specialized unit declined to prosecute. [68]

5.3. Do they Influence Victim Behavior?

Specialized police response is more likely to see victims leave their abusers sooner - within four months, compared to an average of 14 months for victims not receiving specialized police response. Specialized police response also results in higher victim reporting of reabuse. Finally, victims handled by specialized police response are more likely to secure protective orders against their abusers. [130] Specialized police services such as serving protective orders and assisting in safety planning also influence victim behavior. By contrast, victim services alone have not been found to be associated with victims leaving abusers, although this may also be due to the quality of the victim services studied. [172, 220]

5.4. Do They Reduce Reabuse?

An early study of a specialized detective unit in Dade County, Fla., found that it did not affect reabuse rates. [174] However, the detective unit focused on referring parties to counseling. Subsequently, specialized units have been found to be more effective: Victims self-report significantly less reabuse but are more likely to report the reabuse they do suffer. [130] Another study found that specialized responses reduce "personal harm" but not nonpersonal harm, such as property damage. The positive effect may be tied to the safety planning offered to victims. [68] By contrast, research found that victim services alone are not associated with increased victim safety. [172, 220] Research in New York City among victims in public housing suggest that specific crime prevention training, as opposed to general victim counseling, may be associated more closely with reduced subsequent victimization. [37]

In North Carolina, 29 percent of the abusers handled by the specialized domestic violence unit had at least one subsequent domestic violence offense during a two-year follow-up period, compared to 37 percent of abusers handled solely by patrol units. This reduced rate was obtained even though the specialized unit handled more serious cases and offenders with more prior offenses. The odds ratio on reoffending for suspects handled by domestic violence units was nearly half that for suspects not handled by these units. Domestic violence suspects who reabused also reabused less often, averaging 0.46 new assaults compared to 0.62. The difference is statistically significant but, because fewer units' abusers reabused, the actual difference in the number of new incidents for just those abusers who reabused was less (1.59 vs. 1.67), not reaching statistical significance. [68]

5.5. Do They Increase Victim Satisfaction?

Victim satisfaction with the criminal justice system is not associated with whether the victim received advocacy per se, but rather with concrete law enforcement activities such as issuance of a warrant against absent abusers or assistance in obtaining protective orders. [220] Similarly, the NVAWS found that stalking victims whose stalkers were arrested were significantly more likely to be satisfied with the police response than those in situations where no arrest was made (76 percent vs. 42 percent). [208]

Studies of victim dissatisfaction generally focus on four major themes: (1) adverse personal outcomes (victim arrested, child protection agency called), (2) the police "made assumptions or did not listen," (3) the police took sides (against her), and (4) nothing happened (a strong court sanction was absent). [151]

Implications for Law Enforcement

The single, most appreciated service that officers can deliver to the greatest number of victims is the arrest of their abusers. Specialized domestic violence law enforcement units that focus on arrests can enhance the likelihood of successful prosecution and increase victim satisfaction and safety. (Research basis: Although specific studies of specialized domestic violence law enforcement units are few, the activities conducted by these units have been more widely studied and supported by extensive research.)

5.6. Should Law Enforcement Agencies Participate in Coordinated Community Responses?

A number of jurisdictions have endeavored to create what have been called *coordinated community responses*, composed of multiple criminal justice and social service agencies that respond to domestic violence. This approach may exert a positive impact on both case processing and reabuse, according to initial research. [118] For example, both arrests and successful prosecutions increased in several Minnesota jurisdictions with the creation of coordinated community responses involving law enforcement. [69] Other studies have found similar promising results [118], although more is required than participation in multidisciplinary task forces for communities to create effective coordinated responses. [227] Personnel of relatively autonomous organizations (both public and private) cannot be presumed to have the organizational capacity or the willingness among their personnel to truly collaborate. [73]

> **Performance Measure:** A total of 65 percent of police departments have established partnerships with community-based victim advocacy groups, according to a national survey of 14,000 police departments. [213] (Research basis: A representative sample drawn from 14,000 law enforcement agencies across the nation.)

5.7. Does Domestic Violence Training Improve Law Enforcement Responses to Victims?

Several studies suggest that general domestic violence training for law enforcement officers does not necessarily change attitudes toward domestic violence or, more important, change police behavior in terms of arrests of abusers or responses to domestic violence incidents. Although knowing a department's policy regarding domestic violence arrest preference increases the likelihood that officers will arrest alleged domestic violence suspects, the amount of domestic violence training received does not. [59, 65, 197] Research suggests that domestic violence arrest decisions are influenced more by an officer's assessment of the legal variables involved than by his or her attitudes. [117] At least one study suggests that failure of police managers to hold police officers accountable for failure to arrest in contravention of statutory requirements is responsible for their poor performance, not their lack of training. [187]

Implications for Law Enforcement

Clear policy pronouncements from the top administration may be more likely to change officer responses to domestic violence than is general domestic violence training aimed at education and attitude change. (Research basis: There is limited research in this area.)

Performance Measure: A survey of a sample of law enforcement departments across the nation finds that three-quarters have written domestic violence policies in place. Most have been in place for six years or longer. A large majority of departments (88 percent) require officers to complete incident reports for all domestic violence calls they are dispatched to, regardless of outcome. Almost wo-thirds of departments (63 percent) require officers to fill out a supplemental form for domestic violence, and most require written justification when no arrest is made (68 percent) or when there is a dual arrest (86 percent). [213] (Research basis: A representative sample drawn from 14,000 law enforcement agencies across the nation.)

6. PROSECUTION RESPONSES

6.1. What Is the Current Level of Domestic Violence Prosecution across the Country?

Although there remain wide disparities in the prosecution of domestic violence cases from one jurisdiction to another, routine prosecution of domestic violence arrests is no longer exceptional or rare. In fact, prosecutors who automatically dismiss or *nolle prosse* almost all domestic violence cases may be increasingly rare and exceptional.

A total of 120 studies from over 170 mostly urban jurisdictions in 44 states and the District of Columbia (and a few foreign countries) of intimate-partner prosecutions between 1973 and 2006 [71] found the average arrest prosecution rate was 63.8 percent, ranging from a low of 4.6 percent of 802 arrests in Milwaukee in 1988-1 989 to 94 percent of 3,662 arrests in Cincinnati in 1993-1996. The rate of offense prosecution was lower, with an average of 27.4 percent, ranging from a low of 2.6 percent for more than 5,000 offenses in Detroit in 1983 to 72.5 percent for more than 5,000 offenses reported in Boulder County, Colo., in 2003-2005.

Several studies demonstrate that domestic violence prosecutions can be routine across entire states, notwithstanding demographic, prosecution and law enforcement variations across counties and localities. A study of 15,000 protective order violations across Massachusetts between 1992 and 1995 found that 60 percent were prosecuted in total. [10] A study of 4,351 felony domestic violence prosecutions in South Carolina between 1996 and 2000 found a 46 percent prosecution rate. [21] Similarly, a study of 238,000 misdemeanor domestic violence charges between 1997 and 2002 in North Carolina found a prosecution rate of 47 percent. [16]

Jurisdictions with specialized domestic violence prosecution programs generally boast higher rates. A study of San Diego's City Attorney's Office documented that prosecutors prosecuted 70 percent of cases brought by police. Similarly, specialized prosecutors in Omaha, Neb., prosecuted 88 percent of all police domestic violence arrests. In several of these sites, comparisons before and after implementation of the specialized prosecution program found marked increases in prosecutions. In Everett, Wash., dismissals dropped from 79 percent to 29 percent, and in Klamath Falls, Ore., they dropped from 47 percent to 14 percent. [196]

On the other hand, not all domestic violence cases are equally likely to be prosecuted. The research indicates that prosecutions of intimate-partner stalking [160] and intimate-partner sexual assault [161] are rare. The research also reflects very low arrest rates for these offenses.

Implications for Prosecutors

Prosecutors who fail to prosecute the *majority* of domestic violence arrests made by police should examine their practices, policies and priorities to determine why they are prosecuting fewer domestic violence arrests than their peers around the country. (Research basis: Multiple studies, including at least three statewide studies.)

6.2. Can Most Domestic Violence Arrest Cases be Successfully Prosecuted in Court?

Not all cases filed by prosecutors go to trial. As with most offenses, most domestic violence prosecutions are disposed of as a result of plea and sentencing negotiations. Of those that go to trial, not all prosecutions result in convictions. However, studies indicate that, in general, domestic violence prosecutions that go to trial routinely result in court convictions. "Not guilty" findings are rare. Studies document findings that range from a high of only 5.0 percent in Ohio [11], to 2.7 percent in Massachusetts [23], to a low of 1.6 percent in North Carolina. [68] A study of felony domestic violence prosecutions in Brooklyn, N.Y., found a similarly low "not guilty" rate of only 2 percent. [164]

For most domestic violence cases that do not go to trial, an analysis of 85 domestic violence prosecution studies found an overall conviction rate of 35 percent, ranging from a low of 8.1 percent of 37 cases prosecuted in Milwaukee between 1988 and 1989 to a high of 90.1 percent of 229 cases in Brooklyn, N.Y., prosecuted in 1997. If one very large study of 123,507 Maryland prosecutions from 1993 to 2003 is removed, the average conviction rate increases to almost half, 47.7 percent. [71] In three statewide prosecution studies of tens of thousands of domestic violence cases, similar conviction rates ranged from one-third in North Carolina to more than one-half in South Carolina. [16, 21]

Jurisdictions with specialized domestic violence prosecution programs boast higher rates: 96 percent in San Diego, 85 percent in Omaha, Neb., 78 percent in Klamath Falls, Ore., and 55 percent in Everett, Wash. The latter rate was the lowest because prosecutors maintained a diversion program that siphoned off 22 percent of the cases prosecuted. [196]

As important, multiple studies also find that convictions can be consistently obtained that include the most intrusive disposition, sentences of incarceration. For example, in the three statewide domestic violence prosecution studies, 12.6 percent of the Massachusetts [10] and 20 percent of the North Carolina [16] misdemeanant domestic violence defendants prosecuted were sentenced to incarceration. In South Carolina, almost half (45 percent) of felony domestic violence defendants prosecuted were sentenced to prison. [21] In Brooklyn Felony Domestic Violence Court, 80 to 85 percent of all convicted offenders were sentenced to incarceration consistently during the study period of 1996 through 2000. [164] Although the latter single court incarceration rate may have been the result of a singular effort on the part of prosecutors and others, the statewide rates include multiple prosecutors across each state.

Many other disparate court studies document incarceration rates ranging from 76 percent to 21 percent: 76 percent in Klamath Falls, Ore. [196]; 70 percent in Cincinnati, Ohio, with the largest number incarcerated between 150 and 180 days [11]; 56 percent in Everett, Wash. [196]; 52 percent in Omaha, Neb. [196]; 39 percent in the Bronx, N.Y. [185]; 35 percent in Brooklyn, N.Y. [31]; 30 percent in Milwaukee [39]; 23 percent in Chicago (including time jailed pending prosecution) [107]; 22.5 percent in Quincy, Mass. [23]; and 21 percent in San Diego, Calif. [196] A study of intimate-partner arrests across three states - Connecticut, Idaho and Virginia - found similarly intrusive dispositions, with three-quarters of those convicted, incarcerated, sentenced to probation or fined. [117]

Implications for Prosecutors

The research suggests that domestic violence cases can be successfully prosecuted at trial, and a large proportion of cases (and most cases in some jurisdictions) can be disposed of before trial, even without removing incarceration as an outcome. (Research basis: Multiple studies in disparate jurisdictions for both felony and misdemeanor domestic violence prosecutions.)

Performance Measure: Norfolk County, Mass., prosecutors brought 505 charges arising out of 342 domestic violence incidents studied, compared to 531 charges initially filed by arresting police departments, a dropoff of only 5 percent. Prosecutors enhanced charges of felony assault from 14.1 percent filed by police to 23.8 percent. Prosecutors proceeded to *nolle prose qui* in 18.5 percent of the cases and asked that an additional 10 percent be dismissed in court. With the exception of 2.5 percent of arrests that resulted in not-guilty findings, the remaining defendants were either found guilty after trial or admitted to sufficient facts for a finding of guilty (although judges initially allowed 25 percent of the cases to be conditionally continued without imposition of a guilty finding). (Research basis: The studies followed 342 arrests that occurred within Eastern Norfolk County and followed them as long as 10 years. [23, 138])

6.3. Will Aggressive Prosecutions or Sentences Increase the Demand for Trials?

A study of four prosecution programs in four states where prosecutors specifically adopted (what they claimed to be) "no drop" prosecution policies (and in fact proceeded with the majority of all cases brought by law enforcement) found that trial rates ranged from a high of 13 percent to just 1 percent. Further research has suggested that the highest rates would recede once the aggressive prosecution programs were more established. In San Diego, which had adopted a no-drop policy a decade earlier, only 2 percent of the cases subsequently went to trial. [196] Furthermore, in these no-drop jurisdictions, sentencing included incarceration in 21 to 76 percent of the four jurisdictions. [196]

Implications for Prosecutors

Increased domestic violence prosecutions may not result in a dramatically increased proportion of trials, although there may be a transitory increase as defenders test prosecution resolve. (Research basis: Although implications are based on only one study, the study looked at four different no-drop prosecution programs in four states.)

Implications for Judges

Judicial administrators can rest assured that aggressive domestic violence prosecution will *not* result in dramatically increased and sustained demand for jury or bench trials. (Research basis: Although implications are based on one study, the study looked at four different no-drop prosecution programs in four states.)

6.4. Do Victims Want Their Abusers Prosecuted?

If asked to declare publicly in court in front of their abusers, victims may express ambivalence about the prosecution and/or sentencing of their abusers. However, in interviews with researchers, often a majority of victims support domestic violence prosecutions and sentencing, especially mandatory referral to batterer programs. In a Chicago misdemeanor court study, approximately two-thirds of victims (67.6 percent) reported that they wanted their abusers to be prosecuted *and* jailed. [107] A study of four prosecution programs in California, Washington, Oregon and Nebraska, found that three-quarters (76 percent) of the victims interviewed wanted their abusers arrested, and 55 percent want them prosecuted. Furthermore, 59 percent expressed satisfaction with the outcome, and 67 percent expressed satisfaction with the judge, once the cases were prosecuted. [196]

Even when the majority of victims oppose prosecution, after trial they may change their minds. In the Quincy arrest study, only 46.8 percent wanted their abusers to be prosecuted as charged or wanted more serious charges filed. However, after trial, 53.4 percent said the court experience gave them a "sense of control," 36.9 percent said it motivated them to end the relationship with their abuser, and 38.8 percent said it "made them safer." Most victims (71 percent) who did not want the case to go to court expressed satisfaction after the trial. [23] Similarly, a study of four specialized prosecution programs in four different states found that although 45 percent did not want their cases prosecuted, once they were prosecuted, only 14 percent tried to stop the prosecutors and only 4 percent said they wanted the court to let the defendant go. About three-quarters (72.1 percent) reported that they wanted the defendant jailed and/or ordered into treatment (79 percent). Sixty-four percent (64 percent) expressed satisfaction with the prosecution, another 9 percent were neutral, and only 27 percent were dissatisfied. Most (85 percent) reported that they felt the prosecution was helpful. [196]

Implications for Prosecutors

Prosecutors should not allow victim opposition to automatically stop them from prosecuting cases. If prosecutors find that the overwhelming majority of victims consistently oppose prosecution, they should examine both their and law enforcement's interaction with victims to increase support of prosecution from victims that is more in line with that found across the rest of the country. (Research basis: Numerous studies from disparate jurisdictions.)

Implications for Judges

Judges should not assume that allowing cases to proceed over victim objections will necessarily embitter victims or jeopardize their safety. (Research basis: Numerous studies from disparate jurisdictions on victim attitudes toward prosecution, and several studies on court sentencing.)

6.5. Why Do a Minority of Victims Oppose Prosecution?

Although studies have found multiple reasons for victim opposition to prosecution, fear is among the leading reasons expressed by victims. Fear of the abuser is first and foremost, followed by fear of testifying in court.

A study of five jurisdictions in three states found that victims across all sites reported that fear of defendant retaliation was their most common barrier to participation with prosecutors. [103] Even in a Chicago study where the majority of Chicago victims wanted their abusers prosecuted, fear was the biggest factor for those who opposed prosecution. A quarter of victims opposing prosecution reported being specifically threatened by their abusers against prosecution. Others expressed fear that their abusers would become more violent. In addition to fear, almost half who wanted the prosecution to be dropped thought it wouldn't make any difference. About a third of the victims opposed prosecution because they depended on their abusers for housing. [107]

In addition to fear of the abuser, an Ohio study found that more victims were actually more afraid of testifying in court than they were of the defendant or compromising their relationship with the defendant. Specifically, victims expressed fear that the prosecutors would not prepare them adequately to testify. They were also concerned that the defendant might not be found guilty. [11]

Implications for Prosecutors

To increase victim cooperation and participation in prosecution, prosecutors must address victim fears of reabuse *and* of testifying in court. (Research basis: Several victim studies in different jurisdictions.)

6.6. Is Victim Fear of Prosecution Well Founded?

Victim fear of their abusers appears to be well founded. Multiple prosecution and arrest studies broadly concur that abusers who come to the attention of the criminal justice system who reabuse are likely to do so sooner rather than later. In the Quincy court study, about 40 percent of the arrested abusers reabused their victims within one year. Forty-four percent did so *before* the study arrest was prosecuted in court. The average case took about six months from arraignment to prosecution. [23] Similarly, in a Cook County study, 30 percent of the defendants were rearrested within six months of their study arrest, and half of the arrests were for a new domestic violence offense. The average rearrest time was only 29 days after initial arrest. In addition, in almost half of the cases (45.9 percent), the defendants tried to talk the female victims out of testifying. Moreover, 29.1 percent of these defendants stalked their victims before the trial, and 8.7 percent specifically threatened them. [107] An Indianapolis prosecution study found that almost a quarter of the defendants reabused their victims before the pending trial. [67]

In the Brooklyn Specialized Felony Domestic Violence Court - where cases took 6.5 to 7.0 months, on average, to be disposed - 51 percent of defendants charged with domestic felonies (other than violation of protective orders) were rearrested before disposition; 14 percent were arrested for a crime of violence; and 16 percent were arrested for violation of a protection order. Among those charged with order violations - a felony in New York - the rearrest rate was 47 percent, including 37 percent for violating the protective order again. [164]

Although these studies do not demonstrate that prosecution causes reabuse, they indicate that pending prosecution by itself may not deter recidivist abusers.

Implications for Prosecutors and Judges

Prosecutors must gauge defendant risk pending trial and take appropriate measures to address it in order to protect victims and to successfully prosecute the case. Judges should insist that police and prosecutors document and inform the court if defendants reabuse, threaten or intimate victims while cases are pending so that possible additional charges can be filed and subsequent absences of victims who are too fearful to testify in court can be justified, allowing for substitute hearsay testimony. The equitable doctrine of forfeiture, affirmed in *Davis* v. *Washington*, 126 S. Ct. 2266, 2280 (2006), precludes a defendant from using his right to confrontation to bar the admission of a victim's statements when his wrongdoing caused her unavailability at trial. (Research basis: Rapid reabuse rates are documented in multiple studies from disparate jurisdictions. Research on the impact of specific prosecution practices is rare. Victim fear is documented in several victim studies in different jurisdictions.)

6.7. Can Prosecutors Increase Victim Cooperation?

Although victims most commonly reported fear of retaliation as a barrier to their participation in prosecution, a three-state study found that the fear was reduced at sites with specialized prosecution programs, increased victim advocacy and specialized domestic violence courts. [103] These specialized response programs generally include fast-track scheduling, reducing victim vulnerability pending trial, increased victim contact pending trial, and victim-friendly proceedings that remove, as much as possible, victim involvement to proceed with prosecution. These measures contrast with those used in some jurisdictions, in which studies indicate some prosecutors treat victims like civil claimants. In a large 45-county study of upstate New York domestic violence prosecutions, researchers found that half of the prosecutors required victims to sign complaints in order to file charges. (On the other hand, two-thirds required victims to sign affidavits to confirm their interest in having charges withdrawn.) [227]

There is more research on what not to do than on what works. Specific studies suggest that the more prosecution-related burdens are placed on victims, the less likely they are to cooperate. In Milwaukee, a study found the majority of cases were dismissed when victims were required to attend a charging conference within days of the arrest of their abusers. However, absolved of this responsibility, Milwaukee prosecution rates increased from 20 percent to 60 percent. [38] In a similar vein, a comparison of protective order violation prosecutions across Massachusetts found a 66 percent dismissal rate when prosecutors routinely provided and encouraged victims to sign waivers of prosecution forms (often in front of defendants), compared to a 33-percent dismissal rate in an adjacent county in which victims were not provided this alternative. [10]

Some prosecutors are better at maintaining contact with victims than others. The Ohio court study found that the majority of victims never received rudimentary information from prosecutors before trial, including court dates. In almost 90 percent of the court cases, prosecutors never spoke with the victim on the phone and, in more than half of the cases (52 percent), never met with them before the trial date. When they did meet, it typically was for no more than a few minutes. [11] The importance of prosecutor-victim contact is underscored by a Toronto study that found if the victim met with a victim/witness representative, victim cooperation increased by a factor of 3.3. [43] In the Ohio court study, the strongest predictor of a guilty verdict in domestic violence misdemeanor cases was how many times the prosecutors met with the victim before trial. [11]

A limited number of studies that looked at the role of court-based victim advocates suggest that they may help in this regard. The studies found that victims appreciated contact with victim advocates/liaisons and reported a high degree of satisfaction. In the Quincy study, 81 percent of the victims reported satisfaction with the time they spent with victim advocates, and three- quarters (77 percent) said they would talk to the advocate again if a similar incident recurred. [23] Chicago domestic violence victims who had contact with victim advocates reported more satisfaction with the proceedings than those who had no contact. However, the same study reported that advocates' contact with victims did not make the victims more likely to come to court. [107]

The seeds for victim contact may be planted before the case even reaches prosecutors. A Portland, Ore., police study found that the following police activities significantly correlated with increased prosecution: (1) police contacted victims, (2) victim accepted services, (3) police provided victims with prosecution information, (4) police helped set up victim appointments with prosecutors, and (5) police helped victims obtain restraining orders and served the orders. [130]

Implications for Prosecutors

Victim cooperation can be enhanced if prosecutors can address victim fear of their abusers as well as their fear around being involved in subsequent legal proceedings. Pretrial conditions or detention and/or speedy trial dates may address victim fear and minimize actions required of victims, and sensitivity to victim needs may address their fear of court proceedings. The quality of police contact with victims may also be important for subsequent successful prosecution. (Research basis: Multiple studies and victim interviews in multiple studies.)

> **Performance Measure:** Over 80 percent of victims were contacted by a prosecutor advocate in the Quincy court arrest and prosecution study; 42 percent of the victims had 45 minutes or more with an advocate, and the remainder had less time with one. [23]

6.8. Should Prosecutors Follow Victim Preferences When Prosecuting Offenders?

Although victim perceptions of the dangerousness of suspects have been found to be good predictors of subsequent revictimization [23, 112, 113], victim preferences on how the case should be prosecuted are not good predictors. The victims in the Quincy study who wanted the charges dropped were as likely to be revictimized (51 vs. 48 percent after one year) as those who did not want the charges dropped. [23] Similarly, studies in New York found that victim cooperation with prosecutors did not predict recidivism. In other words, if prosecutors proceeded with uncooperative victims, these victims were no more or less likely to be revictimized than victims who cooperated with prosecutors. [145]

Implications for Prosecutors

Although prosecutors should listen to victims, they should explain to victims (and, as important, to defendants) that the decision to prosecute cannot be based solely on victims' preferences.

6.9. What Evidence is Typically Available to Prosecute Domestic Violence Cases?

One of the challenges domestic violence prosecutors face is the lack of evidence accompanying their cases. A study of domestic violence across Rhode Island in 2002, based on 6,200 police incident reports involving adult victims under 50 years of age, found the following evidence reported in cases: victim photos (17 percent), crime scene photos (16 percent), suspect photos (3 percent), physical evidence (8 percent) and weapons collected (11 percent), medical reports (9.4 percent), witnesses' interviews (37 percent: adults 24 percent, children 12 percent), suspect statements (18 percent) and signed victim statements (53 percent). [138] The Rhode Island data are not unique.

In the Mecklenburg County, N.C., study, researchers found that presentation of physical evidence to the special domestic violence prosecution unit was rare. Photos were available in only 15 percent of the cases submitted by patrol officers and only 30.5 percent of cases submitted by the police department's specialized domestic violence unit. Medical evidence was available in less than 10 percent of the patrol cases and 34 percent of the special-unit cases, which selected out the more serious cases such as those involving injuries. Given the fact that most domestic violence incidents occur in private, it is not surprising that witnesses were available in only 16 percent of the patrol cases and 19 percent of the special-unit cases. [68] Similarly, the Ohio court study found that photos of injuries and damages were available in only 14.3 percent of the cases, 911 tapes in only 2.2 percent, medical records in 1.7

percent, eyewitness testimony in only 1.6 percent, and police officer testimony in only 6.7 percent of the cases. [11]

One reason medical evidence may be limited is because of medical staff's poor handwriting. A study found that in records of medical visits containing indications of abuse or injury, one-third of the notes written by the doctors or nurses contained vital information that was illegible. [127]

Implications for Prosecutors

Especially in light of *Crawford* v. *Washington*, 541 U.S. 36 (2004), prosecutors must work with law enforcement to gather as much evidence as possible and accurately identify all potential witnesses and ways to contact them, or identify third parties who will remain in touch with them. Vital witnesses may include third parties whom victims spoke to at the time of the incident. Statements that victims make to third parties are generally nontestimonial and therefore admissible at trial. Children may also be potential witnesses. The presence of children may also allow prosecutors to file additional charges against abusers for endangering the welfare of the child or allow them to file a similar charge that can go forward, even if the original charges cannot. (Research basis: Few studies review domestic violence evidence as a separate issue; these studies suggest that evidence collection can be dramatically improved.)

Consequently, prosecutors must rely on victims. In the Ohio court study, victim testimony was the evidence most frequently relied upon by prosecutors, available in 48 percent of the 2,952 domestic violence cases studied. [11] In Rhode Island, victims provided signed statements in 53 percent of the incident reports. [139] A Canadian study of a Toronto Domestic Violence Court found that, although having witnesses or corroborating evidence does not increase the likelihood of prosecution, if the victim cooperates, the odds of prosecution increase by a factor of 8, compared to cases in which the victim does not cooperate. [43] In Chicago, prosecutors achieved a 73-percent conviction rate for domestic violence cases when the victim showed up in court, and significantly less (only 23 percent) when they did not show. [107]

Generally, lack of cooperative or available victims is cited as the prime reason prosecutors drop or dismiss domestic violence cases. In the Quincy, Mass., arrest study, a quarter of the arrested abusers were not prosecuted by the district attorney's office. When indicated in the court file, the most common reason given was "victim denies abuse" (18.8 percent), married victims invoked their marital privilege not to testify against their husband suspects (12.9 percent), or the victim could not be located (10.6 percent). [23] In the large Ohio study, 70.5 percent of cases were dismissed because of victim "unavailability/failure to attend." [11] In another Ohio study, in Toledo, analysis of a sample derived from 1,982 misdemeanor domestic violence cases before the municipal court found that 70 percent of dismissed cases were dismissed because the "victim failed to appear." [216] In North Carolina, victim opposition was reported as the key factor in reducing the likelihood of prosecution. [119]

Implications for Law Enforcement

Prosecutors must work with local law enforcement to identify and obtain critical evidence whenever it is available, including information on how to locate and contact victims and other potential witnesses. (Research basis: Several large court and statewide studies in disparate jurisdictions indicate law enforcement's failure to provide available evidence.)

6.10. Can Cases be Successfully Prosecuted without the Victim?

Despite the fact that most prosecutors see the lack of victim cooperation as the reason why domestic violence prosecutions cannot proceed, both individual-jurisdiction and comparative studies clearly suggest that either lack of victim cooperation is exaggerated or victims are not the key variable in successful prosecution programs.

A study of almost 100 domestic violence trials in San Diego found that uniformly high conviction rates were obtained independent of victim or defendant statements, witness testimony and corroborating evidence. In fact, outcomes were also independent of whether the victim testified for the prosecution or for the defense. [196]

Other comparative studies consistently found that the determination of prosecutors rather than the availability of victims or other evidence accounted for varying rates of prosecution. For example, in the three statewide examinations of tens of thousands of domestic violence prosecutions, researchers documented widely varying rates of prosecution across equivalent counties. In Massachusetts, county prosecution rates ranged from 82 percent to 25 percent. [10] In South Carolina, prosecution rates varied from 69 percent to 22 percent from one prosecution district to another. [21] Similarly, in North Carolina, prosecution rates ranged from 57 percent to 21 percent in specific prosecution districts. [16] Although some of the counties or prosecutorial districts differed in terms of demographics and population density, even among those that did not, prosecution rates varied greatly. In fact, in South Carolina, after the study was published in the newspaper and the state's attorney general ordered prosecutors to prosecute all cases, the statewide dismissal rate dropped by 29 percent the next month. [20]

Studies confirm that jurisdictions with specialized domestic violence prosecution programs generally support the highest rates of successful prosecution. [196] These specialized programs apparently create their own momentum. For example, they either help create or are associated with courts that create expedited domestic violence dockets. As a result of the specialized prosecution in San Diego, processing time for domestic violence cases decreased to 32 days, with almost half of the defendants (46 percent) pleading at the arraignment. Similarly, in Everett, Wash., time to trial was 80 days, and in Omaha, Neb., it was 43 days. Shortened trial times reduce both victim vulnerability to threats and chances of reconciling with the abuser pending trial. In both San Diego and Everett, bails were regularly set at $10,000 per domestic violence charge (with no cash alternative in the latter location). As a result, for defendants unable to raise bail, the incentive is to plead guilty to get *out* of jail.

In these jurisdictions, researchers found that evidence (eyewitnesses, photos, admissions, excited utterances, medical evidence and physical evidence) was *not* uniformly the most powerful predictor of prosecutors' decisions to proceed without victims and was not significantly associated with the decision to prosecute at all in Klamath Falls, Ore. [196]

Supporting the contention that prosecutorial determination is a powerful predictor of prosecutorial success, the Ohio court study found that increased time the prosecutor spent with victims while preparing the case was positively associated with successful prosecution, and large prosecution caseloads were negatively associated with successful outcomes. The availability of evidence (911 tapes, photographs, medical records and police testimony) was *not* associated with the likelihood of a conviction. Researchers did not suggest that only victims with strong cases self-selected to approach prosecutors. [11]

Implications for Prosecutors

Lack of evidence may be more likely to deter prosecutors from going forward than deterring juries from convicting defendants or deterring defendants from pleading guilty. (Research basis: Multiple studies have found prosecutors able to consistently achieve high conviction rates, notwithstanding consistently limited evidence. The analysis of San Diego trials specifically suggests that convictions may be obtained with varying types of evidence, notwithstanding absence of types of other evidence, including that from victims.)

Implications for Prosecutors

Parity should exist between prosecutors and defenders as well as between prosecutors and crimes to be prosecuted. In the Ohio study, where large prosecution caseloads were associated with unsuccessful domestic violence prosecution, the court had 31 public defenders but only 18 prosecutors. (Research basis: Only one study.)

6.11. Can Successful Prosecutions be Increased?

There have been multiple studies of specific prosecution efforts to significantly increase prosecution by adopting no-drop policies. Although the concept of a no-drop policy has proven elastic, the success of these programs in significantly increasing prosecution has been demonstrated in multiple jurisdictions. In the Queens Borough of New York City, prosecutors increased convictions from 24 to 60 percent. Research suggests that much of the increase was the result of increased follow-up with victims, and prosecutor's improved linkage with police (e.g., monitoring the same case log, and asking whether each of eight evidentiary items were covered in police incident reports, including photos and witness, victim and suspect statements). [159] A study of domestic violence prosecutions in two other states similarly found greatly increased conviction rates as a result of adopting no-drop policies accompanied by increased coordination with police. [196]

A study of specialized prosecution programs in Oregon and Washington that instituted no-drop policies found that increased use of evidence-based prosecution dramatically increased conviction rates, reduced processing time and initially increased trials. Dismissal rates more than halved in Everett, Wash., from 79 to 29 percent, and guilty findings increased from 10 to 53 percent (although diversion increased from 2 to 22 percent), whereas processing time declined from 109 days to 80 days. Trials increased from 1 percent to 10 percent. Conviction rates at trial were 80 percent. In Klamath Falls, Ore., only 10 to 20 percent of cases were screened out by prosecutors. Dismissals dropped from 47 to 14 percent, and convictions rose from 47 to 86 percent after introduction of evidence-based prosecution. Unlike in Everett, diverted cases dropped from 6 percent to none. Trials rose from 1 percent to 13 percent, and prosecutors won 63 percent of them. [196]

6.12. What Does Adoption of No-Drop Policies Actually Mean?

The most comprehensive study of model no-drop prosecution programs, including several that received large Justice Department grants, found that no-drop policies meant that approximately 30 percent of cases brought by police were screened out, but most of the remaining cases proceeded. Even when victims were not present at the time of trial, prosecutors typically were still able to proceed with 60 to 70 percent of the cases. [196]

Implications for Prosecutors

Although *Crawford* v. *Washington* further inhibits domestic violence prosecutors, the dramatic increase in successful prosecutions, with implementation of specialized domestic violence prosecution programs, suggests that most prosecutors should be able to significantly increase successful prosecutions but perhaps not as much as documented in these pre-*Crawford* studies. (Research basis: Multiple studies in disparate jurisdictions before the U.S. Supreme Court decided *Crawford*.)

6.13. What Kind of Dispositions Do Most Suspects Receive?

Just as prosecution rates vary widely, so does sentencing of domestic violence perpetrators, even though the vast majority of domestic violence defendants are prosecuted for misdemeanor assaults. Disparate studies from various jurisdictions illustrate some of the variety of sentences imposed.

In Quincy, where almost three-quarters of the suspects were charged with some form of assault and/or battery, about one-quarter of the defendants were diverted after a plea to sufficient facts, another quarter were sentenced to probation, and a little over one-tenth were imprisoned. The remainder defaulted or had their cases filed. [23] In Ohio, of those found guilty, almost 70 percent were incarcerated. The largest number were incarcerated between 30 and 45 days, but 18.8 percent were incarcerated for 150 to 180 days. A little more than 60 percent of those found guilty were placed under probation supervision. The largest number of defendants (30.8 percent) were incarcerated between 360 and 499 days. [11] In the Brooklyn misdemeanor domestic violence court study of 9,157 cases in 2002, of those defendants pleading or found guilty, 51 percent received a conditional discharge, 35 percent received a jail sentence, 7 percent received probation, 5 percent were ordered to complete community service and 1 percent were fined. [31] In Milwaukee, in the mid-1990s, out of 669 sample cases prosecutors accepted for prosecution, 30 percent were convicted with a jail sentence, and a little less than one-quarter were sentenced to probation. [39] In Chicago, a little less than one-third of the defendants were given conditional discharges, 24 percent were placed on probation or under court supervision and 23 percent received a jail sentence (including time served pending trial). [107] A study of more than 1,000 domestic violence arrests across three states (Connecticut, Idaho and Virginia) found that, of those convicted, three-quarters were incarcerated, sentenced to probation and/or fined. A little less than half (46.7 percent) were ordered into either anger management or batterer programs. [117]

A study of three domestic violence courts with specialized prosecutors in three different states found augmented probation conditions as compared to jurisdictions without domestic violence specialization. Augmented conditions included drug and alcohol abstinence and testing, batterer intervention programs that lasted longer and were more expensive, more no-contact protective orders, attendance at fatherhood programs or women's groups for female offenders, more mental health evaluations, mandatory employment and restrictions on weapons. [103]

Studies of four jurisdictions with specialized prosecution programs in as many states document that incarceration rates ranged from 20 to 76 percent. Most offenders were placed on probation and had to agree to no victim contact and attendance in a batterer treatment program. [196]

In at least one state, imprisonment of domestic violence felons has mushroomed over the last decade and a half. The number of domestic violence offenders sent to Ohio prisons increased nine-fold between 1991 and 2005. [225]

> **Performance Measure:** By statute, Calif. Penal Code §1203.097, California batterers must be sentenced to three years probation; criminal protective orders must be incorporated to protect victims from further violence, threats, stalking, sexual abuse and harassment; the defendant must complete a batterer program of no less than one year, make a minimum $200 payment, perform a specified amount of community service, attend a substance abuse treatment program as needed, pay restitution and, in lieu of a fine, pay up to $5,000 to a battered Women's shelter.

6.14. Does Prosecuting Domestic Violence Offenders Deter Reabuse?

The research is fairly consistent. Simply prosecuting offenders without regard to the specific risk they pose, unlike arresting domestic violence defendants, does not deter further criminal abuse. [11, 39, 55, 68, 96] The minority of abusers arrested who are low risk are unlikely to reabuse in the short run, whether prosecuted or not. Alternatively, without the imposition of significant sanctions including incarceration, the majority of arrested abusers who are high risk will reabuse regardless of prosecution - many while the case against them is pending.

A study of a large number of arrests in three states (Connecticut, Idaho and Virginia) found that those who were prosecuted and convicted for domestic violence were *more* likely to be rearrested than offenders who were not convicted. However, in this study, those prosecuted and convicted were significantly more likely to be higher risk offenders as measured by prior criminal history. [117]

A number of studies have found that prosecution can reduce subsequent arrests and violence. [66, 91, 130, 211, 225, 226] The key to reducing reabuse may depend not on whether the case is prosecuted but on the dispositions imposed. For example, a Toledo, Ohio, misdemeanor court study found that conviction was significantly associated with reduced rearrests for domestic violence one year following court disposition, even when controlling for batterers' prior history of domestic violence arrests, age, gender, education, employment, and marital status. However, the details of the specific disposition mattered. The more intrusive sentences - including jail, work release, electronic monitoring and/or probation - significantly reduced rearrest for domestic violence as compared to the less intrusive sentences of fines or suspended sentences without probation. The difference was statistically significant: Rearrests were 23.3 percent for defendants with more intrusive dispositions and 66 percent for those with less intrusive dispositions. [216]

Another study of 683 defendants in Hamilton County (Cincinnati), Ohio, who were arrested for misdemeanor domestic violence also confirmed that sentence severity was significantly associated with reduced recidivism, especially for unmarried defendants, although in this study the actual sentence length (number of days in jail) was not found to be significant. [206] Similar research looking at the cumulative effects of arrest followed by prosecution and court dispositions (including those receiving batterer treatment) has found modest reductions in reabuse to be associated with greater post-arrest criminal justice involvement. [163, 204] Research of almost 2,000 domestic violence defendants in Alexandria, Va., found that, over a period of three and one-half years, repeat offenders were associating with those who had a prior criminal history and were *not* sentenced to incarceration for the study arrest during that period. This led researchers to recommend jail sentences for domestic violence defendants with any prior criminal history. [1 72]

The Ohio felony study, however, found mixed results between jail sentences and prison sentences. Although jail sentences were significantly related to lower odds of subsequent misdemeanor or felony intimate-partner assaults after two years, prison sentences were not significantly related. Although the likelihood of new charges was 9 percent less for those jailed (compared to those sentenced to probation), the likelihood was only 2 percent lower for those imprisoned, compared to those placed on probation. [225] This may simply reflect that the sample size in the study was too small to produce a statistically significant effect.

Implications for Prosecutors

Prosecution deters domestic violence if it adequately addresses abuser risk by imposing appropriately intrusive sentences, including supervised probation and incarceration. (Research basis: Although studies conflict with each other on the subject of abuse prosecution, those studies that researched prosecutions, and the resulting dispositions that addressed defendant risk, suggest that domestic violence prosecution can significantly deter reabuse.)

6.15. When Does Sentencing of Domestic Violence Defendants Not Necessarily Prevent Reabuse?

Some dispositional studies suggest that domestic violence sentencing patterns differ from standard sentencing patterns. Surprisingly, domestic violence sentences often do not reflect defendants' prior criminal history, suggesting that prosecutors and/or judges may disregard prior records that are not domestic-violence-related. In the Ohio study, for example, researchers found no correlation between offenders' prior criminal histories and sentence severity. [11] Similarly, the Toledo, Ohio, study found that defendants with prior *felony* convictions were the *least* likely to be prosecuted and sentenced. [216] In contrast, in both Quincy, Mass., and Rhode Island, prior criminal history was significantly associated with severity of sentences. [23, 141] Sentences that do not reflect a defendant's prior criminal history (and prior sentences) may suggest to the defendant that domestic violence offenses are not taken as seriously as other offenses.

Implications for Prosecutors

Domestic violence sentencing should reflect defendants' prior criminal histories as well as abuse histories, as both indicate risk of reabuse as well as general criminality. (Research basis: Disparate sentencing studies found inconsistent variables, including consideration of prior records.)

6.16. Are Defendants Who Don't Show up in Court More at Risk for Reabusing than Those Who Do?

A Chicago study found that no-show defendants prosecuted by a specialized prosecution team had a significantly greater number of post-arrests than those that showed up in court (0.78 vs. 0.46). [107] Although this has not been examined elsewhere, in a Berkeley arrest study, researchers similarly documented that having a pending warrant at the time of the domestic violence incident was a significant predictor of reabuse. [228] The Quincy, Mass., arrest study also found that suspects who fled the scene before the police arrived were significantly more likely to reabuse than those suspects arrested at the scene. [23]

Implications for Prosecutors

If defendants default in court before their sentencing, prosecutors should consider them at higher risk for reabusing. (Research basis: Although only one study looked at this issue directly, several others found the same association between defendant conduct - not showing up in court - and risk of reabusing their victim before being prosecuted for the original abuse.)

6.17. Can "First" Offenders be Safely Diverted or Discharged?

In many jurisdictions, a substantial proportion of domestic violence defendants are diverted or given dispositions without having guilty findings imposed. Often, these dispositions are given to "first" offenders. Notwithstanding this trend, a trio of studies has found that a minimum of a quarter of defendants so sentenced reabuse or violate the terms of their conditional release.

In the Quincy, Mass., arrest study, a quarter of the arrested defendants were continued, without a finding to be dismissed, if they remained arrest free for six months to one year. These dispositions were reserved for defendants with less serious prior criminal and domestic abuse histories. These defendants were half as likely to have had prior records for domestic violence or crimes against persons or to have been sentenced to probation previously. Unlike those sentenced to probation or jailed who began their criminal careers as teenagers, these defendants began theirs at an average age of 25. Nonetheless, a quarter of those continued without a finding were arrested or had new protective orders taken out against them within two years of their study arrest. Although this reabuse rate was still half that of defendants with more substantial prior criminal histories, it was substantially higher than prosecutors and judges had anticipated. [138] Similarly, a little more than a quarter of the abusers (27.5 percent) who were given a conditional discharge in Cook County violated the conditions. [107]

In Rhode Island, probationary sentences for domestic violence cases without underlying suspended sentences constitute an in-court diversion much like cases continued without a finding in Massachusetts. (A probationary sentence in Rhode Island does not constitute a conviction under state law and therefore does not count as a sentence enhancement to a former or subsequent conviction. In the study, those sentenced to probationary sentences were most likely to be "first" domestic violence offenders.) Although the average defendant given a suspended or split sentence had 1 .1 and 1 .9 prior domestic violence arrests, respectively, those sentenced to probation had 0.5 prior arrests. Nevertheless, the rearrest rate for domestic violence for probated defendants was 34.8 percent, compared to 43.6 percent for those given suspended sentences and 48.1 percent given split sentences. [141]

Implications for Prosecutors

Prosecutors must exercise caution in recommending case diversion or conditional discharges, even if abusers have minimal prior criminal histories. (Research basis: Limited site studies and broader research on offender risk previously cited.)

6.18. Do Specialized Prosecution Units Work?

There are a limited number of studies specifically devoted to specialized domestic violence prosecution programs. Because specific programs vary, including the resources expended, it is difficult to pinpoint what works and what does not. Also, in many instances, these programs coexist with specialized domestic violence courts and other programs that may affect outcomes independent of the prosecution programs. However, in general, the research suggests that these programs work well on a number of levels.

First, research indicates that victims generally report satisfaction with domestic violence prosecutions conducted by specialized prosecution teams. Increased satisfaction may translate into increased victim cooperation. For example, in Alexandria, Va., a study revealed that 90.2 percent of victims found prosecutors either very or somewhat helpful, a higher rating than that given to the police or a victim support service agency. The 90.2 percent satisfaction rate reported by Alexandria victims compares to only 67.3 percent for victims in Virginia Beach, a jurisdiction that did not have a specialized domestic violence response program by police, prosecutors or victim advocates. [172]

Similarly, in Cook County (Chicago), victims reported higher satisfaction with the specialized domestic violence prosecution unit than with the prosecutors who handled domestic violence outside the unit. The unit featured specially trained prosecutors and vertical prosecution, where one prosecutor handles the case from arraignment through final disposition. This unit also had its own victim advocates. The victims were also more likely to appear in court: 75 percent compared to 25 percent in domestic violence cases in jurisdictions with no specialized domestic violence unit. [107]

The latter finding was not unique. Although victims most commonly reported fear of retaliation as a barrier to their participation in prosecution, a three-state study found that the fear was reduced in sites with specialized domestic violence courts that also contained specialized prosecution programs and increased victim advocacy. [103] However, the same study found equal satisfaction with prosecutors in both demonstration sites and comparison sites that had no specialized court domestic violence programs. [103]

Second, specialized prosecution programs have significantly increased prosecution and conviction rates. The specialized prosecution unit in Cook County (Chicago) obtained a conviction rate of 71 percent compared to 50 percent obtained by the rest of the office for domestic violence cases. [107] In Milwaukee, the specialized domestic violence prosecution unit increased felony convictions five times over, once the unit was established. [104] Implementation of a specialized domestic violence prosecution unit in Champaign County, Ill., increased prosecutions by 18 percent, and overall domestic violence case dismissals decreased by 54 percent. Convictions increased by 22 percent. [109]

However, other studies suggest that specialized prosecution units must be adequately staffed to make a difference. The specialized prosecution unit in Mecklenburg County (Charlotte), N.C., obtained a much lower conviction rate (38 percent), akin to that obtained without specialized units. However, researchers noted that the unit was significantly understaffed, with only two prosecutors assigned to hundreds of cases annually. [68] Brooklyn's specialized felony prosecution program within the Borough's special felony domestic violence court increased convictions from 87 percent to 94 percent for felonies other than protection order violations and to 93 percent for violations. Although the rate was higher than before, the difference was not statistically significant. [164]

Third, specialized prosecution programs appear to be associated with more robust dispositions that also appear to be better monitored and enforced. A study of three domestic violence courts with specialized prosecutors in three different states found augmented probation conditions as compared to jurisdictions without domestic violence specialization. Augmented conditions included drug and alcohol abstinence and testing, batterer intervention programs that lasted longer and were more expensive, more no-contact protective orders, attendance at fatherhood programs or women's groups for female offenders, more mental health evaluations, mandatory employment and restrictions on weapons. [103]

Implications for Prosecutors

If adequately funded, specialized domestic violence prosecution units, especially if associated with specialized domestic violence law enforcement units and courts, should increase domestic violence prosecutions and convictions, victim cooperation and satisfaction and, if dispositions are geared to defendant risk of reabuse, more victim safety. (Research basis: Multiple studies in disparate jurisdictions.)

Performance Measure: Most large prosecutors' offices have special domestic violence units, allowing for innovations such as vertical prosecution for misdemeanors, improved case preparation, greater contact with victims, reduced caseloads and more malleable court scheduling. [160] One-third of prosecutors in small and medium-sized cities across upstate New York also had specialized domestic violence prosecution programs, half of which made victim advocates available to victims. [227] (Research basis: A 2000 mail survey of 200 of the largest jurisdictions in 45 counties of upstate New York.)

6.19. What Characterizes Specialized Prosecution Units?

An analysis of dozens of responses of prosecutors' offices to domestic violence found that the following dimensions characterized their responses: (1) responsiveness to victims (treating them as if they were civil plaintiffs as opposed to treating them dispassionately as witnesses to a crime), (2) treatment of suspects, (3) expectations for victim participation in prosecution, (4) specialization, and (5) information utilization. [227] The specialized units in upstate New York, unlike in other prosecutors' offices, were more likely to track: (1) cases for specialized prosecution, (2) data to inform the pressing of charges for recidivists, (3) data to inform sentencing recommendations, and (4) routinely received police incident reports as well as police arrest reports. In addition, specialized domestic violence units were more likely to participate in task forces or coalitions involving other criminal justice and community agencies involved in responding to domestic violence. [227]

7. JUDICIAL RESPONSES

7.1. Does Sentencing Domestic Violence Offenders Deter Reabuse?

The research is fairly consistent. Simply prosecuting offenders without regard to the specific risk they pose, unlike arresting domestic violence defendants, does not deter further criminal abuse. [11, 39, 55, 68, 96] The minority of abusers arrested who are low risk are unlikely to reabuse in the short run, whether prosecuted or not. Alternatively, without the imposition of significant sanctions including incarceration, the majority of arrested abusers who are high risk will reabuse regardless of prosecution - many while the case against them is pending.

A study of a large number of arrests in three states (Connecticut, Idaho and Virginia) found that those who were prosecuted and convicted for domestic violence were *more* likely to be rearrested than offenders who were not convicted. However, in this study, those prosecuted and convicted were significantly more likely to be higher risk offenders as measured by prior criminal history. [117]

A number of studies have found that prosecution can reduce subsequent arrests and violence. [66, 91, 130, 211, 225, 226] The key to reducing reabuse may not depend on whether or not the case is prosecuted but on the dispositions imposed. For example, a Toledo, Ohio, misdemeanor court study found that conviction was significantly associated with reduced rearrests for domestic violence one year following court disposition, even when controlling for batterers' prior history of domestic violence arrests, age, gender, education, employment and marital status. However, the details of the specific disposition mattered. The more intrusive sentences - including jail, work release, electronic monitoring and/or probation - significantly reduced rearrest for domestic violence as compared to the less intrusive sentences of fines or suspended sentences without probation. The difference was statistically significant: rearrests were 23.3 percent for defendants with more intrusive dispositions and 66 percent for those with less intrusive dispositions. [216]

Another study of 683 defendants in Hamilton County (Cincinnati), Ohio, who were arrested for misdemeanor domestic violence also confirmed that sentence severity was significantly associated with reduced recidivism, especially for unmarried defendants, although in this study the actual sentence length (number of days in jail) was not found to be significant. [206] Similar research looking at the cumulative effects of arrest followed by prosecution and court dispositions (including those receiving batterer treatment) has found modest reductions in reabuse to be associated with greater post-arrest criminal justice involvement. [163, 204] Research of almost 2,000 domestic violence defendants in Alexandria, Va., found that, over a period of three and one-half years, repeat offenders were associating with those who had a prior criminal history and were *not* sentenced to incarceration for the study arrest during that period. This led researchers to recommend jail sentences for domestic violence defendants with any prior criminal history. [172]

The Ohio felony study, however, found mixed results between jail sentences and prison sentences. Although jail sentences were significantly related to lower odds of subsequent misdemeanor or felony intimate-partner assaults after two years, prison sentences were not significantly related. Although the likelihood of new charges was 9 percent less for those jailed (compared to those sentenced to probation), the likelihood was only 2 percent lower for those imprisoned, compared to those placed on probation. [225] This may simply reflect that the sample size in the study was too small to produce a statistically significant effect.

Implications for Judges

Simply imposing guilty findings may not reduce the risk of reabuse. Judges should consider more intrusive sentences, including incarceration, for repeat abusers and those with prior criminal histories. (Research basis: Although studies conflict with each other on the subject of abuse prosecution, several sentencing studies suggest that more intrusive sentences may significantly deter reabuse.)

7.2. Should Judges Follow Victim Preferences When Determining Sentences?

Although victim perceptions of the dangerousness of suspects have been found to be good predictors of subsequent revictimization [23, 112, 113], victim preferences on how the case should be disposed are not good predictors. The victims in the Quincy, Mass., study who wanted the charges dropped were as likely to be revictimized (51 percent vs. 48 percent after one year) as those who did not want the charges dropped. [23] Similarly, studies in New York found that victim cooperation with prosecutors did not predict recidivism. In other words, when judges imposed sentences to which victims objected, these victims were no more or less likely to be revictimized than victims who wanted their abusers to be prosecuted and sentenced. [145]

Implications for Judges

Although judges should be open to victims' views, they should explain to victims (and, as important, to defendants) that the court is obligated to determine sentences as it deems best, with or without victims' agreement. (Research basis: Only one study directly compared victim prosecution wishes and subsequent reabuse.)

7.3. What Should the Response be When the Suspect is Brought in on an Arrest or Court-Default Warrant?

A large percentage of alleged abusers leave the crime scene before law enforcement arrives. Where noted, absence rates range from 42 to 66 percent. [23, 50, 117, 227, 228] Pursuing them, including the issuance of warrants, is associated with reduced revictimization. [50] Pursuing absent suspects may be of particular utility because limited research finds that suspects who flee the scene before police arrive are significantly more likely to have prior criminal histories and higher reabuse rates than those arrested at the scene. [23] Similarly, another study also finds higher reabuse if the *victim* is gone when officers arrive. [228]

Similarly, decreasing defendant defaults may also be associated with reduced reabuse. A study of Cook County's four misdemeanor domestic violence courts found that no-show defendants had a significantly greater number of new arrests than those who showed up in court (0.78 vs. 0.46). [107]

Implications for Judges

Judges should treat alleged abusers who are brought to court on warrants at least as seriously as those arrested at the scene, even if the defendant appeared "voluntarily" to clear up the warrant. (Research basis: Numerous studies confirm that a large proportion of abusers flee the scene; only one study has looked at differences in records of those who fled the scene and those who didnot.)

7.4. What Are Current Abuser Sentencing Practices?

Just as prosecution rates vary widely, so does sentencing of domestic violence perpetrators, even though the vast majority of domestic violence defendants are prosecuted for misdemeanor assaults. Although the United States Civil Rights Commission and National Council of Juvenile and Family Court Judges have opposed the practice [57, 214], many jurisdictions routinely divert abuse cases. In the Brooklyn Misdemeanor Domestic Violence Court study of 9,157 cases in 2002, of those pleading or found guilty, 51 percent received a conditional discharge, 35 percent received jail, 7 percent received probation, 5 percent were ordered to complete community service and 1 percent were fined. [31]

In Chicago, a little less than a third were given conditional discharges, 24 percent received probation or court supervision, and 23 percent were sent to jail (including time served pending trial). [107] While in Massachusetts, where three-quarters of the suspects (74.1 percent) were charged with some form of assault and/or battery, a quarter of the defendants were diverted, a quarter placed on probation and 13.5 percent imprisoned. [23] In Ohio, of those found guilty, almost 70 percent were incarcerated, with the largest number incarcerated between 30 and 45 days, although 18.8 percent were incarcerated 150 to 180 days. [11] The number of domestic violence offenders sent to Ohio prisons increased nine-fold between 1991 and 2005. [225] In three different states with specialized prosecution programs, 52 percent to 76 percent of convicted abusers were incarcerated. [196]

If placed on probation, supervision ranges from unsupervised to intensive, with a variety of special conditions. Most defendants in the specialized prosecution courts along with jail were placed on probation with a condition of no victim contact, undergoing batterer treatment, drug and alcohol abstinence and testing, attendance at fatherhood programs or women's groups for female offenders, mental health evaluations, mandatory employment and restrictions on weapons. [103] A study of over a thousand domestic violence arrests across three states, Connecticut, Idaho and Virginia, found that, of those convicted, a little less than half (46.7 percent) were ordered into either anger management or batterer programs. [117]

By statute, Cal. Penal Code §1203.097, California batterers must be sentenced to three years probation; criminal protective orders must be incorporated to protect victims from further violence, threats, stalking, sexual abuse and harassment; the defendant must complete a batterer program of no less than a year, make a minimum $200 payment, and perform a specified amount of community service as well as attending substance abuse treatment as needed, pay restitution and, in lieu of a fine, pay up to $5,000 to a battered women's shelter. However, a 2005 study revealed widespread variance with the law in practice by allowing defendants to plead guilty to nondomestic violence crimes such as assault or trespass. [149]

7.5. What Accounts for Dispositions?

The research suggests that domestic violence dispositions do not always follow standard sentencing patterns, often not reflecting defendants' prior criminal histories, suggesting that prosecutors and judges disregard prior records that are not related to domestic violence charges. In a large Ohio court study, for example, researchers found no correlation between offenders' prior criminal histories and sentence severity. [11] Similarly and surprisingly, the Toledo, Ohio, study found defendants with prior *felony* convictions were the least likely to be prosecuted and sentenced. [216] In contrast, in both Quincy, Mass., and Rhode Island, prior criminal history was significantly associated with the severity of sentences. [23, 141]

Victim preference was not found to be a significant factor in sentencing in Quincy, Mass., Everett, Wash., Klamath Falls, Ore., Omaha, Neb., San Diego, Calif., or Ohio. [11, 23, 196] In these jurisdictions, factors associated with more severe sentences varied considerably and included whether there was strangulation, the gender of the defendant, whether the defendant and victim were living together, the size of the prosecutor's caseload, and so on. No consistent patterns were noted from study to study.

Implications for Judges
Sentences should reflect defendants' prior criminal histories as well as abuse histories, as both indicate risk of reabuse as well as general criminality. It is a mistake for judges to consider abusers with prior criminal histories as "first offenders" simply because they have no prior record specifically for domestic violence. (Research basis: Disparate sentencing studies find inconsistent variables including consideration of prior records.)

7.6. Are Defendants Who Don't Show up in Court More at Risk for Reabuse than Those Who Do?

The Chicago study found that no-show defendants prosecuted by a specialized prosecution team had a significantly greater number of post-arrests than those that showed (0.78 vs. 0.46). [107] While this has not been examined elsewhere, in a Berkeley arrest study, researchers similarly documented that having a pending warrant at the time of the domestic violence incident was a significant predictor of reabuse. [228] The Quincy, Mass., arrest study also found that suspects who flee the scene before police arrived were significantly more likely to reabuse than those arrested at the scene. [23]

Implications for Judges

If defendants default in court prior to sentencing, judges should consider them higher risk for reabuse for purposes of bail, fashioning civil orders and sentencing. (Research basis: Although only one study looked at this issue directly, several others found the same association between defendant conduct and reabuse pre-prosecution.)

7.7. Can "First" Offenders be Safely Diverted or Discharged?

The few studies that have examined reabuse among diverted or discharged abusers have consistently found that a steady minority continued to reabuse, notwithstanding no or minimal prior records. In the Quincy arrest study, for example, a quarter of the arrested defendants were continued, without a finding to be dismissed, if they remained arrest free for six months to a year, a disposition reserved for first or lesser defendants. A quarter were arrested or had new protective orders taken out against them within two years of their study arrest. Although this reabuse rate was still half that of defendants with more substantial prior criminal histories, it was substantially higher than prosecutors and judges had anticipated. [138] Similarly, a little over a quarter of the abusers (27.5 percent) given a conditional discharge in Cook County violated the conditional discharge. [107] While those placed on probation in Rhode Island with guilty findings was higher than those placed on probation without guilty findings, the rearrest rate for domestic violence over one year was still 35 percent. [141]

Implications for Judges

Judges cannot assume that defendants with no or limited prior records for domestic violence can be diverted pre-adjudication or given conditional discharges without consistently compromising safety for at least a quarter of their victims. (Research basis: Limited site studies as well as broader research on offender risk previously cited.)

7.8. Who Obtains Civil Protective Orders?

The research suggests that abusers brought to court for civil protective orders differ little from their peers arrested by police for domestic abuse. Studies have found that they have equivalent criminal histories, ranging from 65 percent in a study of respondents in Denver,

Delaware and the District of Columbia [133] to a little more than 70 percent in a Texas study [26] and 80 percent in a Massachusetts study. [134] Another Massachusetts study of protective order violators found that 80 percent had a prior record, including 69 percent who were charged for a prior nondomestic but violent offense. [2]

One of the reasons for the substantial overlap between abusers brought to court for civil orders and those arrested for abuse by police is that many petitioners come to civil court as a result of police encouragement following an abuse incident involving police. In a multicourt study, 43 percent of victims who obtained civil protective orders said they either learned of the orders or were encouraged to apply for them by police responding to a domestic violence incident. [182]

Implications for Judges

Victims seeking civil remedies for abuse are at the same level of risk for reabuse as victims of abusers arrested for abusing them. (Research basis: Extensive research of civil petitioners that was conducted in disparate jurisdictions.)

7.9. When and Why Do Victims Ask for Orders?

Researchers agree that most victims do not request civil orders after the first abuse incident or assault. According to the NVAW survey, only 16.4 percent of rape victims, 17.1 percent of assault victims, and 36.6 percent of stalking victims petitioned for protective orders following an abuse incident. [209] A survey of victims in battered women's shelters found that only 40 percent had obtained protective orders before fleeing their homes and entering the shelter. [178] Finally, several studies based on samples of women who reported abuse to police found that only 12 to 22 percent had secured protective orders. [120, 220]

Often, victims petition courts for orders after failing to stem the abuse through other means. In a multicourt study involving both an inner city minority jurisdiction and a suburban nonminority city south of Boston, female victims had tried to protect themselves in a variety of other ways before petitioning court for an order. Perhaps most significantly, 68 percent had left their abuser at least once, and 15 percent had kicked their abuser out of the home at least once before petitioning the courts for orders. In addition, 78 percent had called police at least once before, 30 percent had obtained counseling, and 25 percent had called a hotline or had gone to a shelter. [182] In a Colorado study, half of the petitioners had left their abusers at the time of the incident that provoked the protective order petition. [105] Studies have found that between 27 and 50 percent of victims are living with their abuser at the time of the incident that prompted the order request [106, 133, 182], whereas between 37 and 46 percent file for orders after they have left. [74, 75]

As a result, most victims who petition courts for protection orders have suffered several years of abuse with the same abuser before coming to court for the first time. In a multistate (and District of Columbia) study, researchers found that only 10 percent sought protection orders after a week of abuse, 15 percent experienced abuse for one to two years, and nearly 25 percent had endured abuse for more than five years. [133] In a Colorado study, the average female petitioner suffered 12.74 abusive behaviors in the year before requesting their orders (e.g., being threatened to being raped). About 20 percent reported that their prior abuse included the more serious behaviors, including strangling, forced sex and beating. The duration ranged from once to 31 years, with a median of 2.4 years. [105]

The specific incident that prompted victims to petition for protective orders generally involved physical abuse. In the multistate (and District of Columbia) study, more than a third had been threatened or injured with a weapon (36.8 percent), more than half (54.4 percent) had experienced severe physical abuse, 83.9 percent experienced mild physical abuse, and almost all (98.9 percent) had been intimidated through threats, stalking and harassment. [133] In Quincy, Mass., almost two-thirds (64.4 percent) of the victims were physically assaulted, and another third had been threatened with death or harm to them, their children or a relative. [134] Similarly, in a Colorado study, 56 percent of the female petitioners had sustained physical injuries during the incident that led to the protective order requests. [105] In the two courts studied in Massachusetts (one located in a minority neighborhood of Boston, the other a south shore mid-sized city), 92 percent of the petitions filed by female victims described incidents that constituted criminal acts, and 70 percent of them constituted assault and battery. Breaking down the affidavits further, the researcher found that 48 percent described separation violence; 22 percent described punishment, coercion and retaliation concerning children; and 12 percent described retaliation for calling police. A total of 65 percent of the female petitioners told the researcher that the abuser had threatened them with death, 35 percent had visited hospitals as a result of prior violence in the past, 30 percent suffered sexual abuse and, of those who were mothers, 51 percent reported threats to take children from them or report them as unfit to child protective services. [182]

On the other hand, the incident that prompts victims to seek orders may not be the most serious incident they experienced at the hand of their abusers. Research has found that the seriousness of the incident itself is not predictive of a future risk of reabuse. [23, 39, 134, 141, 145, 172]

Implications for Judges

Although petitions focus on the most recent, discrete incident, the incident rarely reveals fully the nature of the abuse suffered by the petitioner or the risk for future abuse. Post-separation abuse frequently involves stalking behavior, a risk factor for further abuse, and even lethality. To obtain more information, judges need to further question victims and review respondents' prior criminal and civil history. (Research basis: Extensive studies of petitioners in disparate jurisdictions as well as many abuser studies.)

7.10. How Many Abusers Violate Court Protective Orders?

Research varies, but violation rates have been found to range from 23 percent over two years [26], 35 percent within six months [133], to 60 percent within twelve months [105], and in between at 48.8 percent within two years. [134] A Rhode Island study found consistent violation of criminal no-contact orders imposed after domestic violence arrests, resulting in subsequent concurrent sentences for both the initial domestic violence offense and the no-contact violation. Furthermore, the study also found that the majority (51 percent) of abusers sentenced concurrently for abuse-related offenses and no-contact violations reabused their victims. The rearrest rate for new abuse for abusers specifically convicted of civil protection order violations was 44 percent, and for criminal no-contact orders it was 48 percent, higher than all other domestic violence offenses, which ranged from 25 to 39 percent. [141]

The actual rates of violation of protective orders are higher if reabuse is measured by new domestic violence arrests or victim self-reports. In addition, order violation rates may not accurately reflect reabuse over a specific period of time because many victims do not retain or decide to drop orders. Although "permanent orders" in Massachusetts are for one year, almost half of the female victims subsequently returned to court to drop their orders before the year ended. [134] A review of disparate jurisdictions revealed that retention rates varied from 16 percent in Omaha, Neb., in 2003 [135] to 69 percent in the District of Columbia in 2000 [200] and 80 percent in East Norfolk, Mass., in 1995. [134]

Implications for Judges

As with the arrest of abusers, the issuance of protective orders alone does not assure victims' safety. Judges should advise victims of their protective order limitations. (Research basis: Multiple studies in disparate jurisdictions.)

7.11. Do Protective Orders Work?

The research has not been able to answer this question definitively, mainly because it is not ethically permissible to randomly grant or deny protective orders to compare results. Furthermore, these orders may "work" at different levels.

First, in terms of their effectiveness in deterring repeat abuse, before and after studies suggest that protective orders may deter certain abusers. In Travis County, Texas, over a period of two years before and after order issuance, physical abuse dropped from 68 percent to 23 percent after the orders were obtained, if victims maintained the order. If the abusers were also arrested at the time of the order issuance, the physical abuse diminished further; if they had children, it diminished less. [26] These studies cannot reveal whether or not the abuse would have naturally declined overtime without the orders because, for example, the victims are more likely to have left their abusers when they obtained the orders.

Several Seattle studies compared women who obtained orders to women who were abused (as indicated by a police incident report) but did not obtain orders. They found that women with permanent orders were less likely to be physically abused than women without them. However, women who had temporary orders that lasted only two weeks were more likely to be psychologically abused than women who did not obtain any orders. The women who did not obtain orders appeared at higher risk for abuse, involvement with alcohol and drugs, more likely to have been assaulted and injured as a result of the study incident, and less likely to have been married to their abuser. The study did not look at violations of protective orders that did not involve physical assaults. [120] The second Seattle study found that the orders were more effective nine months after they were obtained than during the first five-month period, significantly reducing the likelihood of contact, threats with weapons, injuries and the need for medical care. [121]

Finally, several other studies that compared women who maintained orders and those who dropped them, or did not return for permanent orders, found that order retention made no difference in reabuse rates. [105, 134] A Rhode Island study involving criminal no-contact orders, issued automatically during a domestic violence arrest, also found that whether victims allowed the orders to be continued for the length of the criminal case and probationary sentences that followed (usually one year) or not, the reabuse rates did not vary. [141]

At least one study suggests that the specific stipulations of the protective orders may make a difference. Specifically, victims are more likely to be reabused if their orders bar abusive contact but not all contact. Compared to women whose orders barred all contact, those that barred only abusive contact were significantly more likely to suffer psychological violence, physical violence, sexual coercion and injuries within one year. [150]

Nonetheless, the research consistently finds that victims largely express satisfaction with civil orders, even if they are violated by their abusers. [134] In the multisite study in Massachusetts, 86 percent of the women who obtained a permanent order said that the order either stopped or reduced the abuse, notwithstanding the fact that 59 percent called police to report an order violation. Upon further questioning, the women expressed the feeling that the order demonstrated to the abuser that the "law was on her side." [182] In a multistate study, victims who obtained orders reported that the orders improved their overall well-being, especially if the abuser had a prior criminal history and were more likely to reabuse. [133] It may be that, even though orders do not stop abuse, they reduce the severity of the reabuse. Alternatively, although they may not affect the extent of reabuse, protective orders make victims feel vindicated and empowered.

Although not studied directly, it appears to be significantly easier for law enforcement to monitor and enforce protective and no-contact orders than to monitor and interrupt abuse in general. This may explain why abusers are significantly more likely to be arrested for protective order violations than other common domestic violence offenses. The rearrest rate for abusers in Rhode Island initially arrested for violation of protection or no-contact orders was 45.6 percent over one year, compared to 37.6 percent for domestic assaults, disorderly conduct or vandalism. [141] Of course, it may also be the case that abusers with orders are generally at higher risk for reabusing than abusers without orders.

Implications for Judges

Victims should be encouraged to take out protective orders and retain them but should also be advised that the orders do not deter all abusers and may be more effective when accompanied by criminal prosecution of the abuser. (Research basis: Numerous studies indicating consistent victim satisfaction with orders, complemented by studies that have consistently found that orders do not appear to significantly increase the risk of reabuse and may deter some abusers.)

7.12. Does Judicial Demeanor Make a Difference?

Although few studies have looked at judicial conduct specifically, a multisite study in Massachusetts found that judges issuing orders fell into three categories: (1) those with "good- natured demeanors," who were supportive and informative with victims and firm with abusers; (2) those with "bureaucratic demeanors," who were firm and formal with all parties; and (3) those with "condescending, harsh and demeaning demeanors" but who were often good- natured with abusers. The research found that victims felt more empowered, listened to, and were more likely to retain orders issued by the first category of judges rather than the two other groups. The first group was also more likely to cooperate with prosecutors on concurrent criminal charges against the abusers. Most of the judges were found to be in the first group. [182]

Another study compared two Massachusetts courts within 10 miles of each other. One court was characterized as "user friendly" for victims, with a special office for victims to complete forms as well as special court sessions so petitioners did not have to wait to see judges. The other court was more bureaucratic, with no special offices or sessions for victims. Victims in the first court had an 80 percent retention rate (i.e., they returned to obtain permanent orders after the temporary orders expired), whereas those in the other court had a 20 percent return rate. [101] Similarly and perhaps for the same reason, specialized domestic violence courts have also been found to increase victim order retention rates. A study of a District of Columbia domestic violence court found that it increased retention from 40 to 55 percent after imposition of the specialized domestic violence sessions. [200]

In a related study of upstate New York courts, a study across multiple jurisdictions found that the demeanor of the judge also reverberated across the criminal justice system. It found that, even compared to a "rights-oriented" judge who held police and prosecutors to a high evidentiary standard (which they often met), a judge who strongly believed that domestic violence cases did not belong in court stifled and discouraged both domestic violence arrests in the community and prosecutions in court. [227]

Implications for Judges

Judges should strive to create user-friendly, safe court environments for petitioners, be sympathetic to the parties before them, but firm with respondents once abuse has been determined. Thus, victim concerns are validated, and respondents' abusive behaviors are clearly condemned. (Research basis: Limited studies confined to three different court jurisdictions in Massachusetts.)

7.13. Do Specialized Domestic Violence Courts Work?

Although relatively new, some research shows that specialized domestic violence courts are associated with decreased reoffending and reabuse. The reduction may be due to reforms of court processes or a corresponding specialization of domestic violence prosecution and/or probation supervision, or all three. A study of Milwaukee's federally funded domestic violence court found that the number of arrests were halved for domestic violence defendants sentenced to probation, compared to those sentenced to probation before court reform. The rearrest rate dropped from 8 percent to 4.2 percent. The average number of new arrests also dropped significantly. Researchers posited that one of the prime explanations for the drop was a corresponding rise in the use of incarceration as a sentence. As a result of tight judicial monitoring and enforcement of release conditions, the post-reform probationers spent 13,902 days confined, compared to the 1,059 days probationers spent jailed in the days before court reform. In other words, those sentenced by the special domestic violence court had less time on the streets to reabuse and reoffend. [104]

Studies also found reduced reabuse rates at one other federally funded domestic violence court, in Dorchester, Mass., over a period of 11 months, but not in a third model domestic violence court examined in Michigan. In all three sites, researchers found that the courts were most effective with 18- to 29-year-old defendants, and offenders with seven or more prior arrests whose victims had moderate to high support, did not have children with their abusers, and whose relationship with them was less than three years. Although reabuse declined in two of the courts, overall new arrests for any offense were not statistically different, although they were in the expected direction: 22 percent for the domestic violence courts, and 28 percent for the nondomestic violence courts. [103]

Three other studies of specialized domestic violence courts have found small but significant reductions in reoffending [79, 91], including a study of the San Diego superior court, in which rearrests dropped from 21 to 14 percent in one year. [180] An evaluation of Cook County's four domestic violence courts, on the other hand, found no differences in rearrest rates over six months. [107]

Apart from reduced reabuse rates, domestic violence courts are associated with increased convictions and decreased dismissals. [40, 104, 115, 164] In Cook County, the four misdemeanor domestic violence courts significantly increased the likelihood of victims appearing in court when compared with their appearance in general courts (73 vs. 40 percent). This, in turn, correlated with increased conviction rates of 73 percent in domestic violence courts compared to 22.9 percent in general courts. [107]

Although domestic violence victims generally rate their court experiences highly, they rate domestic violence courts even more highly. [52, 91, 124] One study found that if victims were aware that there was a domestic violence court, three-quarters of the victims were more likely to report future violence. [196] One of the reasons that victims may prefer domestic violence courts may be the court contacts providing increased victim services and referrals to victim advocates, documented in several of the studies. [103, 115, 164] This may be why the District of Columbia domestic violence court was able to report an increased rate of civil protective order retention from 40 to 55 percent. [200] Domestic violence courts are also associated with more efficient processing of cases. The study of Manhattan's domestic violence misdemeanor court experienced faster case processing as well as improved identification of domestic violence cases. [179]

The research also finds that domestic violence courts increase offender compliance by imposing court-ordered conditions and by increasing in the penalties for noncompliance. [104, 164] The study of Manhattan's domestic violence misdemeanor court documented enhanced monitoring of offenders after their convictions. [179] Defendants in Milwaukee were required to attend post- disposition court reviews 60 to 90 days after disposition. In 2002, the court conducted 1,347 such reviews, and probation revocations increased dramatically. [104]

Implications for Judges

Specialized domestic violence courts are associated with beneficial reforms in several areas, including victim safety and satisfaction, offender accountability, and more efficient case-flow processing. (Research basis: The research is based mainly on disparate process evaluations of specialized domestic violence courts. The research does not suggest, however, that judges presiding over general trial courts cannot adopt similar practices and thereby achieve the same results in each case.)

7.14. What Makes Specialized Domestic Violence Courts Different?

A 2004 study found 160 jurisdictions across the country with specialized domestic violence courts. The majority of these courts had the following traits in common: (1) effective management of domestic violence cases, coordinating all of the cases involving the relevant parties and integrating requisite information for the court; (2) specialized intake and court staffing for domestic violence cases; (3) improved victim access, expedited hearings, and assistance for victims by court staff, often assisted by related specialized, vertical domestic violence prosecution units; (4) court processes to ensure victims' safety (e.g., court metal detectors, separate waiting rooms, specialized orders and victim referrals; (5) increased court monitoring and enforcement of batterer compliance with court orders, often exercised by specialized probation supervision units; (6) consideration of any children involved in the domestic violence; and (7) enhanced domestic violence training for judges. [132]

Pretrial Monitoring of Defendants
In the specialized domestic violence court in San Diego, Calif., a bail amount of $10,000 surety or $1,000 cash is standard for each misdemeanor domestic violence charge. In Everett, Wash., $10,000 is the typical bail, without a cash alternative. Increases in the holding of defendants pretrial has been shown to increase plea bargains at arraignment. In San Diego, 46 percent of defendants were found to plead at arraignment. [196] After establishment of a specialized domestic violence court in Milwaukee, 20 percent plead guilty before they were assigned a trial date. [103, 104] Increased restrictions on defendant-victim contact have also been found to increase the likelihood of conviction. [103, 104]

Decreasing defendant defaults may also be associated with reduced reabuse. A study of Cook County's four misdemeanor domestic violence courts found that no-show defendants had a significantly greater number of new arrests than those who showed in court (0.78 vs. 0.46). [107] This is consistent with research that found that defendants who flee the abuse incident before police arrive are twice as likely to reabuse than those who remain at the scene of the incident. [23]

As a result of enhanced pretrial processing after the establishment of the specialized court, convictions through guilty pleas increased and trials decreased in the Brooklyn (Kings County), N.Y., felony domestic violence court, while the conviction rate remained the same. [164]

Implications for Judges
Judicial attention before trial to address the risk to victims posed by alleged abusers will result in quicker case resolution and decrease reabuse by defendants who fail to show for trial. (Research basis: Multiple studies from multiple jurisdictions.)

Enhanced Court Dispositions
Court dispositions in specialized domestic violence courts tend to be more substantial than elsewhere and more rigorously enforced. In Everett, Wash., and Klamath Falls, Ore., defendants were more likely to be ordered to attend batterer intervention programs and drug counseling and to be ordered to abstain from drugs and submit to testing. Furthermore, the batterer intervention programs increased in length and cost. At these and other sites with

specialized court programs, defendants were more likely to be ordered to have no contact with their victims. [196] In terms of enforcement, in Milwaukee, a study revealed that after implementation of the specialized domestic violence court system, there was a dramatic increase in probation revocations (27 percent compared to the previous 2 percent). Most revocations (70 percent) were for technical violations such as failure to attend batterer intervention programs. [104]

In Massachusetts and Cook County, Ill., specialized domestic violence courts reduced deferred prosecutions and increased the percentage of defendants who were sentenced to jail time. Court conviction rates in the latter rose from 50 percent to 71 .4 percent; the likelihood of jail increased significantly from 6.7 percent to 31 .3 percent. [107]

Implications for Judges

Judges presiding over specialized domestic violence courts appear more likely to impose more intrusive sanctions against convicted abusers. (Research basis: Disparate studies demonstrate a correlation, although specialized domestic violence courts may offer judges enhanced dispositional options, including specialized probationary supervision programs for abusers. These specialized courts may also have judges who are better informed about domestic violence than other judges.)

7.15. Do Enhanced Domestic Violence Dispositions Require Enhanced Postdisposition Court Time and Resources?

Studies have found that enhanced sentencing of abusers involving probation with relevant conditions (e.g., batterer programs, abstinence or no-contact orders) requires enhanced monitoring because many abuser probationers typically fail to comply.

Studies have documented that noncompliance rates prompting formal revocations of probation ranged from 12 percent in the Dorchester, Mass., courts to 27 percent in Milwaukee misdemeanor domestic violence courts. [103] In Cook County's four misdemeanor domestic violence courts, the revocation rate was 27.5 percent. [107] Higher rates were found in a series of other studies of domestic violence supervision programs across Illinois: 38.5 percent in Sangamond (Springfield) County, 33 percent in Peoria, and 22.8 percent in Tazewell County. The revocation rate was more than 50 percent in Quincy, Mass. [108, 109, 138] In Brooklyn's felony domestic violence court, the rate was 33 percent. [164]

Revocation rates may reflect probation resources and policies as much as they reflect Probationers' conduct. For example, an evaluation of Rhode Island's specialized domestic violence probation supervision unit found that the unit's probation revocation rate was 44 percent, whereas the rate for comparable abuse probationers supervised in larger mixed caseloads during the same period was only 24.7 percent. Almost all of the violations were for noncompliance with the state's mandated batterer intervention program. [141]

Implications for Judges

Enhanced dispositions increase the likelihood of technical violations, which require additional judicial time if defendants are to be held accountable. (Research basis: Multiple studies in disparate jurisdictions.)

7.16. Does the Type of Postdispositional Monitoring Matter?

Studies are mixed concerning the impact of postdisposition judicial monitoring, which probably should not be surprising because the quality of judicial monitoring is undoubtedly mixed as well. For example, a quasi-experimental study involving the Bronx domestic violence court found that judicial monitoring did not reduce recidivism, although there was a modest but transitory one- year reduction in domestic violence arrests. However, the same study found the quality of the monitoring program to be problematic. [185] A study of the San Diego court system attributed a decrease in rearrests, from 21 to 14 percent in one year, to judicial monitoring. [180] Other studies also suggest that a longer period of court control is associated with reduced reabuse. [42] Increased pretrial court appearances have also been associated with decreased reabuse. [179]

Studies have also found that probation supervision increases the number of offenders who complete batterer intervention programs. A multiyear study across Massachusetts found that the batterer program completion rate was 62 percent for those offenders whose cases were supervised but was only 30 percent for those whose cases were unsupervised. [18]

Implications for Judges

Postdispositional patterns of compliance and enforcement should be reviewed periodically to ensure that the crucial role of judges' postdisposition is being fulfilled. (Research basis: Several studies in disparate jurisdictions are suggestive but, given the variety of court contexts, no specific model of a postdispositional monitoring program has emerged, or is likely to emerge, as better than any other.)

7.17. Does Probation Supervision of Abusers Reduce Likelihood of Reabuse?

A few studies of probation supervision of abusers have been conducted. A quasi-experimental study across the state of Rhode Island found that those abusers who were supervised in a specialized domestic violence probation program - featuring victim contact, slightly more intensive supervision of abusers (twice a month), intensive monitoring of mandated batterer intervention programs, and probation officers who volunteered to supervise these caseloads - were significantly less likely to commit new offenses and abuse within one year, but this applied only to those probationers who had not been on probation previously. [137, 141]

Although specialized domestic violence courts often involve specialized probation supervision programs, probation's contribution to these courts' successes (and failures) has not been studied separately. The cumulative effect of probation monitoring and counseling completion has been found to significantly lower recidivism. [163] Another researcher has found that enhanced domestic-violence supervision programs have reduced reoffending compared to nonenhanced supervision. [108]

Implications for Judges

Specialized supervision of abusers may help reduce reabuse. (Research basis: Tentative findings based on only limited studies.)

8. INTERVENTION PROGRAMS

8.1. Do Batterer Intervention Programs Prevent Reabuse?

Commonly, whether diverted, probated or jailed, many domestic violence offenders are required to attend batterer intervention programs. These programs have increased dramatically over the past several decades. [110]

During this time, there have been more than 35 evaluations of batterer intervention programs, but they have yielded inconsistent results. Two meta-analyses of the more rigorous studies find the programs have, at best, a "modest" treatment effect, producing a minimal reduction in rearrests for domestic violence. [8, 62] In one of the meta-analyses, the treatment effect translated to a 5-percent improvement rate in cessation of reassaults due to the treatment. [8] In the other, it ranged from none to 0.26, roughly representing a reduction in recidivism from 13 to 20 percent. [62]

On the other hand, a few studies have found that batterer intervention programs make abusers more likely to reabuse [90, 102] or have found no reduction in abuse at all. [36, 42, 61]. The multistate study of four batterer programs concludes that approximately a quarter of batterers appear unresponsive and resistant to batterer intervention. In this long-term study, based on victim and/or abuser interviews and/or police arrests, approximately half of the batterers reassaulted their initial or new partners sometime during the study's 30-month follow- up. Most of the reassaults occurred within the first six months of program intake. Nearly a quarter of the batterers repeatedly assaulted their partners during the follow-up and accounted for nearly all of the severe assaults and injuries. [84, 85, 88]

Implications for Prosecutors and Judges

Batterer programs, in and of themselves, are not likely to protect most victims or new intimate partners of referred abusers from further harm from higher risk abusers. Consequently, if mandated or utilized, batterer intervention programs should be supplemented by other measures to assure victim safety from these abusers. (Research basis: Multiple single studies as well as two meta-analyses of studies from disparate jurisdictions in different contexts across the country.)

8.2. Does the Type or Length of Batterer Intervention Program Make a Difference?

Several studies have found that the type of batterer intervention program, whether feminist, psycho-educational, or cognitive-behavioral, does not affect reabuse. [8, 51, 88] One study also found that a "culturally focused" program specifically designed for black male abusers did no better than the program offered to all abusers. In fact, those assigned to a conventional, racially mixed group were half as likely to be arrested for reassaults compared to those assigned to a black culturally focused counseling group or a conventional group of all blacks. [87]

However, a rigorous study based in New York City found the length of the program (26 weeks compared to 8 weeks) may make a difference, with the longer program proving more effective at deterring reabuse. The researchers suggest that the longer program's increased effectiveness was due to its longer suppression effect while abusers were mandated to attend, whether or not they actually attended. [42] On the other hand, a multistate study of four programs ranging in length from 3 to 9 months found no difference in subsequent reabuse. [84, 85, 88]

Implications for Prosecutors and Judges

As long as the batterer intervention program is focused on preventing reabuse, the type of program makes no difference. However, longer batterer programs may be better than shorter programs. (Research basis: Although only one study speaks to the suppression effects of batterer programs, the finding that batterer programs provide little treatment effect suggests that programs' effectiveness may result from their suppression effect and/or the context in which they operate, including probation supervision or periodic court compliance hearings. These findings argue for longer programs.)

Performance Measure: By statute, batterer intervention programs mandated for convicted abusers in California Penal Code §1 203.097(A)(6) must be conducted for two hours each week and for a minimum of 52 consecutive weeks.

8.3. Do Couples Counseling or Anger Management Treatment Programs Prevent Reabuse?

There has been little recent research on the application of couples counseling involving batterers and their victims [201] as most batterer treatment standards prohibit couples counseling. [7] While an early study in 1985 found it ineffective, with half of the couples reporting new violence within six weeks of couples counseling [148], other studies found lower reabuse rates. [47] A small study suggests that couples counseling *after* separate counseling for batterers and victims may be safe and beneficial for couples who want to remain together. [129]

Although anger management is often part of batterer intervention programs based on cognitive psychology, most state batterer treatment standards prohibit generic anger management programs or couples counseling as alternative forms of treatment on their own. [7]

In one of the largest studies to date, the Office of the Commissioner of Probation in Massachusetts studied a sample of 945 defendants arraigned for violating a protective order. As part of their subsequent disposition, they were ordered into a certified batterer intervention program, anger management program, and/or a mental health treatment or substance abuse treatment program; 13 percent were sent to multiple programs. The study found that those referred to 12- to 20-week anger management programs had a higher completion rate than those referred to the much longer 40-week batterer intervention programs. Higher completion rates notwithstanding, there was no difference in rearrest rates for those who completed anger management programs and those who failed to complete one. Furthermore, those who completed anger management programs recidivated at higher rates than those who completed batterer intervention programs, even though those referred to batterer intervention programs had significantly more criminal history, including more past order violations, more long-standing substance abuse histories, and less education than those referred to anger management programs. [18]

An earlier study of a program in Pittsburgh found that abusers who relied on anger management control techniques were more likely to reabuse their partners than those who relied on increased empathy, a redefinition of their manhood, and more cooperative decisionmaking as a means to ending their abuse. [80]

Implications for Prosecutors and Judges

There is no evidence that couples counseling or anger management programs effectively prevent court-referred batterers from reabusing or committing new offenses after treatment. (Research basis: The limited research conducted thus far has been, at best, inconclusive regarding the effectiveness of these programs. One large state study found that court-referred batterers are less apt to commit new offenses [including both domestic and nondomestic violence offenses] if they completed batterer programs rather than anger management programs. The difference, however, may be because the batterer programs were twice as long as the anger control programs.)

8.4. Does Alcohol and Drug Treatment Prevent Reabuse?

The correlation between alcohol and drug treatment has been confirmed in numerous studies cited previously (also see question referring to perpetrators, "Are they likely to be drug and/or alcohol abusers?"). These studies find substance abuse treatment can be effective in reducing domestic violence. [203] In one such study, for example, researchers found that among 301 alcoholic male partner abusers, of whom 56 percent had physically abused their partners the year before treatment, partner violence significantly decreased for half a year after alcohol treatments but still was not as low as the nonalcoholic control group. Among those patients who remained sober, reabuse dropped to 15 percent, the same as the nonalcoholic control group and half that of treated alcoholics who failed to maintain sobriety. [169] As this study suggests, however, alcohol and drug treatment, in and of itself, may not be sufficient for all abusers. Supporting this is a Massachusetts treatment study of 945 defendants convicted of violating protective orders and subsequently ordered into a program. The study found that those who completed a variety of alcohol and drug treatment programs had higher rates of rearraignment over six years, for any crime or for violations of protective orders, than those who completed batterer intervention programs (57.9 vs. 47.7 percent for any crime, and 21 .1 vs. 17.4 percent for violation of protective orders). Furthermore, there was no significant difference in rearraignment rates between those who completed the substance abuse treatment and those who did not. [18]

On the other hand, studies suggest alcohol and drug treatment may be a necessary component of successful intervention to prevent reabuse. The multistate study of four batterer programs found that, among those who completed the program, those who became intoxicated within a three-month period were three times more likely to reassault their partners than those who did not. [84, 85, 88]

Implications for Prosecutors and Judges

Incorporating alcohol and/or drug treatment as a standard component of batterer intervention programs adds to the likelihood of reductions in reabuse among batterers, many of whom abuse alcohol and drugs. Effective treatment should include abstinence testing to assure sobriety and no drug use. (Research basis: Extensive research in both clinical and court settings confirms the correlation between substance abuse and the increased likelihood of reabuse as well as the reduction in reabuse among offenders successfully treated for drug abuse.)

8.5. Are Court-Referred Batterers Likely to Complete Batterer Programs?

Multiple studies of disparate programs around the country have found high noncompletion rates ranging from 25 percent to 89 percent, with most at around 50 percent. [36, 87, 183] Rates vary because different programs have different standards for monitoring attendance as well as different policies regarding re-enrollment, missed meetings, and so on. A study in California found that, of 10 counties examined, only one maintained a database to track offender participation in the mandated batterer intervention program; it reported that 89 percent did not complete the program. [149]

Not surprisingly, adding on additional treatment programs increases noncompletion. For example, although 42 percent of the referred batterers in the Bronx court study failed to complete the batterer intervention program, that number increased to 67 percent for those also required to complete drug treatment. For those required to complete drug treatment alone, the noncompletion rate was 60 percent. [183]

High rates of technical violations are common for probationers sentenced for domestic violence, including violations of no-contact orders and drug abstinence, and failure to attend batterer intervention programs. Various probation studies found technical violation (noncrime) rates ranging from 34 percent of those sentenced in the Brooklyn felony domestic violence court [164], 41 percent in Colorado [125], 61 percent in Champaign County, Ill. [109], and 25 to 44 percent in Rhode Island (regular vs. specialized domestic violence supervision). [141]

Implications for Prosecutors

Prosecutors should be reluctant to recommend court-ordered conditions including batterer intervention programs unless the violators are closely monitored and enforced. If prosecutors are involved in the enforcement process, and bringing violators back to court, they must commit the time and resources required to enforce compliance and hold violators accountable. (Research basis: Multiple studies from disparate jurisdictions across the country.)

Implications for Judges

Judges should take all appropriate steps to ensure that court conditions are enforced, violators are returned to court promptly, and violation cases (i.e., revocation hearings) are heard expeditiously. (Research basis: Multiple studies from disparate jurisdictions across the country.)

8.6. Do Those Who Complete Batterer Programs Do Better Than Those Who Fail?

Abusers who complete batterer programs are less likely to reabuse than those who fail to attend, are noncompliant, or drop out. [9, 30, 48, 54, 87, 90, 183] The differences can be substantial.

A Chicago study of more than 500 court-referred batterers referred to 30 different programs found that recidivism after an average of 2.4 years was 14.3 percent for those who completed the program, whereas recidivism for those who did not complete the programs was more than twice that (34.6 percent). [12] Those who did not complete their program mandate in the Bronx court study were four times more likely to recidivate than those who completed their program. [183]

The multistate study of four programs found that abusers who completed the programs reduced their risk of reassault in a range of 46 to 66 percent. [86] A Florida study found that the odds that abusers who completed the program would be rearrested were half those of a control group not assigned to the program, whereas the odds of rearrest for those who failed to attend were two and one-half times higher than the control group. [60]

A Massachusetts study found that, over a six-year period, those who completed a certified batterer intervention program were significantly less likely to be rearraigned for any type of offense, a violent offense or a protection order violation. (Massachusetts does not have a domestic violence statute, so researchers could not differentiate domestic from nondomestic violence offenses.) The rate differences for these offenses, between those who completed a program and those who did not, was as follows: 47.7 vs. 83.6 percent for any crime, 33.7 vs. 64.2 percent for a violent crime, and 17.4 vs. 41.8 percent for violation of a protective order. [18] The Dallas study found that twice as many program dropouts as program completers were rearrested within 13 months: 39.7 vs. 17.9 percent for any charge, and 8.1 vs. 2.8 percent for assault arrests. [53] An Alexandria, Va., study of almost 2,000 domestic violence defendants found that noncompliance with court-ordered treatment was associated significantly with being a repeat offender. [172]

While some studies have found reduced reabuse for abusers who completed treatment programs, a few studies have found less dramatic reductions, for example, in Broward County, where the difference was only 4 percent vs. 5 percent [61], and in Brooklyn, where it was 16 percent vs. 26 percent. [205]

Implications for Prosecutors and Judges

Compliance with mandated batterer intervention programs provides prosecutors and judges with a dynamic risk instrument based on a defendant's ongoing current behavior. Reabuse can be prevented if prosecutors and courts respond appropriately and expeditiously to batterers who fail to attend or to comply with court-referred batterer intervention programs. (Research basis: Multiple studies of batterer intervention programs in diverse jurisdictions across the country.)

8.7. Can Court Monitoring Enhance Batterer Intervention Program Attendance?

Court monitoring can increase batterer intervention program attendance rates, specifically through periodic court compliance hearings. In the multistate evaluation of four different programs, researchers found that batterer intervention program completion rates rose from under 50 percent to 65 percent after a court introduced a mandatory appearance 30 days following imposition of a batterer intervention program mandate. [82] Similarly, implementation of a specialized domestic violence court in San Diego significantly increased attendance. Among other changes, the court instituted postdispositional compliance hearings. [180] Other domestic violence courts across the country have demonstrated completion rates of more than 50 percent, including the Brooklyn misdemeanor domestic violence court, where completion rates for batterers referred to two different batterer programs was documented at 68 and 77 percent. [31]

In a related finding, a large Massachusetts study found that those defendants ordered to attend programs as a condition of probation had a completion rate of 62 percent, whereas those ordered to attend without probation supervision had a completion rate of only 30 percent. [18] A Rhode Island study found that a specialized probation domestic violence supervision program more aggressively monitored and enforced program compliance, as measured by the number of violation hearings brought to court, than the state's regular probation program involving officers with mixed caseloads. [141] A study of three domestic violence courts in Michigan, Wisconsin and Massachusetts found significantly increased offender compliance with batterer intervention programs, both in showing up and staying enrolled. All three courts featured postdispositional review hearings. [103]

Implications for Prosecutors and Judges

To increase program participation, prosecutors should recommend and judges should hold postdispositional compliance hearings as well as placing abusers on supervised probation, even if their convictions were for misdemeanors or ordinance violations. (Research basis: Limited research has been conducted on this issue, but no research suggests that increased judicial monitoring does anything besides increasing batterers' attendance in the programs.

> **Performance Measure:** A 75-percent completion rate has been documented for batterers referred from the Circuit Court of Cook County (Chicago) to 30 area batterer intervention programs. (Research basis: A single study of 549 male domestic violence probationers who were referred to 30 area batterer intervention programs and completed them or were terminated at the time of the study. [12])

8.8. Which Batterers are Likely to Fail to Attend Mandated Batterer Intervention Treatment?

Researchers generally agree that there are a number of variables associated with failure to complete programs. They include being younger, having less education, having greater criminal histories and violence in their family of origin, being less often employed and less motivated to change, having substance abuse problems, having children, and lacking court sanctions for noncompliance. [15, 45, 46, 61, 86, 97, 98, 181, 194] A number of studies emphasize the positive correlation between program completion and "stakes in conformity," including the variables of age (being older), marital status (being married) and employment (being employed). [12, 61]

Studies also find that many of the same variables that predict noncompletion also predict reabuse or general recidivism. In the Florida probation study, an examination of court-referred batterers found that the same characteristics that predicted rearrest (including prior criminal history and stakes in conformity) also predicted missing at least one court-mandated program session. [61] Other studies, including a study of two Brooklyn batterer intervention programs, also found that employment correlated both positively with completion and negatively with rearrest. [31]

However, prior criminal history remains the strongest and most consistent predictor of noncompletion and new arrests. In the Brooklyn study, defendants with a prior arrest history were found to be four times more likely to fail to complete programs than defendants without prior arrests. [31] The Bronx court study similarly found that prior arrests as well as a history of drug abuse predicted both noncompletion and recidivism and found background demographics to be less important. [183]

Implications for Prosecutors and Judges

Screening referrals based on the common variables found to correlate with successful completion - age, prior criminal history and substance abuse - can reduce program failure. Alternatively, supplemental conditions targeting abusers with these characteristics may be necessary to assure successful program participation. (Research basis: Although not all studies find the same array of variables that predict program completion, reabuse and/or general recidivism, almost all of them find overlapping variables of age, prior criminal history and substance abuse.)

8.9. When are Noncompliant Abusers Likely to Drop out of Batterer Programs?

Several studies have found that batterers who do not complete batterer intervention programs are likely to be noncompliant from the start. Furthermore, these studies found that noncompliance at the first court monitoring predicted both program failure and recidivism. In the Brooklyn study, the strongest predictor of program failure was early noncompliance. Defendants who had not enrolled in a program by the time of their first compliance hearing were significantly less likely to complete the program than those enrolled by the first hearing. [31] These findings are similar to those found in the Bronx study. Defendants who were not in compliance at their first monitoring appearance were six times more likely to fail to complete the program than those in compliance at that time. [183]

These findings are consistent with extensive research indicating that the largest proportion of court-identified abusers who reabuse are likely to reabuse sooner rather than later. (See question, "When are abusers likely to reabuse?")

Implications for Prosecutors and Judges

To safeguard victims and/or new partners, prosecutors and courts should respond immediately to an abuser's first failure to enroll in or attend a court-mandated batterer intervention program. (Research basis: Although most studies do not report when noncompliant abusers failed their programs, the consistent findings among abusers referred to multiple programs, utilized by two different courts in New York, strongly support their findings.)

8.10. What Should the Prosecutor's Response be if Court-Referred Abusers are Noncompliant with Programs?

The Rhode Island probation study that compared probationers in specialized probation supervision caseloads with those in less stringent general caseloads found that the former committed significantly less reabuse over one year. The difference, however, applied only to what researchers called "lower risk" probationers, those without prior arrest histories. Although there were several differences in how the two caseloads were supervised, enforcement of batterer intervention program attendance was one of the major differences. The specialized Group's program was more rigidly enforced, as measured by significantly more violations for nonattendance. As a result of the court violation hearings, most of the noncompliant probationers were required to attend weekly compliance court sessions until they completed the program. [141]

An evaluation of two model domestic violence courts found that victims in the court with significantly more probation revocations for noncompliance (12 percent vs. only 1 percent in the other court) reported significantly less reabuse than in the comparison court. In the court with more revocations, victims reported a lower frequency of physical assaults for up to 11 months after the study incident. The defendants in the court with the higher revocation rates had a significantly higher number of prior arrests than the defendants in the comparison court (8.3 vs. 3.7 percent). Researchers posited that lower domestic violence arrests were obtained primarily through early detection and incarceration of probationers who either continued to reabuse or failed to comply with conditions. [103]

Broward County probation study researchers concluded the following correlation between program noncompliance and reabuse: If abusers are not afraid of violating their court orders, they are also not afraid of the consequences of committing new offenses. [60]

Implications for Prosecutors

Prosecutors should recommend increased sanctions for noncompliant abusers. Incarceration will assure immediate victim protection at least for the length of the incarceration. Short of this, increased surveillance may be effective at reducing risk of reabuse for lower risk abusers. (Research basis: Multiple studies have found that doing nothing in regard to noncompliant, court-referred abusers results in significantly higher rates of reabuse. Two studies involving jurisdictions across four states suggest that vigorous enforcement of conditions is the key in deterring reabuse.)

8.11. What Should the Judge's Response be if Court-Referred Abusers are Noncompliant with Programs?

Among lower risk abusers on probation for domestic violence, one study cited increased enforcement of batterer program compliance (as indicated by significantly more violators brought into court by probation officers for noncompliance) as one major factor correlating with reduced reabuse over a two-year period. This was compared to a control group of probationers who were also referred to batterer intervention programs but were not monitored as rigorously or brought back to court because of noncompliance. As a result of court violation hearings, most noncompliant probationers were required to attend weekly compliance court sessions until they completed the program. Lower risk abusers included those who had not previously been probated for domestic violence. In addition to attending more revocation hearings, these probationers had slightly more contact with probation officers, officers attempted to contact victims at least once, and the probation officers supervised specialized domestic violence caseloads. [141]

An evaluation of two model domestic violence courts found that victims in the court with significantly more probation revocations for noncompliance (12 percent vs. only 1 percent in the other court) reported significantly less reabuse than in a comparison court. Victims from the other model court reported no difference with victims in a comparison court. In the court with more revocations, victims reported a lower frequency of physical assaults up to 11 months after the study incident. The defendants in the court with the high revocation rate had a significantly higher number of prior arrests than defendants in the comparison court (8.3 percent vs. 3.7 percent). Researchers posited that lower domestic violence arrests were obtained primarily through the early detection and incarceration of probationers who either continued to reabuse or failed to comply with conditions. [103]

Broward County probation study researchers concluded the following correlation between program noncompliance and reabuse: If abusers are not afraid of violating their court orders, they are also not afraid of the consequences of committing new offenses. [60]

Implications for Judges

Judges should respond to noncompliant abusers immediately to safeguard victims. (Research basis: Multiple studies have found that doing nothing with regard to noncompliant, court-referred abusers results in significantly higher rates of reabuse. Two studies involving jurisdictions across four states suggest that vigorous enforcement of conditions is the key in deterring reabuse.)

8.12. What Should the Prosecutor's or Judge's Response be to Abusers Who Reoffend While Enrolled or after Completing a Batterer Intervention Program?

Batterers rearrested while enrolled or after completing a batterer intervention program are at high risk for reabusing (also see question, "How many abusers are likely to do it again?"). The multistate batterer intervention program study found that the majority of court-referred batterers who reassaulted did so more than once. [84] Similarly, a Rhode Island probation study found that batterers who were arrested for domestic violence while their prior arrest was still pending, or while they were still on probation for an earlier offense (domestic or nondomestic), had the highest reabuse rates of any probated abuser, averaging over 50 percent. [141]

Implications for Prosecutors and Judges

Prosecutors should recommend incarceration, and judges should incarcerate, any offenders who reabuse while enrolled in batterer programs or after having completed the programs. Due to their limited "treatment effect," simply re-enrolling high-risk abusers in these programs endangers victims. Those abusers who reabuse are likely to continue doing so if left on their own. (Research basis: Both batterer program studies and general studies of court-identified batterers have found that repeatedly arrested abusers are chronic in their abusive behavior.)

8.13. What Effect Do Batterer Intervention Program Referrals Have on Victims?

Studies find that most victims are satisfied with their abuser's referral to a batterer intervention program. In the Bronx study, 77 percent of victims were satisfied with the case outcome if the abuser was ordered to attend a program, compared to only 55 percent of victims who were satisfied when the abuser was not required to attend a program. [145] A survey of victims of men attending batterer intervention programs throughout Rhode Island found most female victims enthusiastic about the batterer programs. Some victims who were enthusiastic were reassaulted but still felt that the program improved their situation. [140] Program enrollment may also influence victims to remain with their abusers. Victims are more likely to remain with their abusers if their abusers are in treatment programs and are hopeful that the abusers will "get better." [58, 81]

Implications for Prosecutors and Judges

Prosecutors, judges, other court personnel and batterer intervention programs should warn victims that batterers' attendance at these programs does not ensure the cessation of abuse during or after the program. (Research basis: Consistent findings of victim surveys in multiple settings across the country as well as a control study of victims whose abusers were not sent to a batterer program.)

Bottom Line: On the whole, unless batterer intervention programs are closely monitored and program compliance is rigorously enforced, batterer intervention programs may be ineffective and give false hope to victims.

REFERENCES

[1]   Adams, D. (2007). *Why Do They Kill? Men Who Murder Their Intimate Partners.* Nashville, TN: Vanderbilt University Press.

[2]   Adams, S. (1999). *Serial Batterers.* Boston, MA: Office of the Commissioner of Probation.

[3]   Albucher, R. & Liberzon, I. (2002). "Psychopharmacological Treatment in PTSD: A Critical Review." *Journal of Psychiatric Research, 36*(6), 355-367.

[4]   Aldarondo, E. (2002) "Evaluating the Efficacy of Interventions With Men Who Batter." In *Programs for Men Who Batter,* ed. E. Aldarondo and F. Mederos. Kingston, NJ: Civic Research Institute,: 3-12.

[5]   Apsler, R., Cummins, M. & Carl, S. (November 2003). "Perceptions of the Police by Female Victims of Domestic Partner Violence." *Violence Against Women, 9*(11), 1318-1335, NCJ 202666. http://www.ncjrs.gov/App/publications/abstract.aspx?ID=202666

[6]   Arias, I. & Pape, K. (1999). "Psychological Abuse: Implications for Adjustment and Commitment to Leave Violent Partners." *Violence and Victims, 14*(1), (Spring), 55-67.

[7]   Austin, J. & Dankwort, J. (1998). *A Review of Standards for Batterer Intervention Programs.* VAWnet Applied Research Forum, National Online Resource Center on Violence Against Women, revised August, available online at http:// new.vawnet. org/AssocFilesVAWnet/ARstandards.pdf

[8]   Babcock, J., Green, C. & Robie, C. "Does Batterers' Treatment Work? A Meta-Analytic Review of Domestic Violence Treatment." *Clinical Psychology Review, 23*(8), (January 2004), 1023-1053.

[9]   Babcock, J. & Steiner, R. (March 1999) "The Relationship Between Treatment, Incarceration, and Recidivism of Battering: A Program Evaluation of Seattle's Coordinated Community Response to Domestic Violence." *Journal of Family Psychology, 13*(1), 46- 59.

[10]   Bass, A., Nealon, P. & Armstrong, C. (2004). "The War on Domestic Abuse." *Boston Globe,* September 25, 1994, quoted in A. Klein, *The Criminal Justice Response to Domestic Violence.* Belmont, CA: Thomson/Wadsworth,: 138.

[11]   Belknap, J., Graham, D., Hartman, J., Lippen, V., Allen, G. & Sutherland, J. (2000) *"Factors Related to Domestic Violence Court Dispositions in a Large Urban Area: The Role of Victim/Witness Reluctance and Other Variables."* Executive summary for National Institute of Justice, grant number 96-WT-NX-0004. Washington, DC: U.S. Department of Justice, National Institute of Justice, August, NCJ 184112. http:// www. ncjrs.gov/App/Publications/abstract.aspx?ID=184112

[12]   Bennett, L., Stoops, C., Call, C. & Flett, H. (2007). "Program Completion and Re-Arrest in a Batterer Intervention System." *Research on Social Work Practice, 17*(42), 42-54.

[13]   Benson, M. & Fox, G. (2004). *"Concentrated Disadvantage, Economic Distress, and Violence Against Women in Intimate Relationships."* Final report for National Institute of Justice, grant number 98-WT-VX-001 1. Washington, DC: U.S. Department of Justice, National Institute of Justice, NCJ 199709. http://www.ncjrs.gov/App/Publications/abstract.aspx?ID=199709

[14] Benson, M., Wooldredge, J., Thistlethwaite, A. & Fox, G. (2004). "The Correlation Between Race and Domestic Violence Is Confounded in Community Context." *Social Problems, 51*(3), (July), 326-342.

[15] Bersani, C. & Chen. (1988). "Sociological Perspectives in Family Violence." In *Handbook on Family Violence,* ed. V. Van Hasselt, R. Morrison, A. Bellack, and M. Hersen. New York: Plenum Press, 57-84.

[16] Bible, A. & Weigl, A. (2004). "Cries of Abuse Unheeded, Assaults Rise to Murders." *News and Observer* [Raleigh, NC], May 18-20, 2003, quoted in A. Klein, *The Criminal Justice Response to Domestic Violence.* Belmont, CA: Thomson/Wadsworth, 139.

[17] Block, C. (2004). *"Risk Factors for Death or Life-Threatening Injury for Abused Women in Chicago."* Final report for National Institute of Justice, grant number 96-IJ-CX-0020. Washington, DC: U.S. Department of Justice, National Institute of Justice, NCJ 199732. http://www.ncjrs.gov/App/Publications/abstract.aspx?ID=199732

[18] Bocko, S., Cicchetti, C., Lempicki, L. & Powell, A. (2004). *Restraining Order Violators, Corrective Programming and Recidivism.* Boston, MA: Office of the Commissioner of Probation, November.

[19] Brookoff, D. (1997). *Drugs, Alcohol, and Domestic Violence in Memphis.* Research Review. Washington, DC: U.S. Department of Justice, National Institute of Justice, October 1997, FS 000172.

[20] Brundrett, R. & Roberts, C. (2004). "Domestic Abuse Cases Go to State." *The State* [Columbia, SC], July 12, 2001, quoted in A. Klein, *The Criminal Justice Response to Domestic Violence.* Belmont, CA: Thomson/Wadsworth, 139.

[21] Brundrett, R., Roberts, C. & Leblanc, C. (2001). "S.C. Dismisses 54 Percent of Worst Domestic Violence Cases," *The State* [Columbia, SC], May 20, quoted in A. Klein, *The Criminal Justice Response to Domestic Violence.* Belmont, CA: Thomson/Wadsworth, 2004: 139.

[22] Buzawa, E. & Buzawa, C. (1992). eds. *Domestic Violence: The Changing Criminal Justice Response.* Westport, CT: Auburn House.

[23] Buzawa, E., Hotaling, G., Klein, A. & Byrnes, J. (1999). *"Response to Domestic Violence in a Pro-Active Court Setting."* Final report for National Institute of Justice, grant number 95-IJCX-0027. Washington, DC: U.S. Department of Justice, National Institute of Justice, July, NCJ 181427. http://www.ncjrs.gov/App/ Publications/ abstract. aspx?ID=181427

[24] Campbell, J., O'Sullivan, C., Roehl, J. & Webster, D. (2005). *"Intimate Partner Violence Risk Assessment Validation Study."* Final report for National Institute for Justice, grant number 2000-WT-VX-001 1. Washington, DC: U.S. Department of Justice, National Institute of Justice, May 2005 (rev. Dec. 2005), NCJ 209731. http://www.ncjrs.gov/App/Publications/abstract.aspx?ID=209731

[25] Campbell, J., Webster, D., Koziol-McLain, J., Block, C., Campbell, D., Curry, M., Gary, F., McFarlane, J., Sachs, C., Sharps, P., Ulrich, Y. & Wilt, S. (2003). "Assessing Risk Factors for Intimate Partner Homicide." *NIJ Journal, 250,* (November), 14-19, NCJ 196547. http://www.ncjrs.gov/App/Publications/abstract.aspx?ID=196547

[26] Carlson, M., Harris, S. & Holden, G. (1999). "Protective Orders and Domestic Violence: Risk Factors for Reabuse." *Journal of Family Violence, 14*(2), 205-226.

[27] Catalano, S. (2007). *Intimate Partner Violence in the United States.* Washington, DC: U.S. Department of Justice, Bureau of Justice Statistics, December, available online at http://www.ojp.usdoj.gov/bjs/intimate/ipv.htm.

[28] Cavanaugh, M. & Gelles, R. (2005). "The Utility of Male Domestic Violence Typologies. *Journal of Interpersonal Violence, 20*(2), 155-166.

[29] Chase, K. O'Leary, K. & Heyman, R. (2001). "Categorizing Partner-Violent Men Within the Reactive-Proactive Typology Model." *Journal of Consulting and Clinical Psychology, 69*, 567-572.

[30] Chen, H., Bersani, C., Myers, S. & Denton, R. (1989). "Evaluating the Effectiveness of a Court Sponsored Abuser Treatment Program." *Journal of Family Violence, 4*(4), (December), 309-322, NCJ 122317. http://www. ncjrs.gov/ App/ Publications/ abstract.aspx?ID=122317

[31] Cissner, A. & Puffett, N. (2006). "Do Batterer Program Length or Approach Affect Completion or Re-Arrest Rates? A Comparison of Outcomes Between Defendants Sentenced to Two Batterer Programs in Brooklyn." New York, NY: Center for Court Innovation, September, available online at http://www. courtinnovation. org/uploads/ documents/ IDCCDCAP percent20final.pdf.

[32] Cochran, D., Adams, S. & O'Brien, P. (1998)"From Chaos to Clarity in Understanding Domestic Violence." *Domestic Violence Report, 3*(5), (June/July): 65.

[33] Cohen, R. (1995). *Probation and Parole Violators in State Prison, 1991.* Bureau of Justice Statistics Special Report. Washington, DC: U.S. Department of Justice, Bureau of Justice Statistics, August, NCJ 149076. http://www. ncjrs.gov/ App/Publications/ abstract.aspx?ID=149076

[34] Collins, J., Spencer, D. Snodgrass, J. & Wheeless, S. (1999). "*Linkage of Domestic Violence and Substance Abuse Services.*" Final report for National Institute of Justice, grant number 97-IJ-CX-0009. Washington, DC: U.S. Department of Justice, National Institute of Justice, May, NCJ 194123. http://www.ncjrs. gov/App/Publications/ abstract.aspx?ID=194123

[35] Dalton, B. (2001). "Batterer Characteristics and Treatment Completion." *Journal of Interpersonal Violence, 16*(12), 1223-1238.

[36] Daly, J. & Pelowski, S. (2000). "Predictors of Dropout Among Men Who Batter: A Review of Studies With Implications for Research and Practice." *Violence and Victims, 15*(2), (Summer), 137-160, NCJ 186644. http://www.ncjrs. gov/App/Publications/ abstract. aspx?ID=186644

[37] Davis, R. & Maxwell, C. (2002). "*Preventing Repeat Incidents of Family Violence: A Reanalysis of Data From Three Field Tests.*" Final report for National Institute of Justice, grant number 2000-WT-VX-0007. Washington, DC: U.S. Department of Justice, National Institute of Justice, July, NCJ 200608. http://www.ncjrs.gov/ App/Publications/ abstract.aspx?ID=200608

[38] Davis, R. & Smith, B. (1995). "Domestic Violence Reforms: Empty Promises or Fulfilled Expectations?" *Crime and Delinquency, 41*(4), (October), 541-552, NCJ 157478. http://www.ncjrs.gov/App/Publications/abstract.aspx?ID=157478

[39] Davis, R., Smith, B. & Nickles, L. (1998). "The Deterrent Effect of Prosecuting Domestic Violence Misdemeanors." *Crime and Delinquency, 44*(3), (July), 434-442, NCJ 173568. http://www.ncjrs.gov/App/Publications/abstract.aspx?ID=173568

[40] Davis, R., Smith, B. & Rabbitt, C. (2001). "Increasing Convictions in Domestic Violence Cases: A Field Test in Milwaukee." *Justice System Journal, 22*(1), 61-72, NCJ 188067. http://www.ncjrs.gov/App/Publications/abstract.aspx?ID=188067

[41] Davis, R. & Taylor, B. (1997) "A Proactive Response to Family Violence: The Results of a Randomized Experiment." *Criminology, 35*(2), (May), 307-333.

[42] Davis, R., Taylor, B. & Maxwell, C. (2000). *"Does Batterer Treatment Reduce Violence? A Randomized Experiment in Brooklyn."* Final report to National Institute of Justice, grant number 94-IJ-CX-0047. Washington, DC: U.S. Department of Justice, National Institute of Justice, January, NCJ 180772. http://www.ncjrs.gov/App/Publications/abstract.aspx? ID=180772

[43] Dawson, M. & Dinovitzer, R. (1997). "Victim Cooperation and the Prosecution of Domestic Violence in a Specialized Court." *Justice Quarterly,* 18(3), (September 2001), 593-622, NCJ 190492. http://www.ncjrs.gov/App/Publications/ abstract.aspx? ID= 190492

[44] de Becker, G. *The Gift of Fear.* Boston, MA: Little, Brown & Co., NCJ 177216. http://www.ncjrs.gov/App/Publications/abstract.aspx?ID=177216

[45] DeHart, D., Kennerly, R., Burke, L. & Follingstad, D. (1999). "Predictors of Attrition in a Treatment Program for Battering Men." *Journal of Family Violence, 14*(1), (March): 19-34, NCJ 177795. http://www.ncjrs.gov/ App/Publications/ abstract.aspx? ID=177795

[46] DeMaris, A. (1989). "Attrition in Batterers' Counseling: The Role of Social and Demographic Factors." *Social Review, 63,* 142-154.

[47] Deschner, J., McNeil, J. & Moore, M. (1986). "A Treatment Model for Batterers." *Social Casework, 67*(1), 55-60, NCJ 105256. http://www.ncjrs. gov/App/Publications/ abstract.aspx?ID=105256

[48] Dobash, R., Dobash, R., Cavanagh, K. & Lewis, R. (1996). "Reeducation Programmes for Violent Men: An Evaluation." *Research Findings, 46,* (October), 1-4.

[49] Dugan, L., Nagin, D. & Rosenfeld, R. (2004). *"Effects of State and Local Domestic Violence Policy on Intimate Partner Homicide."* Final report for National Institute of Justice, grant number 97-WT-VX-0004. Washington, DC: U.S. Department of Justice, National Institute of Justice, NCJ 199711. http://www.ncjrs.gov/ App/publications/ abstract.aspx?ID=202666

[50] Dunford, F. (1990). "System Initiated Warrants for Suspects of Misdemeanor Domestic. Assault: A Pilot Study." *Justice Quarterly, 7*(4), 631-653.

[51] Dunford, F. (2000). "The San Diego Navy Experiment: An Assessment of Interventions for Men Who Assault Their Wives." *Journal of Consulting and Clinical Psychology, 68*(3), 468-476.

[52] Eckberg, D. & Podkopacz, M. (2002). *"Domestic Violence Court in Minneapolis: Three Levels of Analysis."* Presentation at American Society of Criminologists annual meeting, Chicago, IL, November 15.

[53] Eckhardt, C. (2003). *"Stages and Processes of Change and Associated Treatment Outcomes in Partner Assaultive Men."* Final report for National Institute of Justice, grant number 99- WT-VX-0012. Washington, DC: U.S. Department of Justice, National Institute of Justice, August, NCJ 205022. http://www.ncjrs.gov/ App/Publications/ abstract.aspx? ID=205022

[54] Edleson, J. & Grusznski, R. (1988). "Treating Men Who Batter: Four Years of Outcome Data from the Domestic Abuse Project." *Journal of Social Service Research, 12*(3), 3-22.

[55] Fagan, J., Friedman, E., Wexler, S. & Lewis, V. (1984). *The National Family Violence Program: Final Evaluation Report.* San Francisco, CA: URSA Institute.

[56] Fals-Stewart, W. (2003). "The Occurrence of Partner Physical Aggression on Days of Alcohol Consumption: A Longitudinal Diary Study." *Journal of Consulting Psychology, 71*(1), 41-52.

[57] Family Violence Project. (1990). "Family Violence: Improving Court Practice." *Juvenile and Family Court Journal, 41*(4), 14-15, NCJ 131619. http://www. ncjrs.gov/App/ Publications/abstract.aspx?ID=131619

[58] Feazell, C., Mayers, R. & Deschner, J. (1984). "Services for Men Who Batter: Implications for Programs and Policies." *Family Relations, 33*(2), (April): 217-223.

[59] Feder, L. (1999). "Police Handling of Domestic Violence Calls: An Overview and Further Investigation." *Women and Criminal Justice, 10*(2), 49-68, NCJ 177884. http://www.ncjrs.gov/App/Publications/abstract.aspx?ID=177884

[60] Feder, L. & Dugan, L. (2004). *"Testing a Court-Mandated Treatment Program for Domestic Violence Offenders: The Broward Experiment."* Final report for National Institute of Justice, grant number 96-WT-NX-0008. Washington, DC: U.S. Department of Justice, National Institute of Justice, NCJ 199729. http://www.ncjrs.gov/ App/Publications/ abstract.aspx?ID=199729

[61] Feder, L. & Forde, D. (2000). *"A Test of the Efficacy of Court-Mandated Counseling for Domestic Violence Offenders: The Broward Experiment."* Final report for National Institute of Justice, grant number 96-WT-NX-0008. Washington, DC: U.S. Department of Justice, National Institute of Justice, June, NCJ 184752. http:// www.ncjrs. gov/App/ Publications/abstract.aspx?ID=184752

[62] Feder, L. & Wilson, D. (2005). "A Meta-Analytic Review of Court-Mandated Batterer Intervention Programs: Can Courts Affect Abusers' Behaviors?" *Journal of Experimental Criminology, 1*(2), (July), 239-262.

[63] Felson, R., Ackerman, J. & Gallagher, C. (2005). *"Police Intervention and the Repeat of Domestic Assault."* Final report for National Institute of Justice, grant number 2002-WGBX-2002. Washington, DC: U.S. Department of Justice, National Institute of Justice, June, NCJ 210301. http://www.ncjrs.gov/App /Publications/ abstract.aspx? ID=210301

[64] Finn, M. (2003). *"Effects of Victims' Experiences With Prosecutors on Victim Empowerment and Re-Occurrence of Intimate Partner Violence."* Final report for National Institute of Justice, grant number 99-WT-VX-0008. Washington, DC: U.S. Department of Justice, National Institute of Justice, August, NCJ 202983. http://www.ncjrs.gov/ App/Publications/ abstract.aspx?ID=202983

[65] Finn, M., Blackwell, B., Stalans, L., Studdard, S. & Dugan, L. (2004). "Dual Arrest Decisions in Domestic Violence Cases: The Influence of Departmental Policies." *Crime and Delinquency, 50*(4), (October), 565-589, NCJ 207463. http://www.ncjrs.gov/App/ Publications/ abstract.aspx?ID=207463

[66] Ford, D. & Regoli, M. J. (1992). "The Preventive Impacts of Policies for Prosecuting Wife Batterers." In *Domestic Violence: The Changing Criminal Justice Response,* eds. E. Buzawa and C. Buzawa. Westport, CT: Auburn House, 181 -208.

[67] Ford, D. & Regoli, M. J. (1993). *"The Indianapolis Domestic Violence Prosecution Experiment."* Final report for National Institute of Justice, grant number 86-IJ-CX-001 2, and National Institute of Mental Health/DHHS, grant number MH-15161-13. Washington, DC: U.S. Department of Justice, National Institute of Justice, CJ 157870. http://www.ncjrs.gov/App/Publications/abstract.aspx?ID=157870

[68] Friday, P., Lord, V. Exum, M. & Hartman, J. (2006). *"Evaluating the Impact of a Specialized Domestic Violence Police Unit."* Final report for National Institute of Justice, grant number 2004-WG-BX-0004. Washington, DC: U.S. Department of Justice, National Institute of Justice, May, NCJ 215916. http://www.ncjrs.gov/ App/Publications /abstract.aspx?ID=237505

[69] Gamache, D., Edleson, J. & Schock, M. (1988). "Coordinated Police, Judicial and Social Services Response to Woman Battering: A Multiple-Baseline Evaluation Across Three Communities." In *Coping With Family Violence: Research and Policy Perspectives,* ed. G. Hotaling, D. Finkelhor, J. Kirkpatrick. and M. Straus. Beverly Hills, CA: Sage, 193-211, NCJ 114456. http:// www.ncjrs. gov/App/ Publications/ abstract.aspx?ID=114456

[70] Garner, J. (2005). "What Does 'the Prosecution' of Domestic Violence Mean?" *Criminology and Public Policy, 4*(3), (August) 567-573.

[71] Garner, J. & Maxwell, C. (2008). *Prosecution and Conviction Rates for Intimate Partner Violence.* Shepherdstown, WV: Joint Centers for Justice Studies, 49.

[72] Gelles, R. (1997). *Intimate Violence in Families* (3rd ed.). Thousand Oaks, CA: Sage.

[73] Giacomazzi, A. & Smithey, M. (2004). *"Collaborative Effort Toward Resolving Family Violence Against Women."* Final report for National Institute of Justice, grant number 97-WE-VX0131. Washington, DC: U.S. Department of Justice, National Institute of Justice, NCJ 199716. http://www.ncjrs.gov/App/ Publications/ abstract. aspx?ID= 199716

[74] Gist, J., McFarlane, J. Malecha, A., Fredland, N., Schultz, P. & Willson, P. (2002). "Women in Danger: Intimate Partner Violence Experienced by Women That Qualify and Do Not Qualify for a Protective Order." *Behavioral Sciences and the Law, 19*(5-6), (January 9), 637-647.

[75] Gist, J., McFarlane, J. Malecha, A., Willson, P., Watson, K., Fredland, N., Schultz, P. T. Walsh, Hall, I. & Smith. S. (2001). "Protection Orders and Assault Charges: Do Justice Interventions Reduce Violence Against Women?" *American Journal of Family Law, 15*(1), 59-71.

[76] Gleason, W. (1993). "Mental Disorders in Battered Women: An Empirical Study." *Violence and Victims, 8*(1), (Spring), 53-68, NCJ 148472. http://www.ncjrs. gov/App/ Publications/abstract.aspx?ID=148472

[77] Golding, J. (1999). "Intimate Partner Violence as a Risk Factor for Mental Disorders: A Meta- Analysis." *Journal of Family Violence, 14*(2), (June), 99-132, NCJ 178109. http://www.ncjrs.gov/App/Publications/abstract.aspx?ID=178109

[78] Goldkamp, J. (1996*). "The Role of Drug and Alcohol Abuse in Domestic Violence and Its Treatment: Dade County's Domestic Violence Court Experiment."* Final report for National Institute of Justice, grant number 93-IJ-CX-0028. Washington, DC: U.S. Department of Justice, National Institute of Justice, NCJ 163410. http://www. ncjrs.gov/ App/Publications/abstract.aspx?ID=163410

[79] Goldkamp, J., Weiland, D., Collins, M. & White, M. (1996*). "The Role of Drug and Alcohol Abuse in Domestic Violence and Its Treatment: Dade County's Domestic Violence Court Experiment."* Appendices to the final report for National Institute of Justice, grant number 93-IJ-CX-0028. Washington, DC: U.S. Department of Justice, National Institute of Justice, NCJ 163408. http://www.ncjrs. gov/App/Publications/ abstract.aspx?ID=163408

[80] Gondolf, E. (1986). "How Some Men Stop Battering: An Evaluation of a Group Counseling Program." Paper presented at Second National Conference on Family Violence, Durham, NH, August 1984, and cited in E. Gondolf and D Russell, "The Case Against Anger Control Treatment Programs for Batterers,". *Response to the Victimization of Women & Children, 9*(3), 2-5.

[81] Gondolf, E. (1987). "Evaluating Programs for Men Who Batter: Problems and Prospects." *Journal of Family Violence, 2*(1), (March) 95-108, NCJ 105396. http://www.ncjrs.gov/App/Publications/abstract.aspx?ID=105396

[82] Gondolf, E. (1997). *The Impact of Mandatory Court Review on Batterer Program Compliance: An Evaluation of the Pittsburgh Municipal Courts and Domestic Violence Abuse Counseling Center (DACC),* Final Report. Harrisburg, PA: Pennsylvania Commission on Crime and Delinquency, May 15, NCJ 214567. http://www.ncjrs.gov/ App/Publications/ abstract.aspx?ID=236118

[83] Gondolf, E. (1997). "Patterns of Reassault in Batterer Programs." *Violence and Victims 12*(4), (Winter), 373-388, NCJ 173329. http://www.ncjrs.gov/ App/Publications/ abstract.aspx? ID=173329

[84] Gondolf, E. (1998). *Multi-Site Evaluation of Batterer Intervention Systems: A 30-Month Follow-Up of Court-Mandated Batterers in Four Cities.* Brief Report. Indiana, PA: Mid-Atlantic Addiction Research and Training Institute, August 18, NCJ 183367. http://www.ncjrs.gov/App/Publications/abstract.aspx?ID=183367

[85] Gondolf, E. (2000). "30-Month Follow-Up of Court-Referred Batterers in Four Cities." *International Journal of Offender Therapy and Comparative Criminology, 44(1),* (February) 111- 128, NCJ 181487.http://www.ncjrs.gov/App/Publications/ abstract. aspx?ID=181487

[86] Gondolf, E. (2002). *Batterer Intervention Systems.* Thousand Oaks, CA: Sage.

[87] Gondolf, E. (2005).*"Culturally-Focused Batterer Counseling for African-American Men."* Final report for National Institute of Justice, grant number 2001 -WT-BX-0003. Washington, DC: U.S. Department of Justice, National Institute of Justice, June 10, NCJ 210828. http://www.ncjrs.gov/App/Publications/abstract.aspx?ID=210828

[88] Gondolf, E. & Jones, A. (2001). "The Program Effect of Batterer Programs in Three Cities." *Violence and Victims, 16*(6), (December): 693-704, NCJ 193654. http://www. ncjrs.gov/ App/Publications/abstract.aspx?ID=193654

[89] Gondolf, E. & White, R. (2001). "Batterer Program Participants Who Repeatedly Reassault: Psychopathic Tendencies and Other Disorders." *Journal of Interpersonal Violence, 16*(4), (April), 361-380, NCJ 208765. http://www.ncjrs. gov/App/ Publications/ abstract.aspx?ID=208765

[90] Gordon, J. & Moriarty, L. (2003). "The Effects of Domestic Violence Batterer Treatment on Domestic Violence Recidivism: The Chesterfield County Experience." *Criminal Justice and Behavior: An International Journal, 30*(1), (February) 118-134, NCJ 198836. http://www.ncjrs.gov/App/Publications/abstract.aspx?ID=198836

[91] Gover, A., MacDonald, J. & Alpert, G. (2003). "Combating Domestic Violence: Findings From an Evaluation of a Local Domestic Violence Court." *Criminology and Public Policy, 3*(1), (November), 109-132, NCJ 203428. http://www.ncjrs.gov/App/Publications/ abstract.aspx?ID=203428

[92] Grau, J., Fagan, J. & Wexler, S. (1985). "Restraining Orders for Battered Women: Issues of Access and Efficacy." In *Criminal Justice Politics and Women: The Aftermath of Legally Mandated Change,* ed. C. Schweber and C. Fein man. New York: Hawthorn Press, 13-28, NCJ 097703.http://www. ncjrs.gov/App/ Publications/ abstract. aspx? ID=097703

[93] Greenfeld, L., Rand, M., Craven, D., Klaus, P., Perkins, C., Ringel, C., Warchol, G. Maston, C. & Fox, J. (1998). *Violence by Intimates: Analysis of Data on Crimes by Current or Former Spouses, Boyfriends, and Girlfriends.* Factbook. Washington, DC: Bureau of Justice Statistics, March, NCJ 167237. http://www.ncjrs.gov/App/Publications/ abstract.aspx?ID=167237

[94] Greenfeld, L. & Zawitz, M. (1995). *Weapons Offenses and Offenders.* Bureau of Justice Statistics Selected Findings. Washington, DC: U.S. Department of Justice, Bureau of Justice Statistics, November, NCJ 155284. http://www.ncjrs.gov/App/ Publications/ abstract. aspx?ID=155284

[95] Grisso, J., Schwarz, D., Hirschinger, N., Sammel, M., Brensinger, C., Santanna, J., Lowe, R., Anderson, E. Shaw, L., Bethel, C. & Teeple, L. (1999). "Violent Injuries Among Women in an Urban Area." *New England Journal of Medicine, 341*(25), (December 16) 1899-1905.

[96] Gross, M., Cramer, E., Forte, J., Gordon, J., Kunkel, T. & Moriarty, L. (2000). "The Impact of Sentencing Options on Recidivism Among Domestic Violence Offenders: A Case Study." *American Journal of Criminal Justice, 24*(2), (Spring) 301-312, NCJ 184477. http://www.ncjrs.gov/App/Publications/abstract.aspx?ID=184477

[97] Grusznski, R. & Carrillo, T. (1988). "Who Completes Batterers' Treatment Groups? An Empirical Investigation." *Journal of Family Violence, 3*(2), (June) 141 -1 50.

[98] Hamberger, K. & Hastings, J. (1988). "Skills Training for Treatment of Spouse Abusers: An Outcome Study." *Journal of Family Violence, 3*(2), (June) 121 -1 30.

[99] Hanson, R. & Wallace-Capretta, S. (2000). *A Multi-Site Study of Treatment for Abusive Men.* Report No. 2000-05. Ottawa, Ontario, Canada: Department of the Solicitor General Canada.

[100] Hanson, R. & Wallace-Capretta, S. (2000). *Predicting Recidivism Among Male Batterers.* Report No. 2000-06. Ottawa, Ontario, Canada: Department of the Solicitor General Canada.

[101] Hardeman, J. (1995). *Implementation of the Abuse Prevention Act (209A).* Waltham, MA: Heller School, Brandeis University.

[102] Harrell, A. (1991). *"Evaluation of a Court-Ordered Treatment for Domestic Violence Offenders."* Final report for National Institute of Justice, grant number 90-12L-E-089. Washington, DC: U.S. Department of Justice, National Institute of Justice. and The Urban Institute, NCJ 139749. http://www. ncjrs.gov/ App/ Publications/abstract. aspx?ID=139749

[103] Harrell, A., Castro, J., Newmark, L. & Visher, C. (2007). *"Final Report on the Evaluation of the Judicial Oversight Demonstration: Executive Summary."* Final report for National Institute of Justice, grant number 99-WT-VX-K005. Washington, DC: U.S.

Department of Justice, National Institute of Justice, and The Urban Institute, June, NCJ 219386, available online at http://www.urban.org/publications/411498.html.

[104] Harrell, A., Schaffer, M., DeStefano, C. & Castro, J. (2006). *"The Evaluation of Milwaukee's Judicial Oversight Demonstration."* Final report for National Institute of Justice, grant number 99-WT-VX-K005. Washington, DC: U.S. Department of Justice, National Institute of Justice, and The Urban Institute, April, available online at http://www.urban.org/ publications/ 411315.html.

[105] Harrell, A. & Smith, B. (1996). "Effects of Restraining Orders on Domestic Violence Victims." In *Do Arrest and Restraining Orders Work?* ed. E. Buzawa and C. Buzawa. Thousand Oaks, CA: Sage, 214-243.

[106] Harrell, A., Smith, B. & Newmark, L. (1993). *Court Processing and the Effects of Restraining Orders for Domestic Violence Victims.* Washington, DC: Urban Institute, May 1, available online at http://www.urban.org/url.cfm?ID=405114.

[107] Hartley, C. & Frohmann, L. (2003). *"Cook County Target Abuser Call (TAC): An Evaluation of a Specialized Domestic Violence Court."* Final report for National Institute of Justice, grant number 2000-WT-VX-0003. Washington, DC: U.S. Department of Justice, National Institute of Justice, August, NCJ 202944. http://www.ncjrs.gov/ App/Publications/ abstract.aspx?ID=202944

[108] Hayler, B. & Addison-Lamb, M. (2000). *"A Process and Implementation Evaluation of the Specialized Domestic Violence Probation Projects in Illinois's Peoria, Sangamon, and Tazewell Counties."* Springfield, IL: University of Illinois at Springfield, November.

[109] Hayler, B., Ford N. & Addison-Lamb, M. (1999). *"An Implementation Evaluation of the Enhanced Domestic Violence Probation Program in Champaign County."* Final report for Bureau of Justice Assistance, grant number 96-DB-MU-001 7. Washington, DC: U.S. Department of Justice, Bureau of Justice Assistance, December, NCJ 188355. http://www.ncjrs.gov/App/Publications/abstract.aspx?ID=188355

[110] Healey, K. Smith, C. & O'Sullivan, C. (1998). *Batterer Intervention: Program Approaches and Criminal Justice Strategies.* NIJ Issues and Practices, February, grant number OJP94-C-007, NCJ 168638. http://www.ncjrs.gov/ App/Publications/ abstract. aspx? ID=168638

[111] Heckert, D. & Gondolf, E. (2000). "Assessing Assault Self-Reports by Batterer Program Participants and Their Partners." *Journal of Family Violence, 15*(2),(June), 181-197.

[112] Heckert, D. & Gondolf, E. (2004). "Battered Women's Perceptions of Risk Versus Risk Factors and Instruments in Predicting Repeat Reassault." *Journal of Interpersonal Violence 19*(7), 778-800.

[113] Heckert, D. & Gondolf, E. (2005). "Do Multiple Outcomes and Conditional Factors Improve Prediction of Batterer Reassault?" *Violence and Victims, 20*(1), (February): 3-24, NCJ 210809.http://www.ncjrs.gov/App/Publications/abstract.aspx?ID=210809

[114] Hendricks, J., (1991). ed. *Crisis Intervention in Criminal Justice and Social Services.* Springfield, IL: Charles C Thomas Publishers.

[115] Henning, K. & Klesges, L. (1999). *Evaluation of the Shelby County Domestic Violence Court.* Shelby County, TN: Shelby County Government.

[116] Hilton, N., Harris, G., Rice, M., Lang, C., Cormier, C. & Lines, K. (2004). "A Brief Actuarial Assessment for the Prediction of Wife Assault Recidivism: The Ontario

Domestic Assault Risk Assessment." *Psychological Assessment, 16*(3), (September), 267-275.

[117] Hirschel, D., Buzawa, E., Pattavina, A., Faggiani, D. & Reuland, M. (2007). *"Explaining the Prevalence, Context, and Consequences of Dual Arrest in Intimate Partner Cases."* Final report for National Institute of Justice, grant number 2001 -WT-BX-0501. Washington, DC: U.S. Department of Justice, National Institute of Justice, April, NCJ 218355. http://www.ncjrs.gov/App/Publications/abstract.aspx?ID=240055

[118] Hirschel, J. & Dawson, D. (2000). *"Violence Against Women: Synthesis of Research for Law Enforcement Officials."* Final report for National Institute of Justice, grant number 98-WTVX-K001. Washington, DC: U.S. Department of Justice, National Institute of Justice, December, NCJ 198372. http://www.ncjrs.gov/App /Publications/ abstract.aspx? ID=198372

[119] Hirschel, J. & Hutchison, I. (2001). "The Relative Effects of Offense, Offender, and Victim Variables on the Decision to Prosecute Domestic Violence Cases." *Violence Against Women, 7*(1), (January), 46-59, NCJ 186664. http://www.ncjrs.gov/App/ Publications/ abstract.aspx?ID=186664

[120] Holt, V., Kernic, M., Lumley, T., Wolf, M. & Rivara, F. (2002). "Civil Protection Orders and Risk of Subsequent Police-Reported Violence." *Journal of the American Medical Association, 288*(5), (August 7), 589-594, NCJ 196566. http://www.ncjrs.gov/ App/Publications/ abstract.aspx?ID=196566

[121] Holt, V., Kernic, M., Wolf, M. & Rivara, F. (2003). "Do Protection Orders Affect the Likelihood of Future Partner Violence and Injury?" *American Journal of Preventive Medicine, 24*(1),16-21.

[122] Holtzworth-Munroe, A. & Meehan, J. (2004). "Typologies of Men Who Are Maritally Violent: Scientific and Clinical Implications." *Journal of Interpersonal Violence, 19*(12), (December), 1369-1389.

[123] Holtzworth-Munroe, A. & Stuart, G. (1994). "Typologies of Male Batterers: Three Subtypes and the Differences Among Them." *Psychological Bulletin, 116*(3), (November), 476-497.

[124] Hotaling, G. & Buzawa, E. (2003). *"Victim Satisfaction with Criminal Justice Case Processing in a Model Court Setting."* Final report for National Institute of Justice, grant number 2000- WT-VX-0019. Washington, DC: U.S. Department of Justice, National Institute of Justice, January, NCJ 195668. http://www.ncjrs.gov/App/ Publications/ abstract.aspx?ID=195668

[125] Huntley, S. & Kilzer, L. (2005). Battered Justice Series (4 parts). *Rocky Mountain News* [Denver,CO] (February 5, 7-9,), available from http://www.rockymoun tainnews.com/news/2005/feb/05/compassions-high-price/, http://www.rockymountain news. com/news/ 2005/Feb/07 /span-classdeeplinksredsecond-ina-seriesspanbr/, http:// www. rockymountain news. com/news/2005/Feb/08/spanclassdeepli nksred battered-justice-part-fast/, and http://www. rockymountainnews. com/news/ 2005/ feb/09/ divclassdeeplinksredbatteredj ustice-part-4div/

[126] Hutchison, I. (1999). *"The Influence of Alcohol and Drugs on Women's Utilization of the Police for Domestic Violence."* Final report for National Institute of Justice, grant number 97-IJ-CX0047. Washington, DC: U.S. Department of Justice, National Institute of Justice, June, NCJ 179277. http://www.ncjrs.gov/App/ Publications/ abstract. aspx?ID=179277

[127] Isaac, N. & Enos, P. (2000). *"Medical Records as Legal Evidence of Domestic Violence."* Final report for National Institute of Justice, grant number 97-WT-VX-0008. Washington, DC: U.S. Department of Justice, National Institute of Justice, May, NCJ 184528. http://www.ncjrs.gov/App/Publications/abstract.aspx?ID=184528

[128] Jacobson, N. & Gottman, J. (1998). *When Men Batter Women.* New York: Simon & Schuster.

[129] Johannson, M. & Tutty, L. (1998). "An Evaluation of After-Treatment Couples' Groups for Wife Abuse." *Family Relations, 47*(1), (January), 27-35.

[130] Jolin, A., Feyerherm, W., Fountain, R. & Friedman, S. (1998). *"Beyond Arrest: The Portland, Oregon Domestic Violence Experiment."* Final report for National Institute of Justice, grant number 95-IJ-CX-0054. Washington, DC: U.S. Department of Justice, National Institute of Justice, NCJ 179968. http://www.ncjrs.gov/App /Publications /abstract.aspx?ID=179968

[131] Jurik, N. & Winn, R. (1990). "Gender and Homicide: A Comparison of Men and Women Who Kill." *Violence and Victims, 5*(4), (Winter), 227-242, NCJ 130043. http://www.ncjrs.gov/App/Publications/abstract.aspx?ID=130043

[132] Keilitz, S. (2004). *"Specialization of Domestic Violence Case Management in the Courts: A National Survey."* Final report for National Institute of Justice, grant number 98-WT-VX0002. Washington, DC: U.S. Department of Justice, National Institute of Justice, NCJ 199724.http://www.ncjrs.gov/App/Publications/abstract.aspx?ID=199724

[133] Keilitz, S., Hannaford, P. & Efkeman, H. (1997). *"Civil Protection Orders: The Benefits and Limitations for Victims of Domestic Violence."* Final report for National Institute of Justice, grant number 93-IJ-CX-0035. Washington, DC: U.S. Department of Justice, National Institute of Justice, NCJ 172223. http://www.ncjrs.gov/ App/ Publications/ abstract.aspx?ID=172223

[134] Klein, A. (1996). "Re-Abuse in a Population of Court-Restrained Male Batterers: Why Restraining Orders Don't Work." In *Do Arrests and Restraining Orders Work?* ed. E. Buzawa and C. Buzawa. Thousand Oaks, CA: Sage, 192-214, NCJ 161527. http://www.ncjrs.gov/App/Publications/abstract.aspx?ID=161527

[135] Klein, A. (2004). *The Criminal Justice Response to Domestic Violence.* Belmont, CA: Thomson/Wadsworth.

[136] Klein, A. (2005). *Rhode Island Domestic Violence Shelter and Advocacy Services: An Assessment.* Waltham, MA: BOTEC Analysis Corporation and Rhode Island Justice Commission, June 29, available online at http://www.rijustice.ri.gov/sac/ Reports/Final%20ShelterEval%209-20-05.pdf. The Rhode Island arrests may include multiple arrests of the same suspects involving incidents with the same victims within that year. It should also be noted that Rhode Island mandates arrest for "domestic violence," which is defined broadly to include any crime committed by current or former intimate partners, family or household members, and dating partners, although most Rhode Island domestic violence arrests are, in fact, for simple assault.

[137] Klein, A. & Crowe, A. (2008). "Findings From and Outcome Examination of Rhode Island's Specialized Domestic Violence Probation Supervision Program: Do Specialized Supervision Programs of Batterers Reduce Reabuse?" *Violence Against Women, 14*(2), (February 1, 2008), 226-246.

[138] Klein, A. & Tobin. T. (2008). "Longitudinal Study of Arrested Batterers, 1995-2005: Career Criminals." *Violence Against Women, 14*(2), (February 2008), 136-157, NCJ 221764. http://www.ncjrs.gov/App/Publications/abstract.aspx?ID=243648

[139] Klein, A., Tobin, T., Salomon, A. & Dubois, J. *"A Statewide Profile of Abuse of Older Women and the Criminal Justice Response."* Final report for National Institute of Justice, grant number 2006-WG-BX-0009, Washington, DC: U.S. Department of Justice, National Institute of Justice, December 2007, NCJ 222460. http://www.ncjrs. gov/App/ Publications/abstract.aspx?ID=244358

[140] Klein, A. & Wilson, D. (2003). *A Victim Survey on the Effects of a Court-Mandated Batterer Intervention Program in Rhode Island.* Waltham, MA: BOTEC Analysis Corporation, April 21, available online at http://www.rijustice.state.ri.us/sac/Reports/BI percent20 Prog ram. pdf.

[141] Klein, A., Wilson, D. Crowe, A. & DeMichele, M. (2005). *"Evaluation of the Rhode Island Probation Specialized Domestic Violence Supervision Unit."* Final report for National Institute of Justice, grant number 2002-WG-BX-001 1, March 31, NCJ 222912. http://www.ncjrs.gov/App/Publications/abstract.aspx?ID=244821

[142] Koziol-McLain, J., Webster, D. McFarlane, J. Block, C. Ulrich, Y. Glass, N. & Campbell, J. (2006). "Risk Factors for Femicide-Suicide in Abusive Relationships: Results From a Multisite Case Control Study." *Violence and Victims, 21*(1), (February): 3-21, NCJ 213274. http://www.ncjrs.gov/App/Publications/abstract.aspx?ID=234770

[143] Kramer, R. (1989). "Alcohol and Victimization Factors in the Histories of Abused Women Who Come to Court: A Retrospective Case-Control Study." *Dissertation AAT* 8923570. Ann Arbor, MI: UMI Dissertation Services.

[144] Kyriacou, D., Anglin, D. Taliaferro, E. Stone, S. Tubb, T. Linden, J. Muelleman, R. Barton, E. & Kraus, J. (1999). "Risk Factors for Injury to Women From Domestic Violence." *New England Journal of Medicine, 341*(25), (December 16), 1892-1898.

[145] Labriola, M., Rempel, M. & Davis, R. (2005). *"Testing the Effectiveness of Batterer Programs and Judicial Monitoring: Results From a Randomized Trial at the Bronx Misdemeanor Domestic Violence Court."* Final report for National Institute of Justice, grant number 2001- WT-BX-0506. New York: Center for Court Innovation, National Institute of Justice, November, available online at http://www.courtinnovation. org/uploads/ documents/ battererprogramseffectiveness.pdf.

[146] Labriola, M., Rempel, M. O'Sullivan, C. & Frank, P. with McDowell, J. & Finkelstein, R. (2007). *"Court Responses to Batterer Program Noncompliance: A National Perspective."* Final report for National Institute of Justice, grant number 2004-WG-BX-0005. New York: Center for Court Innovation, March, available online at http://www. courtinnovation. org/uploads /documents/CourtResponsesMarch2007.pdf.

[147] Lane, E., Greenspan, R. & Weisburd, D. (2004). *"The Second Responders Program: A Coordinated Police and Social Service Response to Domestic Violence."* Final report for National Institute of Justice, grant number 98-WT-VX-0001. Washington, DC: U.S. Department of Justice, National Institute of Justice, NCJ 199717. http://www.ncjrs.gov/App/Publications/abstract.aspx?ID=199717

[148] Lindquist, C., Telch, C. & Taylor, J. (1983). Evaluation of a Conjugal Violence Treatment Program: A Pilot Study." *Behavioral Counseling and Community Interventions, 3*(1), 76-90.

[149] Lockyer, B. (2005). *Domestic Violence: Keeping the Promise, Victim Safety and Batterer Accountability.* Report to the California Attorney General from the Task Force on Local Criminal Justice Response to Domestic Violence. Sacramento, CA: Office of the Attorney General, June, available online at http://www.safestate.org/ documents / DVReportAG.pdf.

[150] Logan, T., Shannon, L. Walker, R. & Faragher, T. (2006). "Protective Orders: Questions and Conundrums." *Trauma, Violence and Abuse, 7*(3), (July), 175-205, NCJ 216026. http://www.ncjrs.gov/App/Publications/abstract.aspx?ID=237623

[151] Lyon, E. (2002). *"Special Session Domestic Violence Courts: Enhanced Advocacy and Interventions,* Final Report Summary." Final report for National Institute of Justice, grant number 98-WE-VX-0031. Washington, DC: U.S. Department of Justice, National Institute of Justice, October, NCJ 197860. http://www.ncjrs.gov/ App/Publications/ abstract.aspx? ID=197860

[152] Lyon, E. (2005). *"Impact Evaluation of Special Session Domestic Violence: Enhanced Advocacy and Interventions."* Final report for National Institute of Justice, grant number 2000-WEVX-0014. Washington, DC: U.S. Department of Justice, National Institute of Justice, April, NCJ 210362. http://www.ncjrs.gov/App/Publications/ abstract.aspx?ID=210362

[153] Macmillan, R. & Kruttschnitt, C. (2004). *"Patterns of Violence Against Women: Risk Factors and Consequences."* Final report for National Institute of Justice, grant number 2002-IJCX-0011. Washington, DC: U.S. Department of Justice, National Institute of Justice, August, NCJ 208346. http://www.ncjrs.gov/App/ Publications/ abstract.aspx? ID=208346

[154] Malcoe, L. & Duran, B. (2004). *"Intimate Partner Violence and Injury in the Lives of Low-Income Native American Women."* Final report for National Institute on Drug Abuse and National Institutes of Health as part of Interagency Consortium on Violence Against Women and Violence Within the Family, including National Institute of Justice, grant number 5R03- DA/AA11154. Washington, DC: U.S. Department of Justice, National Institute of Justice, NCJ 199703. http://www.ncjrs.gov/ App/Publications/abstract.aspx?ID=199703

[155] Maxwell, C., Garner, J. & Fagan, J. (2001). *The Effects of Arrest on Intimate Partner Violence: New Evidence From the Spouse Assault Replication Program.* Research in Brief. Washington, DC: U.S. Department of Justice, National Institute of Justice, July, NCJ 188199. http://www.ncjrs.gov/App/Publications/abstract.aspx?ID=188199

[156] McFarlane, J., Campbell, J. & Wilt, S. (1999). "Stalking and Intimate Partner Femicide." *Homicide Studies, 3*(4), (November), 300-316, NCJ 179872. http://www. ncjrs. gov/App/Publications/abstract.aspx?ID=179872

[157] McFarlane, J. & Malecha, A. (2005). *"Sexual Assault Among Intimates: Frequency, Consequences and Treatments."* Final report for National Institute of Justice, grant number 2002-WG-BX-0003. Washington, DC: U.S. Department of Justice, National Institute of Justice, October, NCJ 211678. http://www. ncjrs.gov/ App/ Publications/ abstract.aspx?ID=232957

[158] Meehan, J., Holtzworth-Munroe, A. & Herron, K. (2001). "Maritally Violent Men's Heart Rate Reactivity to Marital Interactions: A Failure to Replicate the Gottman et al. (1995) Typology." *Journal of Family Psychology,15*(3), 394-424.

[159] Miller, N. (2000). *"Queens County, New York, Arrest Policies Project: A Process Evaluation."* Final report for National Institute of Justice, grant number 98-WE-VX-0012. Washington, DC: U.S. Department of Justice, National Institute of Justice, February 8, NCJ 201886. http://www.ncjrs.gov/App/Publications/abstract.aspx?ID =201886

[160] Miller, N. (2001). *"Stalking Laws and Implementation Practices: A National Review for Policymakers and Practitioners."* Final report for National Institute of Justice, grant number 97-WT-VX-0007. Washington, DC: U.S. Department of Justice, National Institute of Justice, October, NCJ 197066. http://www.ncjrs. gov/App/Publications/ abstract.aspx?ID=197066

[161] Miller, N. (2005). *"What Does Research and Evaluation Say About Domestic Violence Laws? A Compendium of Justice System Laws and Related Research Assessments."* Alexandria, VA: Institute for Law and Justice, December, available online at http://www.ilj.org/publications/dv/DomesticViolenceLegislationEvaluation.pdf.

[162] Miller, S. & Meloy, M. (2006). "Women's Use of Force: Voices of Women Arrested for Domestic Violence." *Violence Against Women, 12*(1), (January), 89-115, NCJ 212762. http://www.ncjrs.gov/App/Publications/abstract.aspx?ID=234245

[163] Murphy, C., Musser, P. & Maton, K. (1998). "Coordinated Community Intervention for Domestic Abusers: Intervention System Involvement and Criminal Recidivism." *Journal of Family Violence, 13*(3), (September), 263-284, NCJ 175131. http://www.ncjrs.gov/App/Publications/abstract.aspx?ID=175131

[164] Newmark, L., Rempel, M., Diffily, K. & Kane, K. (2001). *"Specialized Felony Domestic Violence Court: Lessons on Implementation and Impacts from the Kings County Experience."* Final report for National Institute of Justice, grant number 97-WT-VX-0005. Washington, DC: U.S. Department of Justice, National Institute of Justice, October (NCJ 191861) and 2004 (NCJ 199723). http://www.ncjrs.gov/ App/Publications/ abstract.aspx?ID=191861 and http://www.ncjrs.gov/ App/ Publications/abstract.aspx? ID=199723

[165] *New York State Division of Criminal Justice Services. "Family Protection and Domestic Violence Intervention Act of 1994: Evaluation of the Mandatory Arrest Provisions,* Final Report." Supported in part by grant number 97-WE-VX-0128 from Violence Against Women Grants Office, Office of Justice Programs, U.S. Department of Justice. Albany, NY: Division of Criminal Justice Services, New York State Office for the Prevention of Domestic Violence, January 2001.

[166] Niemi-Kiesiläinen, J. (2001). *"The Deterrent Effect of Arrest in Domestic Violence: Differentiating Between Victim and Perpetrator Response."* +DIACOM FP I-CIVI DZ F9rnDl, 12(2), 283-305.

[167] Norwood, W., Jouriles, E. McDonald, R. & Swank, P. (2004). *"Domestic Violence and Deviant Behavior."* Final report for National Institute of Justice, grant number 98-WT-VX-0005. Washington. DC: U.S. Department of Justice, National Institute of Justice, NCJ 199713. http://www.ncjrs.gov/App/Publications/abstract.aspx?ID=199713

[168] O'Farrell, T., Fals-Stewart, W., Murphy, M. & Murphy, C. (2003). "Partner Violence Before and After Individually Based Alcoholism Treatment for Male Alcoholic Patients." *Journal of Consulting & Clinical Psychology,71*(1), (February), 92-102.

[169] Office of the Commissioner of Probation. (1992). *Over 8,500 Domestic Restraining Orders Filed Since September in Massachusetts.* Boston, MA: Office of the Commissioner of Probation, November.

[170] Olson, L., Crandall, C. & Broudy, D. (1998). *"Getting Away With Murder: A Report of the New Mexico Female Intimate Partner Violence Death Review Team."* Albuquerque, NM: Center for Injury Prevention Research and Education, University of New Mexico School of Medicine,.

[171] Olson, D. & Stalans, L. (2001). "Violent Offenders on Probation: Profile, Sentence, and Outcome Differences Among Domestic Violence and Other Violent Probationers." *Violence Against Women, 7(10)*, (October), 1164-1185, NCJ 192015. http://www.ncjrs. gov/App/Publications/abstract.aspx?ID=192015

[172] Orchowsky, S. (1999). *"Evaluation of a Coordinated Community Response to Domestic Violence: The Alexandria Domestic Violence Intervention Project."* Final report for National Institute for Justice, grant number 95-WT-NX-0004. Washington, DC: U.S. Department of Justice, National Institute of Justice, September, NCJ 179974. http://www.ncjrs.gov/App/Publications/abstract.aspx?ID=179974

[173] Ostrom, B. & Kauder, N. (1999). *Examining the Work of State Courts, 1998: A National Perspective From the Court Statistics Project.* Williamsburg, VA: National Center for State Courts.

[174] Pate, A., Hamilton, E. & Annan, S. (1991). *"Metro-Dade Spouse Abuse Replication Project Technical Report."* Final report for National Institute of Justice, grant number 87-IJ-CXK003. Washington, DC: U.S. Department of Justice, National Institute of Justice, NCJ 139734. http://www.ncjrs.gov/App/Publications/abstract.aspx?ID=139734

[175] Pattavina, A., Hirschel, D. Buzawa, E. Faggiani, D. & Bentley, H. (2007). "Comparison of the Police Response to Heterosexual Versus Same-Sex Intimate Partner Violence." *Violence Against Women, 13*(4), (April): 374-394, NCJ 218287. http://www.ncjrs.gov/ App/Publications/ abstract.aspx?ID=239986

[176] Paulkossi, L. (2001). "Surveillance for Homicide Among Intimate Partners: United States, 1991-1998." *Morbidity and Mortality Weekly Surveillance Summaries, 5*, (October), 1-16.

[177] Pence, E. & Dasgupta, S. (2006). *"Re-Examining "Battering': Are All Acts of Violence Against Intimate Partners the Same?"* Final report to Office on Violence Against Women, U.S. Department of Justice, grant number 1 998-WR-VX-K001. Duluth, MN: Praxis International, June.

[178] Pennel, S., Burke, C. & Mulmat, D. (2000). *"Violence Against Women in San Diego." Final report for National Institute of Justice,* grant number 97-IJ-CX-0007. Washington, DC: U.S. Department of Justice, National Institute of Justice, March, NCJ 191838. http://www.ncjrs.gov/App/Publications/abstract.aspx?ID=191838

[179] Peterson, R. & Dixon, J. (2005). *"Examining Prosecutorial Discretion in Domestic Violence Cases."* Paper presented at the American Society of Criminology, Toronto, Ontario, Canada, November.

[180] Peterson, W. & Thunberg, S. (2000). *"Domestic Violence Court: Evaluation Report for the San Diego County Domestic Violence Courts."* Report submitted by San Diego Superior Court to State Justice Institute, grant number SJI-98-N-271. San Diego, CA: San Diego Superior Court, September, NCJ 187846. http://www.ncjrs.gov/ App/Publications/ abstract.aspx?ID=187846

[181] Pirog-Good, M. & Stets, J. (1986) "Programs for Abusers: Who Drops Out and What Can Be Done?" *Response to the Victimization of Women & Children*, 9(2), 17-19.

[182] Ptacek, J. (1999). *Battered Women in the Courtroom: The Power of Judicial Responses.* Northeastern Series on Gender, Crime, and Law. Boston, MA: Northeastern University Press, NCJ 183008. http://www.ncjrs.gov/App/ Publications/ abstract. aspx? ID =183008

[183] Puffett, N. & Gavin, C. (2004). *"Predictors of Program Outcome and Recidivism at the Bronx Misdemeanor Domestic Violence Court."* Funded by grants from Violence Against Women Office and New York State Office of Court Administration. New York, NY: Center for Court Innovation, April, available online at http://www. courtinnovation. org/ uploads/ documents/predictorsbronxdv.pdf.

[184] Raiford, L. (2004). "Report of the New York City Police Department Domestic Violence Unit." New York, NY: New York City Police Department, Domestic Violence Unit, March 2002, cited in A. Klein, *The Criminal Justice Response to Domestic Violence.* Belmont, CA: Wadsworth/Thomson, 90.

[185] Rempel, M., Labriola, M. & Davis, R. (2008). "Does Judicial Monitoring Deter Domestic Violence Recidivism? Results of a Quasi-Experimental Comparison in the Bronx." *Violence Against Women,14*(2), (February), 185-207, available online at http://vaw.sagepub.com/ cgi/content/abstract/14/2/185.

[186] Rennison, C. & Welchans, S. (2000). *Intimate Partner Violence.* Special Report. Washington, DC: U.S. Department of Justice, Bureau of Justice Statistics, May, NCJ 178247. http://www.ncjrs.gov/App/Publications/abstract.aspx?ID=178247

[187] Rigakos, G. (1997). "Situational Determinants of Police Responses to Civil and Criminal Injunctions for Battered Women." *Violence Against Women*, 3(2), (April), 204-216, available online at http://vaw.sagepub.com/cgi/content/abstract/3/2/204.

[188] Roehl, J. (1997). *"Police Use of Domestic Violence Information Systems."* Final report for National Institute of Justice, grant number 95-IJ-CX-0097. Washington, DC: U.S. Department of Justice, National Institute of Justice, February, NCJ 182435. http://www.ncjrs.gov/App/Publications/abstract.aspx?ID=182435

[189] Roehl, J. & Guertin, K. (2000). "Intimate Partner Violence: The Current Use of Risk Assessments in Sentencing Offenders." *Justice System Journal*, 21(2), 171-198, NCJ 183443. http://www.ncjrs.gov/App/Publications/abstract.aspx?ID=183443

[190] Roehl, J., O'Sullivan, C., Webster, D. & Campbell, J. (2005). *"Intimate Partner Violence Risk Assessment Validation Study: The RAVE Study - Practitioner Summary and Recommendations: Validation of Tools for Assessing Risk From Violent Intimate Partners."* Final report for National Institute of Justice, grant number 2000-WT-VX-001 1. Washington, DC: U.S. Department of Justice, National Institute of Justice, May, NCJ 209732. http://www.ncjrs.gov/App/Publications/abstract.aspx?ID=209732

[191] Rothman, E., Hemenway, D., Miller, M. & Azrel, D. (2004). "Batterers' Use of Guns to Threaten Intimate Partners." *Journal of the American Medical Women's Association*, 60(1), (Winter), 62-67.

[192] Salomon, A., Bassuk, E., Browne, A., Bassuk, S., Dawson, R. & Huntington, N. (2004). *"Secondary Data Analysis on the Etiology, Course, and Consequences of Intimate Partner Violence Against Extremely Poor Women."* Final report for National Institute of Justice, grant number 98-WT-VX-0012. Washington, DC: U.S. Department of

Justice, National Institute of Justice, NCJ 199714. http://www.ncjrs.gov/ App/Publications/ abstract.aspx? ID=199714

[193] Saunders, D. (1992). "Typology of Men Who Batter: Three Types Derived From Cluster Analysis." *American Journal of Orthopsychiatry*, *62*(2), (April), 264-275, NCJ 139828. http://www.ncjrs.gov/App/Publications/abstract.aspx?ID=139828

[194] Saunders, D. & Parker, J. (1989). "Legal Sanctions and Treatment Follow-Through Among Men Who Batter: A Multivariate Analysis." *Social Work Research and Abstracts*, *25*(3), 21-29.

[195] Smith, A. (2001). "Domestic Violence Laws: The Voices of Battered Women." *Violence and Victims*, *16*(1), (February), 91-111, NCJ 187744. http://www.ncjrs.gov/ App/ Publications/abstract.aspx?ID=187744

[196] Smith, B., Davis, R. Nickles, L. & Davies, H. (2001). *"Evaluation of Efforts to Implement No- Drop Policies: Two Central Values in Conflict."* Final report for National Institute of Justice, grant number 98-WT-VX-0029. Washington, DC: U.S. Department of Justice, National Institute of Justice, March, NCJ 187772. http://www.ncjrs.gov/ App/Publications/abstract.aspx?ID=187772

[197] Smithey, M., Green, S. & Giacomazzi, A. (2000). *"Collaborative Effort and the Effectiveness of Law Enforcement Training Toward Resolving Domestic Violence."* Final report for National Institute of Justice, grant number 97-WE-VX-0131. Washington, DC: U.S. Department of Justice, National Institute of Justice, November, NCJ 191840. http://www.ncjrs.gov/App/Publications/abstract.aspx?ID=191840

[198] Stark, E. (2007). *Coercive Control: How Men Entrap Women in Personal Life.* New York: Oxford University Press.

[199] Starr, K., Hobart, M. & Fawcett, J. (2004). *"Every Life Lost Is a Call for Change: Findings and Recommendations From the Washington State Domestic Violence Fatality Review."* Seattle, WA: Washington State Coalition Against Domestic Violence, December, available online at http://www.wscadv.org/ pages.cfm? ald = 9BF3F91C - C298- 58F608 C8E95 2508 A 52AD.

[200] Steketee, M., Levey, L. & Keilitz, S. (2000). *"Implementing an Integrated Domestic Violence Court: Systemic Change in the District of Columbia."* Final report for State Justice Institute, grant number SJI-98-N-01 6. Williamsburg, VA: National Center for State Courts, and Alexandria, VA: State Justice Institute, June 30, NCJ 198516. http://www. ncjrs. gov/App/Publications/abstract.aspx?ID=198516

[201] Stith, S., Rosen, K. & McCollum, E. (2003). "Effectiveness of Couples Treatment for Spouse Abuse." *Journal of Marital and Family Therapy*, *29*(3), 407-426.

[202] Straus, M., Gelles, R. & Steinmetz, S. (1980). *Behind Closed Doors: Violence in the American Family.* Garden City, NY: Doubleday, NCJ 148986. http:// www. ncjrs. gov/App/Publications/abstract.aspx?ID=148986

[203] Stuart, G. (2005). "Improving Violence Intervention Outcomes Integrating Alcohol Treatment." *Journal of Interpersonal Violence*, *20*(4), 388-393.

[204] Syers, M. & Edleson. J. (1992). "The Combined Effects of Coordinated Criminal Justice Intervention in Women Abuse." *Journal of Interpersonal Violence,* *7*(4), (December), 490-502, NCJ 139788. http://www.ncjrs.gov/App/ Publications/ abstract. aspx? ID=139788

[205] Taylor, B., Davis, R. & Maxwell, C. (2001). "The Effects of a Group Batterer Treatment Program: A Randomized Experiment in Brooklyn." *Justice Quarterly,18*(1),

(March), 171-201, NCJ 187428. http://www.ncjrs.gov/App/ Publications/ abstract.aspx? ID=187428

[206] Thistlethwaite, A., Wooldredge, J. & Gibbs, D. (1998). "Severity of Dispositions and Domestic Violence Recidivism." *Crime and Delinquency*, *44*(3), (July), 388-398, NCJ 173565. http://www.ncjrs.gov/App/Publications/abstract.aspx?ID=173565

[207] Tjaden, P. & Thoennes, N. (1998). *Stalking in America: Findings From the National Violence Against Women Survey.* Research in Brief. Washington, DC: U.S. Department of Justice, National Institute of Justice, grant number 93-IJ-CX-001 2, April, NCJ 169592. http://www.ncjrs.gov/App/Publications/abstract.aspx?ID=169592

[208] Tjaden, P. & Thoennes, N. (1998). *Prevalence, Incidence, and Consequences of Violence Against Women: Findings From the National Violence Against Women Survey.* Research in Brief. Washington, DC, and Atlanta, GA: U.S. Department of Justice, National Institute of Justice, and Centers for Disease Control and Prevention, grant number 93-IJ-CX-001 2, November, NCJ 172837. http://www.ncjrs.gov/ App/Publications/ abstract.aspx? ID=172837

[209] Tjaden, P., & Thoennes, N. (2000). *"Extent, Nature, and Consequences of Intimate Partner Violence: Findings From the National Violence Against Women Survey."* Final report for National Institute of Justice, grant number 93-IJ-CX-0012. Washington, DC: U.S. Department of Justice, National Institute of Justice, July, NCJ 181867. http://www.ncjrs.gov/App/Publications/abstract.aspx?ID=181867

[210] Tjaden, P. & Thoennes, N. (2001). *"Stalking: Its Role in Serious Domestic Violence Cases."* Final report for National Institute of Justice, grant number 97-WT-VX-0002. Washington, DC: U.S. Department of Justice, National Institute of Justice, January, NCJ 187346. http://www.ncjrs.gov/App/Publications/abstract.aspx?ID=187346

[211] Tolman, R. & Weisz, A. (1995). "Coordinated Community Intervention for Domestic Violence: The Effects of Arrest and Prosecution on Recidivism of Woman Abuse Perpetrators." Bureau of Justice Assistance and Illinois Criminal Justice Information Authority, grant number 90-DB-CX-0017. *Crime and Delinquency*, *41*(4), (October), 481-495, NCJ 157475. http://www.ncjrs.gov/App/ Publications/ abstract.aspx?ID= 157475

[212] Torres, S. & Han, H. (2000). "Psychological Distress in Non-Hispanic White and Hispanic Abused Women." *Archives of Psychiatric Nursing*, *14*(1), (February), 19-29.

[213] Townsend, M., Hunt, D. Kuck, S. & Baxter, C. (2005). *"Law Enforcement Response to Domestic Violence Calls for Service."* Final report for National Institute of Justice, grant number 99- C-008. Washington, DC: U.S. Department of Justice, National Institute of Justice, February, NCJ 215915. http://www.ncjrs.gov/ App/Publications/ abstract.aspx? ID=237504

[214] (1982). U.S. Commission on Civil Rights. *Under the Rule of Thumb: Battered Women and the Administration of Justice*, Washington DC: U.S. Department of Justice, NCJ 082752. http://www.ncjrs.gov/App/Publications/abstract.aspx?ID=82752

[215] Ursel, J. & Brickey, S. (1996). "The Potential of Legal Reform Reconsidered: An Examination of Manitoba's Zero-Tolerance Policy on Family Violence." In T. O'Reilly-Fleming, ed., *Post- Critical Criminology*. Scarborough, Ontario, Canada: Prentice-Hall, 6-77.

[216] Ventura, L. & Davis, G. (2005). "Domestic Violence: Court Case Conviction and Recidivism." *Violence Against Women*, *11*(2), (February), 255-277, NCJ 208869. http://www.ncjrs.gov/App/Publications/abstract.aspx?ID=208869

[217] Vigdor, E. & Mercy, J. (2006). "Do Laws Restricting Access to Firearms by Domestic Violence Offenders Prevent Intimate Partner Homicide?" *Evaluation Review*, *30*(3), (June), 31 3-346.

[218] Websdale, N., Sheeran, M. & Johnson, B. (1998). *"Reviewing Domestic Violence Fatalities: Summarizing National Developments."* Final report to Office on Violence Against Women, Office of Justice Programs, U.S. Department of Justice, grant 98-WT-VX-K001, and Minnesota Center Against Violence and Abuse, University of Minnesota. Violence Against Women Online Resources, available online at http://www.vaw.umn.edu/documents/fatality/fatality.html.

[219] Weiss, H., Lawrence, B. & Miller, T. (2004). *"Pregnancy-Associated Assault Hospitali zations: Prevalence and Risk of Hospitalized Assaults Against Women During Pregnancy."* Final report for National Institute of Justice, grant number 1998-WT-VX-001 6, Washington, DC: U.S. Department of Justice, National Institute of Justice, NCJ 199706. http://www.ncjrs.gov/App/Publications/abstract.aspx?ID=199706

[220] Weisz, A., Canales-Portalatin, D. & Nahan, N. (2001). *"Evaluation of Victim Advocacy Within a Team Approach."* Final report for National Institute for Justice, grant number 97-WT-VX0006. Washington, DC: U.S. Department of Justice, National Institute of Justice, January, NCJ 187107. http://www.ncjrs.gov/App/Publications/ abstract.aspx?ID=187107

[221] Wekerle, C. & Wall, A. (2002). *The Violence and Addiction Equation: Theoretical and Clinical Issues in Substance Abuse and Relationship Violence.* New York, NY: Brunner-Routledge.

[222] White, J. & Smith, P. (2004). *"A Longitudinal Perspective on Physical and Sexual Intimate Partner Violence Against Women."* Final report for National Institute of Justice, grant number 98-WT-VX-001 0. Washington, DC: U.S. Department of Justice, National Institute of Justice, NCJ 199708. http://www.ncjrs.gov/App/ Publications/ abstract.aspx?ID=199708

[223] Williams, K. & Houghton, A.-M. (2004). "Assessing the Risk of Domestic Violence Reoffending: A Validation Study." *Law and Human Behavior*, *28*(4), (August), 437-455.

[224] Wilson, D. & Klein, A. (2006). *"A Longitudinal Study of a Cohort of Batterers Arraigned in a Massachusetts District Court 1995 to 2004."* Final report for National Institute of Justice, grant number 2004-WB-GX-001 1. Washington, DC: U.S. Department of Justice, National Institute of Justice, May, NCJ 215346. http://www.ncjrs. gov/App/Publications/ abstract.aspx?ID=236929

[225] Wooldredge, J. (2007). "Convicting and Incarcerating Felony Offenders of Intimate Assault and the Odds of New Assault Charges." *Journal of Criminal Justice*, *35*(4), (July/August), 379-389, NCJ 219877. http://www.ncjrs.gov/App /Publications/ abstract. aspx?ID=241675

[226] Wooldredge, J. & Thistlethwaite, A. (2005). "Court Dispositions and Rearrest for Intimate Assault." *Crime and Delinquency*, *51*(1), (January), 75-102, NCJ 208203. http://www.ncjrs.gov/App/Publications/abstract.aspx?ID=208203

[227] Worden, A. (2001). *"Models of Community Coordination in Partner Violence Cases: A Multi-Site Comparative Analysis."* Final report for National Institute of Justice, grant number 95-WTNX-0006. Washington, DC: U.S. Department of Justice, National Institute of Justice, February, NCJ 187351. http://www.ncjrs.gov/ App/Publications/ abstract.aspx? ID=187351

[228] Wordes, M. (2000). *"Creating a Structured Decision-Making Model for Police Intervention in Intimate Partner Violence."* Final report for National Institute of Justice, grant number 96- IJ-CX-0098. Washington, DC: U.S. Department of Justice, National Institute of Justice, February, NCJ 182781. http:// www.ncjrs.gov/ App/Publications/ abstract.aspx? ID=182781.

In: Domestic Violence: Law Enforcement Response...   ISBN: 978-1-60876-774-8
Editor: Mario R. Dewalt   © 2010 Nova Science Publishers, Inc.

Chapter 4

THE JUDICIAL OVERSIGHT DEMONSTRATION: CULMINATING REPORT ON THE EVALUATION[*]

United States Department of Justice

ABOUT THIS REPORT

The Judicial Oversight Demonstration (JOD) was designed to test the feasibility and impact of a coordinated response to intimate partner violence (IPV) that involved the courts and justice agencies in a central role. A national evaluation of JOD began in 2000 with the start of demonstration activities and continued throughout and beyond the intervention period. This report presents an overview of the entire evaluation and presents specific findings from the three JOD sites and from comparison sites.

WHAT DID THE RESEARCHERS FIND?

Highlights of the findings include:

- Victims in all sites were generally satisfied with the response of police, prosecutors and the court, and rated their fairness and impact on future violence positively.
- Victims identified some problems in interactions with justice agencies (such as scheduling conflicts that made court attendance difficult).
- Victims in all sites reported moderately high levels of safety and well-being 11 months after the initial IPV incident.
- JOD reductions in victim reports of repeat IPV were stronger for some types of victims and offenders (see page 11).

---

[*] This is an edited, reformatted and augmented version of a U. S. Department of Justice publication dated February 2009.

- JOD increased offender accountability (e.g., more probation requirements, increased likelihood of conviction).
- JOD did not decrease offender perceptions of the fairness of judges or probation departments, and also did not increase offenders' perceptions of the certainty and severity of the penalties for violations of some court orders.

WHAT WERE THE STUDY'S LIMITATIONS?

The JOD Initiative

In 1999, the Office on Violence Against Women selected three sites for the implementation of a Judicial Oversight Demonstration (JOD) project. In each of these sites — Dorchester, Mass., Milwaukee, Wisc., and Washtenaw County, Mich. — criminal justice agencies and community- based agencies serving victims and offenders formed partnerships to work collaboratively to support an effective response to intimate partner violence (IPV) incidents. The partnerships differed from earlier coordinated community responses to domestic violence (DV) [please see margin note on terminology] by placing special focus on the role of the court, and specifically the judge, in facilitating offender accountability in collaboration with both nonprofit service providers and other criminal justice agencies.

In this report, the terms intimate partner violence (IPV) and domestic violence (DV) are used interchange-ably to mean violence that occurs between intimate partners.

The JOD core elements included:

- *Uniform and consistent initial responses to DV offenses,* including: a) pro- arrest policies, b) arrest of the primary aggressor, and c) a coordinated response by law enforcement and victim advocates.
- *Coordinated victim advocacy and services,* including: a) contact by victim advocates as soon as possible after a DV incident, b) an individualized "safety plan" for the victim, and c) provision of needed services.
- *Strong offender accountability and oversight,* including: a) intensive court-based supervision, b) referral to appropriate batterer intervention programs (BIPs), and c) administrative and judicial sanctions and incentives to influence offender behavior.

Each site implemented the core JOD elements within the context of its local resources, needs and priorities; expanded its existing coordinated community response to include criminal justice agencies; and established regular meetings to develop and implement strategies for interagency coordination. Guided by technical assistance teams and the needs of its jurisdiction, each site reviewed and developed model policies and programs based on experiences in other jurisdictions, recent research and other best practices for IPV cases. Details of these demonstrations can be found in the NIJ Research for Practice, *Pretrial Innovations for Domestic Violence Offenders and Victims: Lessons From the Judicial*

Oversight Demonstration Initiative (September 2007, NCJ 216041, available online at http://www.ncjrs.gov/ pdffiles1/nij/21 6041 .pdf).

A national evaluation of JOD began in 2000 with the start of demonstration activities and continued throughout and beyond the intervention period. Initial findings of the evaluation are discussed in *The Evaluation of the Judicial Oversight Demonstration: Findings and Lessons on Implementation* (June 2008, NCJ 219077, available online at http://www.ncjrs.gov/ pdffiles1 /nij/21 9077 .pdf). This report presents an overview of the entire evaluation and presents more specific findings from all three sites.

THE EVALUATION OF JOD

Two JOD sites — Dorchester and Washtenaw County — participated in a quasi-experimental evaluation of the impact of the program. IPV cases reaching disposition during JOD were compared to similar cases reaching disposition in Lowell, Mass., and Ingham County, Mich. All IPV cases reaching disposition during the sampling periods were reviewed and included in the sample, if appropriate.[1] To be eligible for the sample, cases had to involve: 1) criminal IPV charges, 2) victims and offenders age 18 or older and 3) victims and offenders who lived in the target jurisdiction at the time of case disposition. Cases that reached disposition more than a year after the incident were excluded to limit loss of data due to poor recall of the facts of the incident and police response. Data for this impact evaluation included: in-person interviews conducted two months after case disposition or sentencing and again nine months later,[2] criminal history records from state and local law enforcement records on arrests before and after the sampled IPV case,[3] and data on JOD victim services and probation supervision.

Interviews were completed with 1,034 victims (526 from JOD sites, 508 from comparison sites) two months after case disposition and 914 victims (90 percent of the initial interview sample) 11 months after case disposition. Further, interviews were completed with 454 offenders (229 from JOD sites, 225 from comparison sites) two months after case disposition and 366 offenders (84 percent of the initial interview sample) 11 months after case disposition. (See exhibits 1 and 2 for victim and offender sample characteristics.)

The evaluation design of JOD in Milwaukee differed from that of the other two sites. The evaluation in Milwaukee was based on a quasi-experimental comparison of offenders convicted of IPV and ordered to probation before and during JOD. This design was selected when early plans for an experimental design had to be abandoned and no contemporaneous comparison group could be identified. Data for this evaluation were collected from court and prosecutors' records of case and defendant characteristics, probation files on offender supervision practices, and official records of rearrest, but do not include interviews with victims or offenders. (See exhibit 3 for offender sample characteristics in Milwaukee. See also "Study Limitations.")

KEY FINDINGS ON THE IMPACT OF JOD

Highlights of findings on the impact of JOD on three primary outcomes — victim well-being, offender accountability and perceptions, and revictimization — are presented in this section. The following sections present findings on JOD implementation and focus groups. The concluding section discusses implications of the findings for policy and practice.

Exhibit 1. Victim Sample Characteristics

	Dorchester (N=307)	Lowell (N=286)	Washtenaw (N=219)	ingham (N=222)
Female	89%	88%	92%	91%
Average age	33.6	34.2	32.1	31.8
Race/ethnicity				
White	10%	67%	50%	49%
Black	64%	4%	39%	32%
Asian	1%	9%	1%	1%
Hispanic	7%	13%	1%	6%
Other/multiracial	18%	6%	10%	13%
Has children	86%	83%	76%	80%
High school graduate	78%	75%	88%	77%
U.s.-born	79%	78%	93%	96%
Employed	47%	58%	74%	61%

Note: Percentages may not add up to 100 percent due to rounding.

Exhibit 2. Offender Sample Characteristics

	Dorchester (N=97)	Lowell (N=82)	Washtenaw (N=83)	ingham N(=103)
Male	79%	84%	84%	90%
Average age	33.9	35.6	32.7	35.1
Race				
White	8%	57%	49%	52%
Black	65%	1%	45%	36%
Other/multiracial	27%	41%	6%	12%
High school graduate	74%	66%	84%	76%
Unemployed at initial Interview	60%	46%	30%	38%
Average number of Prior arrests	8.3	3.7	1.9	2.9
Lived with victim at Time of incident	61%	77%	66%	79%

Note: Percentages may not add up to 100 percent due to rounding.

Exhibit 3. Offender Sample Characteristics in Milwaukee

	pre-JoD *N* (=289)	JoD (*N*=333)
Male	96%	93%
Average age (rounded)	35	34
Race		
White	32%	32%
Black	56%	49%
Other/multiracial	13%	19%
Average number of prior arrests	5.1	5.2

Note: Percentages may not add up to 100 percent due to rounding.

STUDY LIMITATIONS

The study was designed to measure the overall impact of the JOD intervention, not to assess the impact of individual strategies or component services. The primary reason for this design is that individuals received various JOD interventions based on need and their particular circumstances, making comparisons to those who did not receive that particular intervention inappropriate. In addition, there was considerable variation within intervention components provided to sample members. For example, in each site, offenders could be referred to one of several BIPs that varied in content and duration. Moreover, victims received services based on their need and interest in participation. Finally, the samples were too small to isolate similar samples that did and did not receive specific interventions.

Another caution is that the samples were carefully selected to create similar JOD and comparison groups, but group members were not randomly assigned to JOD as in a true experiment. With random assignment, sample groups can be assumed to vary only by chance. With the quasi-experimental design in this study, the validity of the results depends on the extent to which differences in sample characteristics can be adequately controlled in the statistical analysis. In the outcome analyses, statistical techniques such as weights and multivariate modeling techniques were used to control for observed group differences and minimize any bias due to selection effects, but could not control for unobserved differences.

Another potential threat to the internal validity of the quasi-experimental comparisons in Massachusetts and Michigan is that pre-existing differences between JOD and comparison sites, not the JOD intervention, might account for differences in outcome. However, in this study, a process evaluation documented differences in the response to IPV in each site, providing supporting evidence that differences in policies and practices impacted outcomes.

The threat that external features of the setting affected the outcomes is minimized in the Milwaukee evaluation by comparing outcomes within a single site before and during JOD. However, this design opens the possibility that changes other than JOD during the demonstration period could account for differences in outcomes. Monitoring of court and other agency responses to IPV during the Milwaukee demonstration period did not identify events other than JOD that were likely to affect the measured outcomes. Still, to avoid the risk that measurement error could distort or attenuate the observed effects of JOD, the study used multiple outcome measures and diverse data sources. This strategy was chosen to avoid relying on any single measure, given the imperfections in measurement associated with any single measure.

Another potential limitation involves the external generalizability of the findings. These evaluations were based on experiences at three carefully selected sites. The extent to which results from these locations can be generalized to other communities cannot be determined.

Victim Services and Well-Being[4]

JOD increased community- based victim services, particularly in Michigan

In Michigan, but not in Massa-chusetts, JOD victims were significantly more likely than comparison victims to report contact with nongovernmen-tal (NGO) victim services. NGO advocates had con-tact with 68 percent of the JOD victims in Washtenaw County, compared to 22 percent of the JOD victims in Dorchester. This differenceresulted in part from the focus in Massachusetts on serving victims in civil cases.

In both JOD sites, victims contacted by NGO service providers received more services and were more likely to receive needs asse-ssments and safety planning than comparison victims contacted by NGO service providers. In both Dorchest-er and Washtenaw County, victim/witness staff in JOD prosecutors' offices or the court[5] contacted at least 80 percent of victims in criminal cases and provided an average of four or more different types of services to those they contacted.

Victims who received NGO victim services were pleased with the quality of those services

Victim ratings of service quality and satisfaction were generally positive. There was no difference in ratings between victims who received services in the JOD program (hereinafter, JOD victims) and comparison samples.

Victims in all sites were generally satisfied with the response of police, prosecutors and the court, and rated their fairness and impact on future violence positively. JOD and comparison victims did not rate official responses differently, despite some differences in patterns of police, prosecution and court practice across sites.

Victims identified some problems in interactions with justice agencies

Victims from all sites reported barriers to participation in prosecutions, with fear of defendant retaliation being the most common. Scheduling conflicts were the most common barrier to court attendance, with comparison victims more likely to cite fear as a court participation barrier than JOD victims.

JOD increased victim contacts with probation agents

Two-thirds to three- quarters of JOD victims in both states reported contact with probation officers, which was about two to three times the proportion of comparison victims reporting such contact. In Michigan, JOD victims with probation officer contact also had more contacts and rated these contacts more favorably than did comparison victims. JOD victims in Michigan, but not in Massachusetts, also reported more contact with BIPs than comparison victims.

Victims in all sites reported moderately high levels of safety and well-being 11 months after the incident

Factors that influenced these victim outcomes included the victims' reports of defendants' psychological or emotional problems; victims' social support resources; and direct consequences of the incident and the subsequent court case, both positive   and negative. No significant differences between JOD and comparison victims in perceptions of safety or well-being were found.

Offender Accountability and Perceptions

JOD increased offender accountability, especially in Dorchester and Milwaukee

In all sites, JOD introduced post-disposition review hearings for IPV offenders placed on probation. Probationers were required to appear before the sentencing judge for review of their compliance with court orders and progress in BIPs, and were aware that their behavior would be scrutinized and violations would be subject to penalties. JOD-sample offenders (hereinafter, JOD offenders) had more probation requirements than comparison offenders, although specific requirements varied by site. In Massachusetts and Michigan, they were more likely to be ordered to attend a BIP, abstain from drug and alcohol use, and undergo substance abuse testing, and they were placed in BIP programs that lasted longer and cost more per session than comparison offenders.

In all three demonstration sites, they were more likely to have court orders specifying no contact with the victim without consent. In Massachusetts, they were more likely to be ordered to substance abuse evaluation or to attend a fatherhood program or (for female offenders) women's group. In Michigan, they were more likely to be ordered to mental health evaluation and to have restrictions on weapons. In Wisconsin, JOD offenders were much more likely to be required to remain sober, stay employed and comply with other specific probation conditions. In Massachusetts, JOD offenders were significantly more likely than comparison offenders to be convicted and sentenced, and more likely to be sent to jail or probation. They were also more likely to have the case continued without a finding, and less likely to be granted deferred prosecution.[6] In Massachusetts, greater offender accountability was not accomplished at the cost of defendant rights: JOD offenders were more likely to have a public defender and had, on average, more defense attorneys than comparison offenders.

In Massachusetts, JOD increased offender understanding of the legal process.[7]

In Massachusetts, Dorchester offenders were significantly more likely than Lowell offenders to report that the legal process was clearly explained by the judge and scored higher on their understanding of the legal process. In Michigan, the only significant difference in understanding of the legal process was that Washtenaw County offenders were significantly more likely than Ingham County offenders to report that the defense attorney clearly explained the charges against them.

JOD did not decrease perceptions of the fairness of judges and probation departments

There were no significant differences between JOD and comparison offenders in Massachusetts and Michigan in ratings of the fairness of the judges, fairness of the probation agents, or in offender satisfaction with the way these officials responded to the IPV incident.

In Massachusetts, offenders in the JOD program rated the police and defense attorneys lower than comparison offenders on fairness and satisfaction; no significant differences between JOD and comparison offenders on these measures were found in Michigan

The lower ratings resulted in lower overall scores by offenders in the JOD program in Massachusetts on ratings of justice system fairness and satisfaction. Reasons for the differences between Dorchester and Lowell offenders are not clear, but may be related to more aggressive enforcement and prosecution under JOD.

JOD increased offender compliance with court orders to report to probation and BIP

Increased offender compliance under JOD was observed in several ways. In both Massachusetts and Michigan and overall, JOD offenders were significantly more likely than comparison offenders to report to a BIP in the first two months after case disposition. Similarly, JOD offenders were less likely to miss a BIP session by the time of the follow- up interview if ordered to attend. In Michigan, but not Massachusetts, JOD offenders were significantly more likely to report to probation in the first two months than comparison offenders. JOD offenders had reported to probation by the time of the follow-up interview at slightly higher rates than comparison offenders in both Massachusetts and Michigan, resulting in a significantly higher reporting rate in the overall sample.

JOD increased the certainty or severity of penalties for violations of some court-ordered requirements

Sanctions for missing BIP sessions were significantly more certain in Dorchester than in Lowell, and slightly more likely in Washtenaw than Ingham, producing an overall significantly higher sanction certainty in JOD than comparison areas. Sanctions for missing probation appointments were significantly more severe in Dorchester than in Lowell, and slightly more severe in Washtenaw than Ingham, producing an overall significantly higher sanction severity in JOD than in comparison areas. These findings must be viewed with some caution, however, because relatively few offenders reported these violations and sanctions, reducing the power of the analysis to detect differences in sanctioning practices.

In Milwaukee, a review of the records showed that during JOD probation, agents were more likely to address problems that came to their attention and imposed more severe penalties for probation violations. Probation revocation, the most severe sanction, was much more frequent during JOD than before in Milwaukee and more widely used in Dorchester than in Washtenaw County. Probation records showed revocations in the first year after case disposition for 27 percent of the Milwaukee IPV probationers and 12 percent of the Dorchester IPV probationers, compared to 1 percent of the Washtenaw IPV probationers. In Milwaukee, probation agents initiated more revocations for technical violations, failure to comply with BIP requirements, unauthorized victim contacts and new criminal activities under JOD than previously.

JOD did not create heightened belief among offenders that IPV would result in negative legal consequences

Criminal justice theory predicts that perceptions of the certainty of negative consequences for illegal behavior will deter illegal behavior. In both sites, offenders rated the certainty and severity of legal penalties for future IPV as high; there was no significant difference in ratings between JOD and comparison offenders. However, in Massachusetts but not in Michigan, JOD significantly increased the perception that future IPV would have negative social consequences for offenders in the form of loss of employment or negative responses from family, friends, children or the victim.

Revictimization

JOD victims in Massachusetts reported significantly lower rates of new IPV

In Massachusetts, JOD victims reported significantly less repeat IPV by the offender than comparison victims in the first two months (initial report) and then 11 months (composite report) since the incident, using multiple measures of revictimization: any threat or intimidation, physical assault, or severe physical assault. In addition, JOD victims in Massachusetts reported lower frequency of physical assault at both time points and lower frequency of severe physical assault at the initial time point. In Michigan, there was no significant difference between JOD and comparison victims in their reports of repeat IPV on any measure at either interview. As a result, no general effects of the JOD model on repeat IPV can be inferred.

JOD reductions in victim reports of repeat IPV were stronger for some types of victims and offenders

- In multivariate models predicting repeat IPV, significant interactions showed that, collectively, JOD had its strongest effect in reducing victim reports of repeat IPV when:

- Offenders were young (age 18 to 29).
- Offenders had a high number of prior arrests (seven or more).
- Victims had moderateto-high social support.
- Victims did not have children in common with the offender.
- The relationship between victim and offender was less than three years in duration.

Offender self-reports of repeat IPV were very low and showed no significant variation between JOD and comparison samples

Overall, very few offenders admitted to repeat IPV at two months post-disposition, and reports at 11 months after disposition were one-third to one-half the rates reported by victims. Earlier research has consistently reported that offenders report significantly lower rates of repeat violence than victims. Based on offender self-reports, there were no significant differences in the prevalence or frequency of physical or severe physical assaults measured at two months and 11 months after case disposition.

Offenders' perceptions of legal deterrence predicted lower frequency of offender reports of repeat IPV

Offenders who reported medium-to-high ratings of legal deterrence reported lower frequencies of physical assault against their victims, although no such differences were observed for other measures of repeat IPV (e.g., prevalence of physical assault, prevalence and frequency of severe physical assault). However, as noted earlier, JOD and comparison offenders did not differ in their perceptions of legal deterrence.

JOD did not reduce the likelihood of offender rearrest in Massachusetts or Michigan when characteristics of the victim, offender and IPV case were controlled

Estimated official rearrest rates from the multivariate models for the JOD and comparison samples ranged from 18 percent of JOD offenders in Michigan to 31 percent of JOD offenders in Massachusetts. These rates are comparable to several studies that have reported about a 25-percent offender recidivism rate in the year following an IPV incident. Unfortunately, IPV arrests could not be distinguished from other arrests in the data made available from Michigan and Massachusetts. Possibly because of the general arrest measure, JOD had no significant effect on offender rearrest rates in the year after case disposition. The likelihood of offender rearrest, using a multivariate model that controlled for characteristics of the victim, offender and IPV cases, was 22 percent for JOD offenders and 28 percent for comparison offenders. Although this result is in the expected direction, it is not statistically significant at conventional levels of hypothesis testing.

In Milwaukee, JOD decreased the likelihood of arrest for domestic violence during the first year of probation

IPV probationers were significantly less likely to be arrested in the year after case disposition for domestic violence during JOD (4 percent) than before JOD (8 percent) in Milwaukee, when only rearrests for IPV and other kinds of domestic violence were counted. As in Massachusetts and Michigan, there was no significant difference between JOD and comparison offenders in the total number of all rearrests. The increase in revocation and the resulting incarceration suggests that the lower DV arrest rates may have been attained primarily through early detection and incarceration of probationers who continued their pattern of domestic violence or otherwise failed to comply with conditions of probation.

LESSONS ON JOD IMPLEMENTATION

Lessons on JOD implementation were drawn from the experiences of all three demonstration sites documented through process evaluation across the entire study period. The process evaluation included regular visits to JOD and comparison sites, semi-structured interviews with JOD partners, observations of court proceedings and other activities, quantitative data on site operations, conference calls, group meetings with sites and national partners, and focus group interviews with offenders and victims in each site. The lessons are intended to assist other jurisdictions that are considering innovative, comprehensive responses to I PV in their communities. The process evaluation identified three principal impacts of JOD on criminal justice and community responses to IPV cases: 1) increased coordination between the judiciary and other justice and community agencies; 2) increased consistency in the justice system response to IPV cases; and 3) lasting changes in the system response to IPV, including judicial review hearings for IPV probationers, improved practices for investigating and prosecuting IPV cases, and increased contact of probation agents with BIPs and IPV victims. The following strategies were identified as particularly helpful in implementing JOD.

Involving all partners in the formal strategic planning process. For all sites, these sessions were the first time that such a diverse group of justice and community agencies had come together to discuss a coordinated response to domestic violence in their communities. These planning sessions highlighted components of the initiative that required more attention, allowed agency partners to discuss their views on their role in the initiative, and led to the development of subcommittees and further technical assistance on specific topics.

Actively managing the collaboration through regularly scheduled meetings and a full-time project director. In each site, the management of JOD required regular team meetings, executive committee meetings and meetings of subcommittees around specific issues. Ongoing meetings increased case-level collaboration and increased understanding among the agencies and confidence among social service providers and probation agencies that their efforts to change offender behavior would be supported.

Building an inclusive set of partners beyond the core criminal justice agencies and giving them a voice in shaping policies and procedures. The sites also found it important to continue adding partners as the partnership grew, developing plans for outreach to specific cultural groups, and adding other types of victim assistance and offender intervention programs available for court referrals.

Using technical assistance by "outsiders" with acknowledged expertise to help promote change. In all demonstration sites, training of personnel in JOD partner agencies and technical assistance in developing new policies and procedures was extensive and ongoing.

Dedicating specialized staff to IPV cases. To act effectively, the police, prosecutors, courts and probation agencies need staff trained in the challenges of these cases, strategies for responding effectively, and personal ties to specialized staff in partner agencies to foster a team approach to managing cases.

JOD partnerships began with a vision of collaborative operations in which agencies would work together seamlessly to protect victims and hold offenders accountable for their violence. Agreements were forged and commitments made. However, the process of actualizing this collaborative vision encountered barriers and challenges that can serve as a lesson and guide to agencies embarking on similar coordinated responses to IPV. Key challenges included:

- Gaps in knowledge about the operations of other partner agencies.
- Understanding the implications of changes on the workload of partner agencies.

- County and state rules governing recruiting and funding of new positions that slowed the start of the project and limited hiring options.
- Inadequate systems for sharing data across justice agencies and with community service providers. Even data systems routinely kept by the courts and other justice agencies are often not adequate or in a form that can be used to provide timely information to other partner agencies.
- Differences in goals, roles and expectations of justice agencies and community-based victim service providers. Issues arose around client confidentiality, encouraging victims to testify in court and the weight to be given to victim preferences during prosecution.

The sites had varying levels of success in meeting these challenges, and other communities are likely to face similar challenges.

LESSONS FROM JOD FOCUS GROUPS

Eight focus groups were conducted in the JOD demonstration sites: four victim focus groups (two in Milwaukee and one each in Dorchester and Washtenaw) and four offender focus groups (also two in Milwaukee and one each in Dorchester and Washtenaw). Victim focus group participants were recruited from lists of victims named in criminal cases filed in JOD courts (Dorchester and Washtenaw) or from lists provided by participating JOD agencies (Milwaukee). Offender focus group participants were recruited from lists of probationers who were convicted of IPV offenses before focus group recruitment began. Characteristics of the focus groups are displayed in exhibit 4 (p. 16).

The focus groups were conducted to supplement the quantitative survey findings by allowing an open discussion on a variety of topics without restricting the type or form of feedback received. This type of information complements quantitative findings and provides important narrative details on the lives of program participants. By design, the focus groups were limited to a small number of participants to permit in-depth discussion. Although potential participants were selected by researchers from lists of victims and offenders in JOD cases without regard to individual or case characteristics, many of those invited did not attend the groups. Thus, there is no way to know if the views of those who did attend are representative of victims and offenders in criminal IPV cases in the JOD jurisdictions.

The discussion focused on victim and offender perceptions of procedural justice with respect to their interactions with police, prosecutors, defense attorneys, probation, the court, the judge, victim service agencies and batterer intervention programs. Understanding procedural justice issues and reflecting such themes in service practices may lead to improved offender compliance with case outcomes, and improved satisfaction and safety for victims. Findings across the sites, for both victims and offenders, indicate the importance of procedural justice concepts when individuals reflect on their IPV cases, services received and related outcomes. Individuals involved in IPV cases, whether victims or offenders, want to feel as though they have been heard and treated with respect and consideration. They want those in the justice system to act impartially and neutrally when responding to IPV incidents. The evaluation produced some recommendations based on the opinions of victims and offenders. Victims generally endorsed the following police practices, which can be strengthened further through ongoing training:

- Victims want the police to show concern for victims by responding quickly and taking appropriate legal steps based on the evidence at the scene, regardless of the abuser's criminal profile (i.e., whether he/she was wanted on other charges).
- Victims want police to avoid engaging in conversations that would put them on the spot, such as asking in the offender's presence whether the victim wanted the offender arrested, since this could trigger retaliation against the victim in the future. Victims felt that off icers should only ask for the victim's input on the arrest decision if there was no clear evidence that a physical assault had occurred.
- Victims want the police to abstain from remarks that appear to trivialize the incident or appear to blame the victim. Such remarks were reported by more than a few victims.
- Victims want more consistent enforcement of protection orders, including those issued by courts outside the local jurisdiction.
- Victims noted that police have difficulty in respond¬ing to IPV calls that, ac¬cording to victims, involved alcohol and sometimes cocaine.

Exhibit 4. Characteristics of JOD Focus Groups

Site	Type of participants	Number of participants	Race/ethnicity of participants	Date of focus group
Dorchester	victims	13	10 african-american 3 White	november 2004
milwaukee	victims	8	4 african-american 3 White 1 asian-american	July 2003
milwaukee	victims	10	6 african-american 4 White	July 2003
Washtenaw	victims	10	4 african-american 5 White 1 hispanic	september 2004
Total victims		41[*]		
Dorchester	offenders	10	9 african-american 1 White	December 2003
milwaukee	offenders	9	5 african-american 3 White 1 unknown	september 2003
milwaukee	offenders	8	4 african-american 4 White	September 2003
Washtenaw	offenders	6	6 White	September 2004
Total offenders		33[†]		

*40 women, 1 man
†32 men, 1 woman

Offenders in all focus groups complained about the police making quick judgments about the incident and not considering their side of the story. A frequent complaint was that officers were quick to judge the male as the primary or only aggressor in the situation, even when physical evidence pointed otherwise. Offenders generally endorsed the following police practices and identified them as areas that should be strengthened:

- Offenders want the police to give them an opportunity to present their side of the story before an arrest decision is made. Several male participants remarked that the police officer took the women's statement but did not take their statement. This may require an extension of training in determining probable cause and the primary aggressor.
- Offenders want to be treated with respect, despite their apparent responsibility for the crime. Some of the offenders felt that their treatment during arrest and pretrial detention violated the legal presumption of "innocent until proven guilty," in that officers' behavior and jail conditions were inappropriately punitive or deliberately and unnecessarily humiliating.

The victim focus groups produced several recommendations for courts:

- Victims, particularly those with children and those with ongoing, long-term relationships with the offender, want the court to consider their individual needs and wishes in setting a no-contact order and its duration and conditions. This would help police enforce these orders more consistently, help ensure respect for court orders and offer greater protection to victims.
- Victims indicated a need for emotional support during the case and greater security during the court process — especially at in-court appearances.
- Victims implicitly supported the concept of evidence- based prosecution that would allow victims to choose whether to testify in court or not, and those who had this choice were grateful.
- Victims varied in whether they wanted the offender penalized or treated. This led to a consensus on wanting greater input into sentencing decisions and more variation in sentences so they could be tailored to the situation.

Offenders in the focus groups were generally less satisfied with their court experience. These perceptions reflect areas in which courts could expand efforts to explain the legal process to the offender:

- Some offenders wanted more opportunity for a strong defense in which their side of the case was explained in court.
- Some offenders did not believe that all IPV offenders were treated equally under the law. Participants cited similar sentences for cases of varying severity and complained that sentences were not tailored to the severity of the incident and criminal history.
- Some offenders thought the financial consequences were more severe (too severe) for low-income working men than for upper- income men (who could afford to pay the fees) and the unemployed (who, by virtue of the sliding scales, paid almost nothing).

Offenders identified two areas of concern about status review hearings. First, the frequency of the hearings put a strain on their employment (particularly for those who were not fully compliant, thereby requiring additional hearings). Second, offenders wanted more opportunity to address the court during their review hearings.

IMPLICATIONS FOR RESEARCH, POLICY AND PRACTICE

Feasibility and Impact of the JOD Model

The implementation study indicates that JOD is feasible and provided many benefits to the justice agencies. The JOD initiatives targeted at court improvement and leadership (greater court specialization, initiation of pretrial monitoring and post-trial compliance reviews, coordination with victim service agencies) and probation improvement and leadership (dedicated DV agents, increased supervision, compliance review preparations, outreach to victims) resulted in significant advances in holding offenders accountable. Improvements were made in monitoring, consistent sanctioning and sentencing decisions, and compliance review (court and probation functions) that were not previously achieved by communities relying on police leadership or coordinated community responses that did not engage these agencies.

The JOD model implementation was tailored to site needs and resources, and specific strategies and arrangements varied from site to site. However, data from multiple sources confirm that significant changes in justice system collaboration and offender accountability occurred in JOD sites. All JOD sites achieved substantial gains in collaboration among justice agencies responding to IPV, expanding participation by law enforcement officers, prosecutors, judges and probation agents. Criminal justice partner agencies in the JOD sites were very enthusiastic about improvements in interagency communication and coordination of efforts that emerged from the joint planning and development of arrangements for sharing information on IPV offender status. They also embraced new JOD innovations. Courts in all three JOD sites hope to continue specialized DV dockets and judicial review hearings. The Milwaukee probation agency has trained all agents working in the county in DV supervision practices, including victim contact.

In all JOD sites, the prosecutors and police were pleased with improvements in evidence collection and investigations to support prosecution. In addition, the increased coordination between the judiciary and other justice and community agencies led to improved consistency and significant changes in the justice system response to IPV. The lessons from the implementation study summarized above provide guidance on building and sustaining coordination across justice and community agencies. These substantial changes in the collaborative response to IPV produced mixed results in terms of project goals.

The project did not achieve gains in victim perceptions of their safety or well-being using survey measures. Gains in offender accountability were significant, but did not translate into perceptions likely to deter future offending. Reductions in victim reports of repeat IPV were found in Massachusetts, but not in Michigan. Reductions in DV arrests were found in Milwaukee, but not in the two jurisdictions that had only measures of rearrest on all charges. This mixed pattern of results points to the need for further efforts in several areas.

The reductions in repeat IPV occurred in the jurisdictions that revoked probationers for noncompliance. The implication is that the reduction resulted from incapacitating abusers who failed to comply with probation conditions rather than from deterring offenders. Despite implementation of strategies for holding offenders accountable through judicial review hearings, specialized prosecution and probation, police training, and increased BIP requirements, there was no significant difference in the perception of risk of legal sanctions for future IPV between JOD and comparison offenders. However, Dorchester offenders scored much higher on a measure of perceived certainty of legal sanctions for repeat IPV than did Washtenaw offenders. To some extent, these perceptions may be related to the higher rate of actual revocation in Dorchester (12 percent) compared to Washtenaw (1 percent). In Milwaukee, much higher revocation rates (27 percent in the first year of probation) were accompanied by a dramatic drop in rearrest rates for IPV, probably due to incarceration of offenders most likely to be arrested. These findings suggest that research is needed on the effectiveness of selective incarceration through probation revocation or other strategies for increasing the perceived threat of legal sanctions in this population.

Like many other studies, JOD found efforts to change offender perceptions and reduce IPV reoffending challenging. The results suggest, like those of other studies, that referral to batterer intervention programs does not have a powerful effect in reducing IPV. Until progress is made in changing offender beliefs and behavior, the implication is that the justice system must continue to focus on protecting victims and using the authority of its agencies to closely monitor offenders and respond rapidly with penalties when violations of court-ordered conditions are detected.

The success of JOD in reducing IPV in selected subgroups may be a fruitful way to begin designing new intervention strategies. There were indications that JOD strategies are particularly effective for some subgroups, including younger offenders with fewer ties to the victim as well as offenders with extensive arrest histories. Further research to confirm these findings may well lead to guidance for the courts on the appropriateness of alternative sentences and supervision conditions.

The lessons on whether a coordinated system response to IPV is beneficial for victims are less obvious. Even in Michigan, where the large majority of JOD victims received a wide range of quality services, JOD victims did not report higher levels of well-being or safety than comparison victims. Survey results indicate that interventions intended to improve victims' safety and overall well-being need to go beyond services centered on cases in the court system to include services that address issues in the victims' lives outside the realm of the court case. Victim service providers' efforts may be most fruitful when they focus on helping victims strengthen their social support networks and augment the positive consequences while attenuating the negative impacts of abuse and its aftermath (such as financial impacts/finding a job, practical issues such as moving, and the emotional trauma of victims and their children). However, despite the efforts of victim service agencies to provide support and encouragement, victims may be unwilling to take actions that would increase their safety. In all sites (JOD and comparison sites), victims who reported that they had lived with their offender or had frequent contact with their offender after the case was disposed were more likely to report repeat victimization, including intimidation, threats and assaults.

Implications for Service Delivery

Survey and focus group results indicate that victims who received victim services were very satisfied with them. However, there were substantial differences in victim services provided across the sites. Most criminal case victims in the focus groups in the two sites with multiple nongovernmental agencies affiliated with JOD said they were not referred to victim services by anyone at the court. These victims were generally unfamiliar with basic safety planning strategies. In some cases, the NGO advocates in these sites focused on providing services in civil matters such as protection orders; in other cases, the advocates targeted special populations or were located off site, making communication with the court more difficult. Most of these victims expressed an interest in services, particularly in receiving emotional support and services for their children. In Washtenaw County, a single victim service agency worked very closely with staff in the prosecutor's office and had contact with a large majority of the victims in criminal cases. This level of close collaboration may be necessary to reach IPV victims. Service gaps in that site seemed to be limited to preferences for more services for children and housing options other than shelters (such as independent, family-style housing, possibly through private arrangements with landlords).

Efforts to improve victim services need to continue. Feedback from victims in the focus groups suggests the existence of unmet needs for better housing options and greater counseling and other service options for their children. Also notable: some victims, if not most, across all three sites were particularly critical of their treatment by the police and prosecutors. Victims described examples in which they felt that these agents failed to treat them with due respect and dignity. The focus groups thus highlight a need for improved training among stakeholders who interact with victims. Concerning the police in particular, most victims indicated that they did not want the police to ask them directly whether to make an arrest (i.e., in front of the offender), but to evaluate the situation thoughtfully and considerately and then attempt to use sound judgment about how to proceed. Concerning prosecution, most victims indicated that they wanted to retain a voice in the prosecution, but most believed that they were not granted such a voice. Some expressed a feeling that prosecutors essentially used them for their own purposes but were not concerned for the victim's individual situation.

Similarly, organizational differences may account for variation in offender experiences with probation. Offenders in areas with specialized probation units or officers praised probation officers for their helpfulness. However, offenders in Milwaukee supervised by a large, nonspecialized agency wanted probation officers to be more service-oriented and less enforcement-oriented. Probationers there discussed incidents where agents enforced rules and court orders differently, leading to feelings of unfair and unequal treatment.

Probationers described incidents where their agents required them to obtain employment but offered no assistance in finding and securing a job. Others were dismayed when their agents refused to schedule appointments around the offender's work schedule, and they did not understand why keeping the offender employed was not a top priority of the agent. This suggests that specialized probation supervision may be more effective in motivating offenders to engage in required services. Overall, the evaluation points to the need for research in several critical areas:

- How to build stronger linkages between courts and NGO victim service providers, given the high levels of satisfaction with services when they are received.

- How to motivate offender compliance and desistance from violence using both sanctions and treatment in combination.
- How to change offender perceptions of the risks of future violence.
- How to engage victims in services that will assist them in staying safe.

PROJECT REPORTS (BY DATE)

DeStefano, Christine Depies, Adele Harrell, Lisa Newmark & Christy Visher. (2001). *"Evaluation of the Judicial Oversight Demonstration: Initial Process Evaluation Report."* Report for National Institute of Justice, cooperative agreement number 99-WT-VXK005. Washington, D.C.: The Urban Institute, August.

Harrell, Adele, Lisa Newmark, Christy Visher & Christine DeStefano. (2002). *"Evaluation of the Judicial Oversight Demonstration Initiative: Implementation Strategies and Lessons."* Report for National Institute of Justice, cooperative agreement number 99-WT-VX-K005. Washington, D.C.: The Urban Institute, September. NCJRS, NCJ 220872.

Harrell, Adele, Megan Schaffer, Christine DeStefano & Jennifer Castro. (2006). *"The Evaluation of Milwaukee's Judicial Oversight Demonstration."* Final report for National Institute of Justice, cooperative agreement number 99-WTVX-K005. Washington, D.C.: National Institute of Justice, April. NCJRS, NCJ 215349.

Harrell, Adele, Lisa Newmark, Christy Visher & Jennifer Castro. (2007). *"Final Report on the Evaluation of the Judicial Oversight Demonstration*: Volume *1.* The Impact of JOD in Dorchester and Washtenaw County." Final report for National Institute of Justice, cooperative agreement number 99-WT-VX-K005. Washington, D.C.: National Institute of Justice, June. NCJRS, NCJ 219382.

Visher, Christy, Lisa Newmark & Adele Harrell, with Emily Turner. (2007). *"Final Report on the Evaluation of the Judicial Oversight Demonstration*: Volume *2.* Findings and Lessons on Implementation." Final report for National Institute of Justice, cooperative agreement number 99-WT-VX-K005. Washington, D.C.: National Institute of Justice, June. NCJRS, NCJ 219383.

Newmark, Lisa, Adele Harrell, Janine Zweig, with Christine Depies DeStefano, Lisa Brooks & Megan Schaffer. (2007). "Final Report on the *Evaluation of the Judicial Oversight Demonstration*: Volume *3.* Findings from JOD Victim and Offender Focus Groups." Final report for National Institute of Justice, cooperative agreement number 99-WTVX-K005. Washington, D.C.: National Institute of Justice, June. NCJRS, NCJ 219384.

Harrell, Adele and Jennifer Castro, with Atlantic Research and Consulting and The Center for Urban Studies, Wayne State University. "Final Report on the *Evaluation of the Judicial Oversight Demonstration*: Volume *4.* Final Report on Survey Methodology." Final report for National Institute of Justice, cooperative agreement number 99-WT-VX-K005. Washington, D.C.: National Institute of Justice, June 2007. NCJRS, NCJ 219385.

The National Institute of Justice is the research, development, and evaluation   agency of the U.S. Department of Justice. NIJ's   development, and evaluation to enhance the administration of justice and public safety.

The National Institute of Justice is a component of the Office of Justice Programs, which also includes the Bureau of Justice Assistance; the Bureau of Justice Statistics; the

Community Capacity Development Office; the Office for Victims of Crime; the Office of Juvenile Justice and Delinquency Prevention; and the Office of Sex Offender Sentencing, Monitoring, Apprehending, Registering, and Tracking (SMART).

End Notes

[1] The sampling periods were: Dorchester, Jan. 29, 2003, to Nov. 11, 2004; Washtenaw County, Feb. 14, 2003, to April 4, 2003, and then from Nov. 21, 2003, to Oct. 29, 2004; Ingham County, March 12, 2003, to March 12, 2004; and Lowell, Jan. 29, 2003, to Aug. 27, 2004.

[2] Atlantic Research and Consulting (now Guidelines) conducted the in- person interviews in Massachusetts. The Center for Urban Studies at Wayne State University conducted the in-person interviews in Michigan.

[3] In Michigan, the Michigan State Police Department of Information Technology provided the criminal history records. In Massachusetts, the information on criminal offender records from Massachusetts Criminal History Systems Board was supplemented by checks of warrants that resulted in arraignments after case disposition to verify that the new incidents occurred during the year after case disposition.

[4] The results in this section are based on the evaluation of JOD in Dorchester and Washtenaw County because interviews were not conducted as part of the evaluation of JOD in Milwaukee.

[5] Based on agency records in JOD sites (not available in comparison sites).

[6] Similar differences were not found in Michigan because all offenders in both sites were convicted (only Massachusetts allowed deferred prosecution and continuation of cases without a finding, although some Michigan convictions were later expunged from the record).

[7] Results for Milwaukee are limited to factors that were captured in the review of probation and court files and do not include offender perceptions measured on surveys in Massachusetts and Michigan.

Chapter 5

Pretrial Innovations for Domestic Violence Offenders and Victims[*]

United States Department of Justice

About This Report

Domestic violence cases involving intimate partners pose challenges for the crimi-nal justice system as the cases move from arrest to adjudication to sentencing. The lengthy time period after arrest but before case dispo-sition (either by plea, trial ver-dict, or dismissal) puts domestic violence victims at high risk. Offenders often vio-late no-contact orders and seek out their victims during this pretrial period, raising the potential for more violence.

State courts in three demon-stration sites are rethinking how they handle domestic violence cases through the Judicial Oversight Demon-stration (JOD) project. The three sites are all seeking to increase victim safety while holding offenders accountable, but each site implemented the project in a slightly differ-ent way.

This report discusses how pretrial innovations were implemented in the three demonstration sites—

Dorchester, MA, Milwaukee, WI, and Washtenaw County, MI. It also describes the pre-trial strategies, key aspects of their implementation, and lessons learned for other jurisdictions wishing to imple-ment innovations in pretrial procedures for domestic violence cases.

Major changes in the opera-tions of the courts at the pre-trial stage entailed—

- Developing consistent and timely procedures for judges to use in handling pretrial matters in domestic violence cases.
- Restructuring court processes to focus on the unique characteristics of domestic violence cases.

---

[*] This is an edited, reformatted and augmented version of a U. S. Department of Justice publication dated August 2007.

- Monitoring defendants prior to trial and respond-ing to violations of bond conditions.
- Connecting victims to support services early in the process.

In this report, the term domestic violence is used to refer to violence that occurs among intimate partners, as this term is most commonly used among practitioners and policymakers. The term intimate partner violence is used as well.

The Judicial Oversight Demonstration (JOD) initiative tests the idea that quick, coordinated responses by the community and the justice system can keep victims safer and hold offenders accountable in intimate partner violence cases.[1]

In 1999, Dorchester, MA, Milwaukee, WI, and Washtenaw County, MI, began integrating better judicial oversight into existing coordinated responses to intimate partner violence. The demonstrations strengthen previous partnerships and build new partnerships between the court and other agencies, including the prosecutor's office, victim service providers, batterer intervention programs, law enforcement, and probation. The goals include greater safety and offender accountability.

Researchers are in the process of evaluating the outcome of the project— whether domestic violence victims are truly safer because of this new approach. The answers will be available in 2009. In the meantime, many jurisdictions are considering putting in place a domestic violence court or enhancing their pretrial responses to this crime. This report describes some of the challenges these jurisdictions may face.

INNOVATIVE PRETRIAL STRATEGIES

The pretrial period can be a high-risk time for domestic violence victims.[2] Their abusers, usually charged with misdemeanor domestic violence, are rarely held in custody before trial in most jurisdictions, though they may be held briefly after arrest (overnight or over a weekend) while awaiting an arraignment hearing. In most jurisdictions, released defendants are not supervised prior to trial. This raises concerns about the safety of their victims. Defendants may retaliate or intimidate their victims into changing their story or not testifying.

Although many jurisdictions prohibit defendants from having any contact with victims while the case is pending, victims still face significant safety risks because no- contact bond conditions are often violated by the defendants. Further, no-contact order violations, even those reported to the police, often go unpunished because of lengthy intervals between court appearances.

The JOD sites addressed both victim safety and offender accountability by increasing the involvement of judges in managing domestic violence cases before trial, restructuring court procedures, and expanding victim services. Dorchester and Washtenaw County dedicated domestic violence dockets within their existing court structures, and Milwaukee added a domestic violence intake court. Washtenaw County and Milwaukee also developed standard policies and protocols for predisposition case processing, and all three sites expanded victim services to improve victim security and participation in the court process.

JUDICIAL INVOLVEMENT AND CONSISTENCY

With multiple judges hearing domestic violence cases at each of the sites, an important goal of the project was to ensure that the new JOD policies and protocols promoted consistent court procedures. This objective was accomplished in a variety of ways.

At each site, at least one judge started using innovative court responses to intimate partner violence before the demonstration began. These judges were instrumental in educating other judges on new approaches and involving the court in a coordinated, systemwide response. Also, all judges (and Milwaukee's court commissioners) involved in JOD participated in a judicial training institute sponsored by the Office on Violence Against Women (OVW). The 5-day curriculum covered a variety of topics including judicial decisionmaking in intimate partner violence cases, review hearings, graduated sanctions, the role of judges beyond the courtroom, immigration law, cultural awareness, risk and lethality assessment, and the effects of domestic violence on children. The judges reported that the training gave them a more detailed understanding of intimate partner violence and the role of the court in adjudicating these offenses.

In Dorchester, judges used peer-to-peer learning to improve consistency in decisionmaking. The judges on the Dorchester JOD bench at the start of implementation had been very active in developing the *Massachusetts Trial Courts' Guidelines for Judicial Practice in Abuse Prevention Proceedings*. As other judges came to that court, the original judges shared their knowledge and expertise in domestic violence case processing through informal, on-the-job training opportunities.

In Washtenaw County, all seven of the county's district court judges signed and adopted a new domestic violence protocol, agreeing on six principles for domestic violence cases:

- Dedicated dockets 1 day per week.
- Priority processing of cases.
- Compulsory bond conditions.
- Use of a designated probation unit.
- Automatic appointment of defense counsel.
- Early subpoenaing of witnesses.

The designated domestic violence judges also developed formal, standardized, written protocols for conducting arraignments, which included obtaining defendants' criminal histories and other background information to use in making bond decisions and using a common conditional bond-release form. This process built consensus and commitment to consistent judicial practices across the county's four district courts.

In Milwaukee, the chief judge carefully selected the new domestic violence court commissioner and the judges to be assigned to the domestic violence court. Judges were assigned to the domestic violence court for a 2-year term and attended special domestic violence training. The judges were rotated periodically to reduce burnout and give more judges the opportunity to receive training and experience in handling domestic violence cases— training and experience that can be applied to other cases, such as homicide and sexual assault. The use of rotation suggests that the specialized judicial training in domestic violence provided by the OVW for the JOD sites should be continued as standard practice.

RESTRUCTURING COURT PROCESSES FOR DOMESTIC VIOLENCE CASES

Two JOD sites, Dorchester and Washtenaw County, dedicated courts or docket days to domestic violence cases (including civil protection orders, misdemeanor criminal cases, and some or all felony cases in Dorchester), and Milwaukee added an intake court. Restructuring depended on each site's existing court structures, characteristics of the community, the size of the intimate partner violence caseload, and judicial practices in these cases. Other jurisdictions interested in replicating this approach could benefit from an examination of their own court organization and contextual factors before deciding how to structure their specialized courts (see "Structure, Schedules, and Staff Issues" on page 5).

In Dorchester, domestic violence cases had been spread across six general sessions or courtrooms. The JOD initiative consolidated domestic violence into a single session for the first time, using a "vertical adjudication" model—the processing of cases by a single prosecutor through a specialized prosecution unit—for cases disposed without trial. Now, one of the general sessions operates as a full-time domestic violence court. This dedicated domestic violence court handles all intimate partner violence civil restraining orders and all criminal court procedures for domestic violence misdemeanors and lower- level felonies, including arraignments, pretrial and other hearings, plea hearings and sentencing, preliminary and final probation violation hearings, and probation reviews. The court also handles preindictment hearings for more serious felonies. Trials are adjourned to another session to help manage caseloads.

STRUCTURE, SCHEDULES, AND STAFF ISSUES

The structure of the domestic violence court in each of the JOD sites proved to be very efficient for coordinating the necessary activities in prosecuting domestic violence cases. Prior to JOD, domestic violence case hearings in two of the three sites (Dorchester and Washtenaw County, except for District 15) were spread across different courtrooms. This meant that the relevant persons—prosecutors, defense attorneys, probation officers, and victim advocates—had different schedules.

During JOD, the dedicated dockets for domestic violence cases ensured that the dedicated staff could be present in the courtroom for all phases of the court process—from arraignment to sentencing. This led to the formation of courtroom teams of staff from different agencies, all dedicated to domestic violence cases. Anecdotal reports from the JOD sites suggest a positive response from staff and successful working relationships resulted from this change.

In Milwaukee, three specialized courts for domestic violence misdemeanor cases operated prior to JOD. With plans under JOD to expand services to these cases and begin hearing felony cases as well, Milwaukee needed an additional specialized court to respond to the anticipated workload. Under the direction of a domestic violence court commissioner, an intake court was established to handle initial appearances for out-of-custody defendants and misdemeanor arraignments, freeing the other three courts for case disposition including pleas, trials, sentencing hearings, postdisposition hearings, and adjudication of felony cases. Milwaukee's domestic violence courts use vertical adjudication with felony cases only.

In Washtenaw County, one of the four district courts (District Court 15, located in Ann Arbor) already had a domestic violence docket day prior to the JOD project. Because Washtenaw County is a larger and less densely populated area compared to urban Dorchester and Milwaukee, it was necessary to maintain domestic violence courts at each of the four district courts located in different areas of the county. The caseload did not require full-time court resources for domestic violence cases in any of the courts, so each court established one domestic violence docket day per week. Washtenaw County District Courts also use a vertical adjudication model.

MONITORING AND EDUCATING DEFENDANTS

Court monitoring of defendants is a delicate legal matter, touching on the "innocent until proven guilty" concept at the heart of the U.S. judicial system. Yet, it is clear that domestic violence victims are at high risk, and defendants can imperil both the victim's safety and the outcome of the criminal case if steps are not taken to deter defendants from further intimidation or violence. At the outset of the demonstration, Dorchester did not plan a pretrial monitoring component because of strong defendants' rights laws and a probation system limited by fiscal constraints. Instead, emphasis was placed on postdisposition supervision. Washtenaw County and Milwaukee struggled with balancing defendants' rights and victim safety in the pretrial period and ultimately addressed this dilemma in different ways.

The Washtenaw County demonstration initially included active monitoring of defendants during the predisposition phase. After objections were received from the defense bar, monitoring activities were redesigned to an in-person review of bond conditions with groups of recently charged defendants and an initial drug test if ordered by the court (with regular testing possible, contingent on the results of the first test). Under this new practice, the courts ordered defendants to contact the Domestic Violence Probation Unit—a newly formed unit under the authority of County Probation—within 24 hours to make an appointment. Several times a week, the probation supervisor reviewed bond conditions with a group of defendants to ensure they understood the conditions and to answer any questions. The group review of bond conditions within a week of arraignment was designed to overcome the pre-JOD problem of defendants and defense attorneys claiming that they were unaware of the bond conditions.

Also in Washtenaw County, responses to violations of bond conditions were improved in several ways. Court officers entered bond conditions into a statewide law enforcement database, so that if a law enforcement officer stopped a defendant anywhere in the State, any violations of release could easily be detected. The courts also put new systems in place to handle pretrial bond violations. If the defendant failed to call or appear for the appointment to review bond conditions with the Domestic Violence Probation Unit, a request for a bench warrant was sent to the judge for review. Washtenaw County streamlined procedures for bringing violations of bond conditions to the attention of prosecutors and the court, so that the courts could issue sanctions for these violations in advance of the trial date. Judges used a variety of sanctions to enforce bond conditions, including fines and weekends in jail. Although it was not possible to enhance activities to detect noncompliance through active, individualized monitoring, strengthened responses to reported violations were intended to increase defendant accountability.

Only Milwaukee was able to implement active, individualized monitoring of released defendants, but defense bar concerns, as well as operational issues, also shaped its new monitoring program. The pretrial monitoring program evolved into an intensive schedule of monitoring activities, but was limited to 30 to 40 high-risk defendants at a time. On average, defendants reported to either the commissioner or the bail monitor every 2 weeks prior to case disposition. The bail monitor also made home visits to defendants to verify their addresses and monitor bail conditions such as absolute sobriety. Violations could be immediately reported to the court commissioner for possible sanctions. In addition, the bail monitor contacted victims regularly to check on their safety, reminding them to report any violations of the no-contact orders to the court. As part of the demonstration, Milwaukee's Office of the District Attorney made enhancements to the prosecution of violations of bond conditions by charging many of those who violated a no-contact order with bail jumping, a criminal offense under Wisconsin law.

INFORMATION AND SERVICE REFERRALS FOR VICTIMS

Another way to guard against the risks posed to victim safety is by improving direct services to victims. While all three JOD sites funded enhanced services by nongovernmental victim service agencies, the Dorchester and Washtenaw County sites also provided additional court- based services. Milwaukee had a longstanding presence in the courthouse with a range of services provided by two nongovernmental agencies, including an onsite restraining order clinic. JOD funds were used to enhance programs for these functions as well as for services in the community provided by four well-established nongovernmental organizations.

The Dorchester site used JOD funds to employ a victim specialist known as the triager, who was based onsite in the restraining order clerk's office to provide early needs assessment, information and referrals, and assistance with restraining orders for victims in criminal and civil cases. The triage function, designed to serve all domestic violence victims who entered the courthouse, increased coordination and cross-referrals among the prosecution-based victim/ witness specialists and the nongovernmental service providers, and encouraged victim participation in the justice system. Dorchester also used JOD funds to staff a Civil Legal Services Office at the courthouse with community-based advocates from four organizations. This office provided restraining order assistance to victims in multiple languages and referrals to culturally appropriate victim services.

Washtenaw County devoted some of its JOD funds to hire two specialists for the prosecutor's victim/witness unit who handled domestic violence cases exclusively. Prior to JOD, victim/witness specialists' major responsibility in intimate partner violence cases was to send letters to all victims informing them of their rights. With the initiation of JOD, the new specialists took a more active role in working with victims. Specialists attempted to reach all victims by phone the day after the defendant's arrest to explain the court process and assess the victims' needs (see "Timing of Intervention" on page 9). They also encouraged victims to participate in the prosecution process, accompanied them in court, and referred them to the local nongovernmental victim support organization for further services.

In planning for JOD in Milwaukee, victim advocates expressed concern that the large urban courthouse posed the risk that domestic violence victims would be confronted with defendants appearing for hearings or trial. The Milwaukee project provided a secured space in the courthouse for victims and their children, staffed by victim/witness specialists who provided information about the court process and service referrals. All subpoenas to victims from the District Attorney's office instructed victims to report to this victim waiting room prior to the court proceeding. This innovation encouraged victim participation by providing information, privacy, and security on site. Anecdotal reports from JOD staff indicate that victims were less likely to leave the courthouse prematurely because the likelihood of an unwanted encounter with the defendant had been sharply reduced.

To encourage victims to testify in court, the new domestic violence court commissioner in Milwaukee implemented new procedures in his courtroom, routinely asking if the victim was present and whether she wished to communicate with the court. Prior to JOD, victim input was not requested. In most jurisdictions, victim testimony is usually only requested at sentencing.

LESSONS LEARNED

Four major lessons emerged from the Judicial Oversight Demonstration site's experiences in developing innovative, pretrial approaches to ensure defendant accountability and victim safety for intimate partner violence cases. These were the importance of—

- Judicial involvement and willingness to coordinate case procedures to enhance consistency.
- Restructuring court processes in domestic violence cases to permit better coordination among agencies.
- Procedures to monitor or educate defendants and provide a quick court response to violations of no-contact orders and other bond conditions.
- Connecting victims to support services early in the process.

TIMING OF INTERVENTION

The JOD sites found that the most feasible first response to domestic violence victims by a victim advocate or law enforcement liaison may occur the day after the incident. Immediate, onscene crisis response to victims of intimate partner violence was attempted in two of the three sites (Dorchester and Milwaukee). Both sites experienced concerns for the safety of the advocate or responder,

and law enforcement agencies were not always able to provide sufficient staffing to ensure their protection. In addition, victims may be more receptive to intervention after the initial crisis has passed—the domestic violence liaison in the Milwaukee Police Department made contact with 82 percent of the victims referred.

Challenges to implementing innovative pretrial practices include—

- Resource limitations for expanding staff and providing training.
- Developing consistent practices among the judiciary.
- Balancing pretrial policies and procedures with due process concerns.
- Defining the roles and mandates of different service providers.

Other states are also experimenting with unique procedures for handling intimate partner violence cases in the period before trial to ensure the safety of the victim. The Pretrial Services Resource Center reports[3] that Illinois has established a rule requiring persons arrested for domestic violence offenses to see a judge before being released so that appropriate release conditions can be set. Mississippi and Washington also have such laws. In Oregon, the pretrial release statute was recently amended to state that when setting terms of release for a person arrested for domestic violence, the judicial officer is to set whatever conditions are necessary "to assure that there is no repeat of the offense." A typical condition is that the defendant provide a verified alternate address to live at until the case is resolved.[4]

As jurisdictions around the country move forward in strengthening pretrial responses to domestic violence, the experiences of the JOD demonstration sites may help guide their efforts and suggest strategies and responses to the challenges they face.

Other Reports on Domestic Violence

DeStefano, Christine, Adele Harrell, Lisa Newmark, & Christy Visher, (2001). *Evaluation of the Judicial Oversight Demonstration Initiative: Baseline and Implementation Report*, Research Report, December, available at www.ojp.usdoj.gov/nij/vawprog/ baselinerpt.pdf.

Harrell, Adele, Lisa Newmark, Christy Visher, & Christine DeStefano, (2002). *Evaluation of the Judicial Oversight Demonstration Initiative: Implementation Strategies and Lessons*, Research Report, September, available at www.ojp.usdoj.gov/nij/vawprog/ lessons. pdf.

Harrell, Adele, Megan Schaffer, Christine DeStefano, & Jennifer Castro, (2006). "*The Evaluation of Milwaukee's Judicial Oversight Demonstration*," Final Report, April, NCJ 215349, available at www.ncjrs.gov/ pdffiles 1 /nij/grants/2 15349. pdf.

Jackson, Shelly, Lynette Feder, David R. Forde, Robert C. Davis, Christopher D. Maxwell, & Bruce, G. (2003). Taylor, *Batterer Intervention Programs: Where Do We Go From Here?*, Special Report, June, NCJ 195079, available at www.ojp.usdoj.gov/nij/ pubs-sum/1 95079. htm.

Healey, Kerry Murphy, & Christine Smith, (1998). *Batterer Programs: What Criminal Justice Agencies Need to Know*, Research in Action, July, NCJ 171683, available at www.ojp.usdoj.gov/ nij/pubs-sum/171 683.htm.

NIJ Journal 250, www.ncjrs.gov/ pdffiles1/jr000250.pdf (special issue containing six articles about homicide committed by the victim's spouse or other intimate partner).

The National Institute of Justice is the research, development, and evaluation agency of the U.S. Department of Justice. NIJ's mission is to advance scientific research, development, and evaluation to enhance the administration of justice and public safety.

The National Institute of Justice is a component of the Office of Justice Programs, which also includes the Bureau of Justice Assistance; the Bureau of Justice Statistics; the Community Capacity Development Office; the Office for Victims of Crime; the Office of Juvenile Justice and Delinquency Prevention; and the Office of Sex Offender Sentencing, Monitoring, Apprehending, Registering, and Tracking (SMART)

End Notes

[1] Although JOD was funded with the goal of improving victim safety and offender accountability in intimate partner violence cases, some of the JOD sites also chose to use JOD enhancements to address other domestic or family violence, including child and elder abuse cases and cases involving nonintimate cohabiting adults.

[2] Erez, Edna, and Joanne Belknap, "In Their Own Words: Battered Women's Assessment of the Criminal Processing System's Responses," Violence and Victims 13 (3) (1998): 251–268; Goolkasian, Gail, Confronting Domestic Violence: The Role of Criminal Court Judges, Research in Brief, Washington, D.C.: U.S. Department of Justice, National Institute of Justice, May 1986, NCJ 102833.

[3] Pretrial Services Resource Center, 2004, www.pretrial.org/faq.html.

[4] After JOD was underway, a similar law was passed in Michigan. As part of the arraignment guidelines developed in Washtenaw County, the judge or magistrate asks whether there are weapons in the home and whether the defendant is moving to a location that complies with the bond conditions.

INDEX

D

T

U

V